Arts and Learning

Arts and Learning

An Integrated Approach to Teaching and Learning in Multicultural and Multilingual Settings

Merryl Goldberg

California State University, San Marcos

 LONGMAN

An imprint of Addison Wesley Longman, Inc.

New York • Reading, Massachusetts • Menlo Park, California • Harlow, England
Don Mills, Ontario • Sydney • Mexico City • Madrid • Amsterdam

Arts and Learning: An Integrated Approach to Teaching and Learning in Multicultural and Multilingual Settings

Longman, 10 Bank Street, White Plains, N.Y. 10606

Associated companies:
Longman Group Ltd., London
Longman Cheshire Pty., Melbourne
Longman Paul Pty., Auckland
Copp Clark Longman Ltd., Toronto

Acquisitions editor: Virginia L. Blanford
Production editor: Linda Moser
Cover design: Joseph DePinho
Production supervisor: Edith Pullman
Compositor: ExecuStaff

Library of Congress Cataloging-in-Publication Data
Goldberg, Merryl Ruth
    Arts and learning : an integrated approach to teaching and
learning in multicultural and multilingual settings / Merryl Goldberg.
      p. cm.
    Includes bibliographical references and index.
    ISBN 0-8013-1607-3
    1. Arts—Study and teaching (Elementary)—United States.
2. Multicultural education—Activity programs—United States.
I. Title.
NX280.G65   1997
372.5'044—dc20   96-3768
                                                      CIP

1 2 3 4 5 6 7 8 9 10-MA-0099989796

Contents

Preface   *ix*

CHAPTER 1   **ART AS KNOWING: A METHODOLOGY
                 FOR LEARNING**   **1**

    Arts and Knowledge   *2*
    Arts and Learning   *4*
    Arts as Language   *8*
    Arts and Culture   *11*
    Goals of Multicultural Education and the Arts   *13*
    Methodology for Learning   *16*
        Learning With *the Arts 17, Learning* Through *the Arts 17,*
        Learning About *the Arts 20*
    Summary   *20*
    Questions to Ponder   *21*
    Explorations to Try   *21*
    References   *22*

CHAPTER 2   **WHAT DOES IT MEAN TO BE LEARNER?
                 INTELLECTUAL DEVELOPMENT REVISITED**   **23**

    Theories of Intellectual Development   *23*
    The Role of "Translation through Representation" in Learning   *26*
    What Does It Mean to Be a Learner?   *29*
    Summary   *37*
    Questions to Ponder   *37*
    Explorations to Try   *37*
    References   *38*

CHAPTER 3 **PIAGET, IMITATION, AND THE BLUES: REFLECTIONS ON IMAGINATION AND CREATIVITY** 41

Creativity *42*
Piaget, Imitation, and the Blues *45*
Imagination *47*
Howard Gardner, Creativity, and the Classroom *49*
Creativity and Technique *53*
Creator and Participant *54*
Summary 55
Questions to Ponder 55
Explorations to Try 56
References 56

CHAPTER 4 **COMMUNICATION, EXPRESSION, AND EXPERIENCE: LITERACY AND THE ARTS** 59

Literacy with the Arts *60*
Cursive Writing through the Arts *61*
Picto-Spelling Learning through the Arts *62*
Story Comprehension Learning through the Arts *63*
    Drama (Visual and Auditory) 65, Movement (Kinesthetic) 66,
    Music (Auditory) 66
Poetry and Language Acquisition through the Arts *66*
Playing with Words *69*
Journals: Working with Ideas over a Period of Time *77*
Copied Poems *79*
Key Elements toward Writing Poetry *83*
Summary 83
Questions to Ponder 84
Explorations to Try 84
References 84

CHAPTER 5 **THE VOICES OF HUMANITY: HISTORY, SOCIAL STUDIES, GEOGRAPHY, AND THE ARTS** 87

Learning with the Arts *89*
    Poetry 90, Visual Arts 92, Music 92, Drama 93
Learning through the Arts *93*
    Presidential Puppetry 94, Mural Making and History 97,
    Geography and Papier Mâché 98
Summary 99
Questions to Ponder 100
Explorations to Try 100
References 100

CHAPTER 6 **THE WONDER OF DISCOVERY: SCIENCE AND THE ARTS   103**

Learning with the Arts   *106*
   Painting 106, Music 107, Poetry 107
Learning through the Arts   *108*
   Dance 108, Ecology: Drawing from Nature 108, The Nature of Poetry: Working with Ideas 112
Summary   125
Questions to Ponder   126
Explorations to Try   126
References   126

CHAPTER 7 **PUZZLES OF THE MIND AND SOUL: MATHEMATICS AND THE ARTS   127**

Learning with the Arts   *130*
   Visual Arts 130, Dance 132, Literature 134, Music 134
Learning through the Arts   *134*
   Distance Estimation 135, Permutations 135, Fractions 135, Shapes, Symmetry, Angles, and Geometry 137, Single-Digit Addition and Subtraction 139, Points and Coordinates, Parallel Lines 140, Drama, Story Problems 141
Summary   142
Questions to Ponder   142
Explorations to Try   142
References   143

CHAPTER 8 **SETTING THE STAGE FOR A TURN OF EVENTS: SUBJECT MATTER INFORMS THE ARTS   145**

Arts Setting the Stage for Learning   *150*
Subject Matter Informing Art   *151*
Art as Subject Matter   *154*
Learning about Arts with Arts   *155*
Learning about Arts through Arts   *158*
Summary   159
Questions to Ponder   160
Explorations to Try   160
References   161

CHAPTER 9   **SEEING A DIFFERENT PICTURE:**
            ASSESSMENT AND THE ARTS   163

The Need for Assessment   *164*
Evidence of Learning   *165*
Content and Concept Assessment   *167*
Incidental Assessment   *168*
Setting Assessment Parameters   *169*
Strategies to Collect Evidence   *171*
   Portfolios Assessment 172, Performance-Based Assessment 172,
   Listening to and Observing Children 175
Summary   177
Questions to Ponder   177
Explorations to Try   178
References   178

CHAPTER 10   **A LITHOGRAPH IN THE CLOSET**
             AND ACCORDION IN THE GARAGE:
             CONNECTING WITH THE ARTS
             AND ARTISTS IN YOUR COMMUNITY   179

Utilizing Community Resources   *180*
The World Wide Web and Arts Education   *182*
SUAVE: A Cultural Partnership for Teachers   *182*
   Description and Overview 182, Background 183, Philosophy and
   Theoretical Underpinnings 185, Goals and Objectives 186,
   Methods 187, Accomplishments of One Year of SUAVE 189,
   Funding and Assessment 190, Beyond the Pilot Year 190,
   Reflections on the Program 191
Summary   193
Questions to Ponder   193
Explorations to Try   193

Index   195

Preface

This book is about children and teachers in some of their most imaginative and creative moments. It is about creating a learning community committed to educational equity. It is about access to knowledge, and it is about the journeys of individuals as they seek adventures in learning. *Arts and Learning* focuses on the multiple roles of the arts as languages of learning and methods for teaching in the multicultural and multilingual classroom.

Educators using this book need not have any arts background or familiarity with specific art techniques. The book will introduce you to the possibilities the arts hold for you and your students. Its motivating philosophy is that the arts are fundamental to education because they are fundamental to human knowledge and culture, expression, and communication. Artistic methods and activities encourage creative and critical thinking skills while at the same time enabling students to imagine possibilities, seek solutions, and be active discoverers of knowledge.

This book is unique in that it does not focus on learning about the arts, as is usually the case in schooling. Instead, it focuses on how teaching and learning can be considerably enhanced through art-based activities. Students can learn *about* the arts, learn *with* the arts, and learn *through* the arts. The most familiar, most common, and least integrated experience students have with the arts is learning *about* them: In classes taught by arts specialists they learn about painting, drawing, music, and perhaps even dance or drama. No doubt these classes enrich the students' lives.

However, learning *about* the arts is not the goal of this text. Rather, its focus is on educating you to help students learn *with* the arts and *through* them. Learning subject matter in this way supports an integrated approach to curriculum development and teaching. Learning *with* the arts occurs when an art

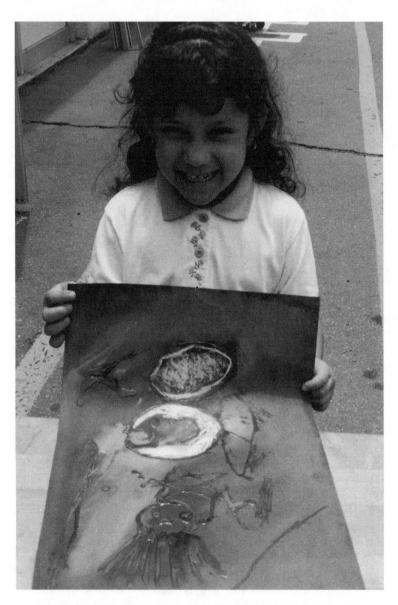

Showing off her oceanography collage, this kindergartener
from Escondido, California, delightfully shares her knowledge
of sea creatures.

form is the source of a study. For example, a teacher may introduce her students
to the songs of the civil rights movement as a method of studying the period,
or to the paintings of Monet or Manet in studying mathematical points and sets.
Likewise, a teacher might use poems written at the time of the American
Revolution as a source to study aspects of the war. Learning *with* an art form

introduces students to real-life applications of the arts in documenting humanity's most personal histories and expressions.

Learning *through* the arts employs artistic mediums as a strategy for learning. For example, students might dramatize the life cycle of a spider or butterfly to better understand it, or they might write a rap script as a way to apply and express their observations of nature. By learning *through* the arts, students are engaging with ideas rather than reporting on them. As they work through the arts to express subject matter, they are stretching their imaginations and pursuing the challenges involved in critical thinking and learning.

The arts are indeed powerful tools for motivating students to apply their knowledge, work cooperatively, and make connections across content areas; and arts integration can become a natural tool for everyday learning. As a teaching methodology, learning with and through the arts encourages imaginative, metaphoric, and creative thinking as well as cultural awareness. Participation with the arts gives children the freedom to learn and explore subject matter, discover the world around them, and venture to new worlds. By integrating learning strategies based on the arts, teachers may tap into multiple learning styles and modes of expression, thereby fulfilling several goals of multicultural education.

The opening chapters of this book offer a theory and philosophy of art as it relates to teaching and learning in multicultural and multilingual settings. To that end, an examination of the goals and strategies of multicultural education are presented as they relate to arts integration. I explore the role of creativity and imagination in learning and knowledge acquisition. In discussing imagination and creativity, I challenge common definitions of creativity that rely on finished products and calls of judgment. Specifically, I examine Howard Gardner's work on creativity and the arts and offer an alternative point of view that focuses on characterizing the processes of creation.

Most of the chapters examine the multiple ways in which the arts can be utilized throughout curriculum content areas of literacy (including second language acquisition), history/social studies, science, mathematics, and the arts (as disciplines themselves). Each chapter includes examples from K–8 classrooms where the methods described were applied to practice. At the end of each chapter the reader is presented with Questions to Ponder and Explorations to Try as a source of further guided reflection. Assessment as it relates to classroom learning and the arts is addressed in a separate chapter, including a discussion of the use of portfolios. Finally, a working model of an integrated program is presented as an example of how to integrate classroom work with local arts centers and community-based organizations.

I focus on many art forms throughout this book, ranging from rap and poetry and the power such few words can capture and convey, to the magic of movement and dance that allows us to experience how simple shapes can become intricate mathematical formulas. I am fortunate in that the arts have been an integral aspect of my own life since childhood. My father is a painter; his father was a musician who played with Benny Goodman, Duke Ellington, Paul Whiteman, and the Boston Pops. My mother crafts jewelry, has worked with stained glass, and is currently learning how to make paper.

I bring additional experience to this discussion as well. Since 1980 I have traveled throughout the world as a professional musician playing the saxophone, performing and recording ethnic music in a variety of settings including the Adelaide World Music festival in Australia, jazz and folk clubs, weddings, and radio shows such as "Prairie Home Companion" with Garrison Keillor. At a certain point in my performing career I decided to give up the stage and applause as a full-time profession and turn my energies to education. Having been a part-time K–8 music educator for seven of the years I was performing, I was able to experience and compare both professions.

Although my love of music never waned, I began to look hard at the life of a performer and decided that it wouldn't fulfill me in the long run. I was bothered by always performing *for* people, whereas in teaching I could work *with* people—forming relationships lasting at least a semester, year, or more. Being fascinated by students and the ways in which they learned captured my attention more than the anonymous audience ever could. In Chapter 9, I address the notion of performance in teaching and learning—a discussion with useful implications for classroom practice especially as it relates to assessment.

Intrigued by the role of making art and its relationship to making meaning for individuals throughout history, I began to investigate the role of the arts in teaching and learning. I became especially interested in the arts as a method for exploring subject matter as students create representations through artwork to express their understandings of the subject matter.

As you consider the ideas and activities in this book, I ask you to a keep a number of things in mind. None of the activities are meant to be prescriptive, or even replicated in their reported form (although they can be). Each classroom teacher should adapt the ideas to her or his situation. Therefore, I see this book as a springboard toward developing a way of teaching and learning that can work for you and the children in your classroom, rather than as a guide for activities.

Like all knowledge, the ideas presented in this book continue to evolve. No doubt, if I were to write this book again in a few years I might have different things to say and other activities propose. In terms of the arts and education, I believe it is especially true that the more you learn and the more you create, the more you understand how much there is to learn and create. I hope this work opens to you, the reader, new worlds to investigate and exciting paths on which to wander.

Finally, a word of encouragement as you consider integrating arts activities into your practice. Be willing to take risks. It can be a bit intimidating to try new activities, especially if you haven't had much experience with the arts. But, I have rarely been in a perfect teaching situation, and I have long gotten over the idea that everything I might do will work or that the art pieces I create will always be magnificent. Fortunately for you, your students will probably jump on the bandwagon immediately. Few children shy away from the opportunity to perform, listen to music, draw a picture, or create a sculpture. Once you get going, the unleashing of your own and your children's creativity not only will surprise you but will expand the expressive opportunities and intellectual musings in your classroom. Often, the greatest successes result from the greatest risks. Be an arts adventurer and invite your students along.

ACKNOWLEDGMENTS

Putting together this book has been a joyful adventure. I am very grateful to many people I have met along the way for their ideas and suggestions. First and foremost, thanks to hundreds of children with whom I worked in the course of gathering ideas and artwork. As well, thanks to their teachers, most notably Cathy Bullock, Karen Burke, Patty Christopher, Michelle Doyle, Judy Leff, Betsey Mendenhall, and the teachers in the SUAVE program. Thanks to California State University, San Marcos and Lesley College students who have enthusiastically learned through the arts with a special mention to Elaine Memmelar for help with music references and Monique Flannagan for scanning artwork into the computer.

Deb Stern is an artist and photographer whose work appears throughout this book. Her artistic eye in capturing the essence and nature of the ideas in this book has been a delight. Credit is also due to artist educators with whom I work, Mindy Donner, Marni Respicio, Eduardo Parra, Eduardo Garcia, Roberta Villaescusa, and Juanita Purner for taking risks in imagining and implementing many creative ideas and artistic activities. CSUSM professors Joe Keating read and commented on the science chapter; Francisco Rios lent many suggestions in integrating multicultural education; Laurie Stowell suggested art-based literature; and Stella Clark helped with Spanish language poetry.

I would also like to thank a few of my teachers who have over the years supported, questioned, and pushed me beyond ordinary boundaries in my thinking. They are Eleanor Duckworth, Maxine Greene, Ken Hale, and Jim and MaryAnn Hoffmann. A special thanks goes to my teacher, friend, and musical partner Carol Chomsky, who after her extraordinary role as thesis advisor at Harvard University remained on the job reading every draft and chapter of this book. Friends and family also deserve mention for living through numerous projects and relishing the excitement with me: Tomé; Sid Storey; Catherine Lacey; P. J. Nomathemba Seme; Xu Di; Don, Carolyn, and Matt Funes; the Goldbergs; and the Rosenbergs. Kudos to the staff and editors at Longman for their ongoing support—most notably to Laura McKenna and Travis Lester for their hard work in the beginning and to Linda Moser for her hard work finishing it all up. Thanks.

Finally, I wish to express my appreciation to the following reviewers whose suggestions and insight contributed to the development of this book:

J. David Betts, University of Arizona

Xu Di, University of West Florida

Barbara F. Rahal, Edinboro University of Pensylvania

P. J. Nomathemba Seme, Old Dominion University

Vivien Marcow Speiser, Lesley College

M. Kay Stickle, Ball State University

Susan L. Trostle, University of Rhode Island

Nancy Whitaker, University of North Carolina, Chapel Hill

Nillofur Zobairi, Southern Illinois University

chapter 1

Art as Knowing: A Methodology for Learning

THE CLIFF

It stands alone in silence
never losing its strength
except sometimes a wave
will come and dig beneath
the sandstone shell

It cannot lose more than a chip
but slowly it disintegrates from
all the time the tide has come and
all the time the wind has gone

Joey Strauss, fifth-grader

Reading poems like this one by Joey, a fifth-grader in southern California, reminds me how fundamental the arts are to human development, expression, and communication. Joey wrote this poem after closely observing the cliffs on a beach near his school as an assignment for his science class. In teaching a unit on ecology, his teacher sought to put her students directly in touch with nature. Having them observe and document aspects of their environment—in this case, the local beach—is important, she argued, to their learning. But what makes this class unusual is that the teacher also used an art form—poetry—as a way to have the students reflect on, work with, and apply their observations. The arts provide a methodology by which her students can transform their observations into a creative form as they learn about nature. The teacher has experienced again and again that using the arts as a teaching methodology allows her students to think more deeply about subject matter.

This integrated poetry activity is representative of the potential of the arts in the construction of knowledge: that of a methodology for exploring subject matter in a deep and meaningful manner. Not only do the arts serve as an engaging medium, but they provide students with the tools to work with ideas as well. In so doing, they also expand the expressive opportunities available to children in the classroom. Whereas traditional schooling relies heavily on testing and writing as the principal modes of assessment and expression, the arts expand the modes available to children as they seek to understand and express their conceptions of the world around them.

In this first chapter, I will outline several theoretical and practical applications that set the stage for integrating the arts as a methodology for learning in the multicultural and multilingual classroom. I will begin with a discussion of the relationships between the arts and knowledge, learning, language, and culture. Following that I will examine the relationship between the arts and multicultural education. Finally, I will present a detailed description of an expanded use for the arts in classroom settings.

ARTS AND KNOWLEDGE

I consider knowledge as an evolving and nonstatic action. As we learn we are constantly changing our understanding of the world. What I think about today will surely change as I gather more and more experiences tomorrow. Bodies of knowledge which often take priority as a focus of study in schooling, should instead serve as a springboard from which children may explore ideas about their relationship to the world. In other words, bodies of knowledge are not fixed. For example, as scientists continue to explore aspects of the natural world, their theories evolve and change accordingly. In the realm of history, events and stories may be interpreted and reinterpreted according to perspective and additional documentation.

In describing knowledge, I do not mean the reiteration of someone else's great ideas. Instead, I would concur with Eleanor Duckworth (1987) when she writes, "By knowledge, I do not mean verbal summaries of somebody else's knowledge. . . . I mean a person's own repertoire of thoughts, actions, connections, predictions, and feelings" (p. 13). Accepting this premise, a teacher may play an important role in the classroom by having her students actively work with knowledge rather than simply mimicking others' knowledge. Here, the arts are important.

Having been on the beach and documented aspects of nature along with Joey (the child whose poem is at the opening of this chapter) and the other children in his class, I have witnessed students as they work toward making sense of their surroundings. Writing poetry gives them a structure through which to apply their observations. In doing this they are actively working with a knowledge base and constructing understandings of nature through an art form. The art form enables each child to apply his or her observations in an imaginative manner, creating a personal connection to the subject matter. At the same time, because students are engaged in the activity they are in a strong position to retain and apply their understandings in the future.

Placing the students directly in touch with nature is a sound pedagogical approach in and of itself, but asking the students to write poetry following their observation activities gives them an opportunity to reflect even more deeply on their work. As the students consider the complex aspects of nature, the poem is a form through which they can actively reflect upon their experiences. In his sketchbook, Joey recorded the following notes based on his observations of that day. It is fascinating to see the leaps Joey made from notes to poem.

Cliffs
   solid sandstone
   full of holes and crevices
   covered with brush
   iceplant

Waves
   forming far away
   it grows to a few feet high
   a surfer catches it
   it crashes
   and turns to foam on the sand

A Rock
   worn smooth
   dark black holes
   streaks of white
   egg shaped
   four small holes

Seagull
   diving
   swooping
   flying far away
   flapping
   soaring high above my head
   spies its prey and dives

It is evident from his notes that Joey paid close attention to his surroundings. As it happens, his observations are recorded in what some might consider a surprisingly poetic manner. I too was surprised in the beginning. But I have learned that when children are constantly engaged in thinking imaginatively, they begin to naturally apply their observations and understandings in creative ways. I have come to learn that applying one's imagination can be a practiced skill.

In writing his poem, Joey has taken his observations, seriously worked with them, and transformed them into something else.

Transformation is a key to knowledge construction and acquisition. The activity of writing a poem has given Joey an opportunity for learning and an outlet for expressing his ideas and questions. At the same time, each student is engaged in "practicing" his or her imagination. By working on something in a manner that stretches his or her thinking, the child is simultaneously engaged in critical and reflective thinking. The arts allow that imaginative and critical thinking to emerge in a personal and creative manner. Consider the following poem written by Rell on the same day, after she documented the rush of incoming waves:

THE WAVE

No one is there to ride it
but the sun
who glimmers with glee
at riding
being closely followed
as it washes to shore
in turn.

Rell Parker

Whereas Joey was fascinated by the cliffs, Rell focused on the waves. Both successfully completed the nature observation assignment by carefully documenting an aspect of the beach. Both used their observation notes to create a unique poem. In this example, the teacher and I know at the very least that the students are engaged in a process of learning through applying observations to a deeper level by using them in a concentrated and serious way. As a byproduct, each child is an emerging poet and can share his or her original compositions with the class, often to the amazement of peers.

ARTS AND LEARNING

When most people think of the arts in education, they think of their own elementary music class in which they probably sang songs accompanied by a teacher on the piano or autoharp. Most of us remember art class where the art teacher had us sculpt a clay bowl or draw a still life. Not many of us were introduced to the arts as a methodology for studying, say, ecology or geometry. The arts have been traditionally taught as something added onto a core of "basics." Although some might argue that the arts *are* basic (as I would), for the most part the arts have remained removed and distant from other learning.

There are three ways in which I will describe the arts as integrated into learning: *learning about* the arts, *learning with* the arts, and *learning through*

the arts. Historically, the most common form ⸺
specialist who teaches *about* the arts. In this f'
usually handles the job: The music teacher takes ⸺
each week and teaches about music; the art teache⸺
separate room teaches about visual arts. If you were l⸺
even been a drama or dance teacher in your school whom ⸺
weekly basis. Although this model has served education since the ⸺
of public education in the United States, we see its importance slow⸺
ing in direct relation to diminishing educational budgets. The arts, oⸯⸯ
sidered a "frill," have been cut as the "basics" receive attention.

There is no doubt that the model of arts education so familiar in traditionaↄ
schooling (learning *about* the arts) is failing—and what a tragedy that is for all
students. However, the traditional model does not take into account the full
potential of the arts in relation to knowledge and intellectual development.
Taught as a subject unto itself, the arts reveal many aspects of human nature
and give students multiple outlets to express their innermost thoughts. Keeping
the arts separate from other subjects, however, severely limits their potential as
a methodology for teaching and learning in general. As taught in traditional
settings, the arts allow students to travel to places of mystery, dreams, adventure.
Left separate from the sciences, math, social studies, or language arts, the arts
are limited in their potential and practical use in the classroom.

The emphasis throughout this book is to broaden the potential of arts in
the classroom by outlining a *methodology* for learning. I define arts in the very
broadest sense to include the performing arts (e.g., music, dance, drama) as well
as the nonperforming arts (e.g., visual arts, photography, literature, sculpture).
I define methodology as a means by which teachers engage students in learning
that is meaningful to them, and that provides a forum through which they
actively grapple with the complexities of knowledge.

Reflecting upon your own and others' knowledge changes you and the way
you perceive the world. According to Karen Gallas (1994), "[creating knowledge]
makes you powerful and gives you authority within community. It enables you
to feel some control over your history as a learner" (p. 111). Using the arts as
a way to teach subject matter places the learner in the position of truly working
with ideas and taking control of learning in a manner that is at once intellectual,
personal, meaningful, and powerful.

The arts, as a methodology for teaching and learning, provide the teacher
with an expanded repertoire of actions and activities to introduce subject matter.
By exercising their imaginations through subject matter–related artwork, children
are more likely to make new connections and transcend previous limitations.
Being imaginative and creative is an attribute that not only serves artists. Being
creative is fundamental to any field. For example, the chief executive officer of
a company must be able to employ his or her imagination to stay competitive.
A computer programmer must be creative to invent new programs. An auto
mechanic must use her or his imagination to solve problems and determine ways
to fix cars. The power of the imagination as a practiced skill must not be

oked or lost in learning. The arts, as a teaching methodology, enable
nts to practice those skills.

The arts are humanity's expression of life itself. Viewed in this manner, they
ve not been used to their fullest in learning and teaching in typical North
merican school settings. Even though many art programs present students with
important lessons concerning techniques such as perspective in drawing, or
singing in tune, history shows us over and over that the arts play an even greater
role in capturing and promoting cultures. The arts present many kinds of
knowledge, and students may learn a tremendous amount by examining their
content. Songs, paintings, or poetry of a culture may represent the history of a
people; drama might explore the political tensions of a community; playing with
the colors in a sand sculpture might provide inspiration for the scientist who
explores different combinations of molecules.

In light of the previous argument, I believe that we should evaluate the
traditional approach to arts in education and consider its limitations as well as
its contributions. In short, I propose an expansion of the role of arts in teaching
and learning such that art be more fully integrated as a methodology for learning
and a language of expression in the general classroom. This approach broadens
the definition of the role of the arts in learning to include their use as a medium
or language to translate, reflect on, and work with ideas and concepts.

As a methodology, the arts become a *process* toward learning. This notion
is parallel to one developed by Sonia Nieto (1996) as she discusses multicultural
education: "Curriculum and materials represent the *content* of multicultural
education, but multicultural education is above all a *process*" (p. 317). Both
multicultural education and "art as a methodology" require an ongoing and
dynamic process. Both involve content, and both stress process through an
attention to active participation, learning environments, learning styles, culture,
and language abilities in the classroom. This is played out in infinite ways.

At the university where I teach we often have special programs. Recently
we received a grant that enabled a group of musicians who play Spanish Jewish
music (Ladino) to be in residence for a week. The premise of their visit was to
engage students in humanities, arts, and education classes with the incredible
vessel of knowledge (content) housed within the songs of the Spanish Jews in
exile, as documented in the Diaspora over the last 500 years. In 1492 Jews and
Muslims were expelled from Spain and many traveled to Bulgaria, Morocco, Eastern
Europe, Mexico, and Greece, among other countries, in a resettlement effort. During
their exile the Jewish Spaniards kept alive their language and history through songs
and poetry. They also created new songs and poetry that reflected and documented
their evolving history and the changes in their lives and cultures.

When the Ladino musicians performed at the university, they offered much
more than entertainment and an eclectic style of music. They engaged the
students in a *process* of learning. Captured in their songs was a rich series of
history lessons, linguistic lessons, musical lessons, and cultural lessons. Their
residency brought them to the Spanish Civilization class, where they presented
a history lesson through song; to the Critical Music Listening class, where they
introduced the students to instruments and music theory as it related to Spanish

songs; to the Linguistics seminar, where the students compared the Spanish of 500 years ago to present-day Spanish; and to the Education class, where student teachers learned how Ladino culture could be introduced to children in multicultural classrooms.

The group also visited a fifth-grade bilingual (Spanish-English) classroom, where they interacted with students and engaged them in writing poetry to a traditional melody. After presenting the fifth-graders with a few songs and stories from their repertoire, they played a haunting, melancholy song without words and asked the students to create a poem to accompany the melody. Engrossed in the activity, the children composed an amazing array of poems, both in English and in Spanish, which they later recited to the accompaniment of the musicians. The level of engagement was phenomenal, and the poems surprised us all. Here are two of the poems written that day:

VOZ DE LA TORTUGA

Triste me siento
No siento alegría
En mi corazón
Mi corazón se parte en dos pedazos
No me siento alegre en este día
Dejenme en paz
No estoy alegre
Me siento decaída
No quiero ver a nadie ahorita
Quiero estar sola
Sin nadie a mi lado
No quiero que nadie venga a mi lado
No quiero
No quiero más dolor
Quiero ver alegría
Mi corazón está derrotado de tristeza
La lluvia está cayendo
El sol no sale
Me siento sola
No hay pájaros en el aire
Todo está solo
No me gusta el día
El día está triste

Jovanna Flores

MY DYING SOUL

Here I am dying
all upon my own
with no one to die with
I am so lonesome so lonesome

whispers of sadness
birds made of stone
gray and black feathers
I am all upon my own
my sadness is too deep to cry
for my soul is spared

Emily Birnbaum

The students continued to talk about their experience with the musical group for months after the visit. Many of the students also chose poems from that day to include in a class publication.

The overall residency proved to be far more than entertainment, and it illustrates the depth with which the arts may engage students in active learning. To each audience, the group offered specific content as well as an opportunity to connect evolving understandings through the arts to history, culture, and their own personal interests.

One might ask why it is any better to learn history through the songs of a people than through a history book. It is better in that it provides an interesting array of authentic historical voices that is perhaps more inviting and aesthetically pleasing than a history text. Songs can provide "feelings" or moods more than the written text through the musical language added to words. Songs often present an authentic point of view drawing on the thoughts and experiences of real people in history. As such, the song texts often provide firsthand accounts of events in history.

Using art forms such as the Ladino musicians provided can be highly effective in the classroom. Karen Gallas (1994) outlines three ways in which art experiences may be placed at the center of a curriculum: (1) the arts representing a methodology for acquiring knowledge; (2) the arts as subject matter for study, in and of themselves; and (3) the arts as an array of expressive opportunities for communicating with others—what she labels "art as story" (p. 116). In the example of the Ladino musicians, all the experiences Gallas outlines were played out. Jovanna and Emily, the fifth-grade students whose poems you just read, accessed the arts as both a methodology for acquiring knowledge and an expressive outlet. The songs and poems presented them with subject matter for study.

Next, we will look a little deeper at the role of art as a *language* for learning.

ARTS AS LANGUAGE

Art is a language of expression and communication that has always been and will always remain a fundamental aspect of the human condition and the perpetuation of cultures. Defining art is a challenging proposition because it can be viewed through so many cultural, theoretical, philosophical, and even geographical perspectives. This does not mean, however, that people have not tried. For our purposes, we will briefly examine how the arts—in their multiple complexities—act as languages of expression for people and cultures throughout the world.

"Art is a mirror of life" or "art imitates life" are common notions of the function of art in experience. The mirror metaphor is of special interest to me. Socrates and Shakespeare (through the voice of Hamlet) both raised the theory that "art is a mirror of reality" (in Danto, 1981). In discussing the two men's views, Arthur Danto concludes that Hamlet "made a far better use of the metaphor: mirrors and then, by generalization, artworks, rather than giving us back what we already can know without the benefit of them, serve instead as instruments of self-revelation" (p. 9).

What intrigues me about the mirror metaphor is that it incorporates the notion of reflection. If art is a mirror—which I believe it can be—it necessitates reflection. And in that reflection we often see things that are or aren't there. Our look in the mirror is discriminating. The same is true of our look at life; it is discriminating according to our experiences, culture, gender, environment, and so on. Art enables us to see things that are both there and not there; it provides us with an opportunity to imagine and reflect on our lives.

Bella Lewitzky (1989), a dancer and philosopher, writes, "Art is a language, a form of communication, a philosophy, a perception of truth" (p. 2). Although I might argue that there are no truths, only complexities (the more we learn, the more we know we have more to learn), I agree that the arts are most definitely a language and that they most certainly communicate. For example, let's think about music. Listening to Tchaikovsky's *1812 Overture* or his *Romeo and Juliet*, I sense definite feelings and images. However, each piece communicates very different images, stories, and feelings. In listening to the *1812 Overture* I can picture cannons and artillery. I imagine troops patriotically marching toward battle. In listening to *Romeo and Juliet* I sense two individuals drawn to each other, longing for each other. I see them trying to get close to one another. Similarly, a popular piece by the Beatles might evoke and communicate very different feelings and images than an Indian raga. Music in Australian traditional Aboriginal communities serves to communicate history, geography, and culture. Catherine Ellis (1985), while doing music research among Aboriginal communities, writes of an Aboriginal man who told her that "the most knowledgeable person in a tribal community was the person 'knowing many songs'" (p. 1).

Mickey Hart (1991), one of the drummers from the group Grateful Dead, describes music as a "reflection of our dreams, our lives, and it represents every fiber of our being. It's an aural soundscape, a language of the deepest emotions; it's what we sound like as people" (p. 7). James Hoffmann (1991) argues that music not only communicates but is a powerful tool, especially in the hands of performers. "Music, a potent social instrument from earliest times, operates not merely in imitation of society but also in dynamic interaction with it. In comprehending this, a performing musician gains power not only over his or her immediate audience, but through contemporary media, over a broader public as well—for good or ill" (p. 270). One could make a similar argument for other art forms as well.

The arts provide humankind with modes for reflecting on, expressing, and documenting experiences, as well as providing a body of knowledge from which to draw upon. The arts provide a method for expressing ourselves, while at the same time they serve as a unique document of cultures and history. As a study, the arts offer historical, emotional, cultural, and personal sources of information and documentation. Lewitzky (1989) continues, "Art can, in the hands of great talent, make beauty which reverberates through our lives and carries us into rarified strata. It can shatter our perceptions. It can clarify our anger. It can help us to understand our sorrow. The arts are a mirror for society—critic, teacher and forecaster—and teach the value of individual differences" (p. 2).

Art can stimulate our imagination or reflect our experiences. Through creating a work in art, a person can explore the complexities of an idea or situation more fully than if they were to read about it or listen to a lecture. As a tool the arts enable us to cross boundaries that are usually closed to us, or to join together in ways that are new. As such, it is not unusual for artists to imagine new ways of being or to invent ways of seeing something anew.

Creating art or experiencing it is an act of what Lucy Lippard (1990) describes as "a process of consciousness" (p. 9) reminiscent of Nieto's characterization of multicultural education. Maxine Greene (1991) writes of encounters with arts as "shocks of awareness" that may, and should, leave persons "less immersed in the everyday, more impelled to wonder and to question." She goes on to tell us how it is not uncommon "for the arts to leave us somehow ill at ease, nor to prod us beyond acquiescence. They may, now and then, move us into spaces where we can create visions of other ways of being and ponder what it might signify to realize them" (p. 27).

I readily admit that I love music—and lots of kinds of music at that. I've imagined living inside of a Bob Marley reggae tune or inside a passage of Stravinsky's *Symphony of Psalms*. I can honestly say that I experience a sense of freedom when I listen to or play a piece of music that enables me to transcend everyday limitations. Music to me is, as Adrienne Rich (1993) refers to in a discussion of the arts, "a vital way of perceiving and knowing" (p. 162). As a child I spent many hours writing song after song from the poignant to the sublime. Growing up during the 1960s, I wrote songs with lyrics ranging from "We need peace, we need love, all over this world, peace love peace to love" to the more whimsical notion of "Flower power is in today." Obviously, neither song made it to the top ten or even a Grammy nomination. However, writing these songs was a truly powerful and empowering activity. I learned to sit for periods of time working in a concentrated manner. I enjoyed the activity of creating. I was encouraged by supportive peers and adults who listened closely to my finished songs and even found opportunities for me to show them off in school cafeterias or during assemblies.

The connection to this discussion is that the language of the arts can be very powerful in the life of a child. Art can be a source of empowerment as children explore their world and personal potential while retaining (and, one hopes, celebrating) a sense of individualism in relating to their community, be it the classroom, neighborhood, clubs, or family. As I have previously written (Goldberg and Phillips, 1992), "For both teachers and students, the arts can be a form of expression, communication, imagination, observation, perception and thought. The arts are integral to the development of cognitive skills such as listening, thinking, problem solving, matching form to function, and decision making. They inspire discipline, dedication and creativity" (p. v.).

Working with the arts opens the classroom to surprises and excitement. As Gallas (1994) writes, "There is an aura of excitement in the classroom engaged in the arts, and also one of serious intent. . . . What I began to see were the surprises: the ways that children could learn to read through their artworks; the potential for communication that painting offered a nonverbal child; the joy that artistic activity brought to children and teachers alike" (p. 112). I, too, am continually amazed as children work and create understandings through the arts. Sometimes they make surprisingly personal statements such as when the class bully wrote a poem about his desire to fly freely as a butterfly. Through their artwork, children introduce themselves to us in deep and meaningful ways that may not ordinarily emerge otherwise.

Perhaps one of the more compelling reasons why the arts, as languages of learning, are fundamental to classroom life is that they give rise to many voices. "They can nurture a sense of belonging, of community; or, they can foster a sense of being apart, of being an individual. The arts also provide a vehicle for individuals, communities, and cultures to explore their own world and journey to new ones, thus enriching their understanding of the varied peoples and cultures that exist on our planet" (Goldberg and Phillips, 1992, p. v.).

Moreover, the arts can reach across boundaries. In a class where many verbal languages are spoken, the arts can be a uniting language. Although a new student from Peru might not be able to communicate in words with a child who just arrived from Vietnam, she can more than adequately communicate through her drawings and dances. Indeed, using the arts of different cultures as primary sources of learning history introduces children to the "feel" of a culture in addition to the "facts" of a culture.

ARTS AND CULTURE

Making art and creating what I refer to as representations or "metaphors for understanding" (see Chapter 2) occurs within a context of ideas and reflection. Presenting and examining art for consideration in a class also occurs within a context. That context may include the sociopolitical atmosphere, economic status, geographical location, or cultural, linguistic, and ethnic identity of the creator or the observer. All work is in some manner shaped by the cultures and communities in which we live and travel.

Art cannot be divorced from culture; it grows from individuals interacting or reacting to their world. So, too, education and culture cannot be separated from one another because both relate to the actions and continuation of a people. Though education often refers to information acquired, culture is often seen as a mode of thought and feeling of groups of people as they evolve through generations, passing down traditions and inventing new ones (Okakok, 1989).

Much of education involves the telling and creating of stories of our global culture. Stories are told through the spoken word, artwork, music, dance, poetry—all these languages are essential as they transmit culture both within various cultures and to people outside of the culture. It is when we begin to tell other people's stories that we must take the utmost care and respect so that our actions adequately reflect the complexities of the culture.

When students work creatively through the arts, they often begin to incorporate their culture into their work. So, too, when teachers present works of art to emphasize a point or to examine a particular issue, context must be a consideration. The arts embody culture; sometimes they even enhance it. The arts are languages that communicate; like words, they are a system of symbols that represent ideas, emotions, feelings, and history. When I was first teaching music, a few teachers in my school asked if I could enhance their work on various subjects, such as the study of Jewish Eastern Europe in the 1800s. I remember feeling annoyed that I was being asked to enhance their curriculum, yet I couldn't quite figure out what bothered me. I understand better now.

The music of the Eastern European Jews in the 1800s didn't simply enhance life at that time; it embodied life. The songs reflect the hardships, the passion, the events of the time. On their own, the songs could easily be a history text— a rich one at that. The writings of Toni Morrison don't simply enhance life (though they might do that as well); they capture and embody experiences, emotions. The same can be said of Diego Rivera's paintings, Michelangelo's wall paintings, Adrienne Rich's poetry, Bill T. Jones's choreography, the Indigo Girls' music, and on and on.

In Australia, where multicultural equity in arts and education has become a national focus, many dedicated educators, artists, and activists have formulated principles with regard to understanding and celebrating the integration of arts, culture, and education. I believe the principles may be helpful in considering the role of culture and arts in education in the United States. I have taken some of those principles and adapted them for consideration here.[1] (1) There is no such thing as a homogeneous culture or community. Thus, there is no such thing as a homogeneous form of communication within a culture or society. The artwork of any society will be diverse and unique. The promotion of a particular culture and that culture's artworks should reflect accurately the diversity of interests of that group. (2) Cultures develop and use their own symbols and methods of operations. These symbols and methods of operation include the arts in their many and varied formats in addition to the written and spoken word. (3) Cultural activities of groups should be represented as dynamic and living.

---

[1] The statements were originally constructed at the Australian Conference in 1988, "Arts Policy for a Multicultural Australia: Towards Cultural Democracy."

In other words, the expressions of a people are continuous and evolving. Artworks fit into a larger contextual framework than more simply a historical artifact. (4) Different cultures have different challenges and problems according to socioeconomic class, whether they are indigenous, voluntary immigrants, or involuntary immigrants; and these challenges and problems might be reflected throughout the artworks. (Later in this chapter, drawing on this work and the work of others, I present my own principles as they relate to multicultural education and the arts.)

Applied to North America, where many schools have a multicultural and multilinguistic student population, the Australian guidelines offer a structure that suggests complexity over simplicity, a certain rigor in thinking about the ways in which we approach arts and culture. The arts potentially offer more than an "awareness" of a culture; they provide authentic voices from a particular culture. To apply some of the Australian guidelines in your class, you might consider the following example. A study of the music of American Indians of the Southwest could provide your students with an important slice of that particular culture. To consider the study with the rigor suggested by the Australian guidelines, one would include traditional and contemporary songs—songs that reflect diversity within the Southwest American Indian experiences. The songs would be presented within the broader context of the society and larger community. The songs would be introduced so as to yield a more complex understanding of the culture.

GOALS OF MULTICULTURAL EDUCATION AND THE ARTS

The arts, as languages and expressions of cultures and peoples throughout the world, provide many concrete opportunities to educators who are dedicated to multicultural education. According to Leonard Davidman and Patricia T. Davidman (1994) (who draw heavily on the conceptions and work of James Banks, Carl Grant and Christine Sleeter, H. Prentice Baptiste Jr., and Mira Baptiste to articulate their goals), multicultural education is defined as a multifaceted, change-oriented process that can be outlined in six interrelated yet distinct goals: (1) providing educational equity; (2) empowering students and their caretakers; (3) valuing cultural pluralism in society; (4) promoting intercultural/interethnic/intergroup understanding and harmony in the classroom, school, and community; (5) developing an expanded multicultural/multiethnic knowledge base for students, teachers, administrators, and support staff; and (6) supporting students, teachers, staff, and administrators who think, plan, and work with a multicultural perspective.

Davidman and Davidman also describe a number of strategies toward attainment of the goals. Among them are the following: student-specific pedagogy (learning-style–informed teaching), bilingual education and specifically designed academic instruction in English (also known as Sheltered English Instruction), self-esteem–oriented education, teaching toward self-directed learning, and cooperative learning.

In considering goals and strategies of multicultural education, one might imagine how the arts can create webs connecting many aspects of their content. I offer seven general principles outlining the connections of multicultural education and the arts. I will return to the principles throughout the chapters as they apply in specific circumstances. The principles relate both to the content of a multicultural education with the arts, and to the process of multicultural education as it incorporates the arts as methodology. I have created the principles by combining goals and strategies presented by Davidman and Davidman, incorporating notions of process as described by Nieto, and integrating the many roles of art when utilized in the classroom as presented in discussions on art and learning. The seven principles are:

- The Arts Expand Expressive Outlets and Provide a Range of Learning Styles Available to Children
- The Arts Enable Freedom of Expression for Second Language Learners
- The Arts Provide a Stage for Building Self-Esteem
- The Arts Encourage Collaboration and Intergroup Harmony
- The Arts Empower Students and Teachers
- The Arts Deepen Teachers' Awareness of Children's Abilities and Provide Alternative Methods of Assessment
- The Arts Provide Authentic Cultural Voices and Add Complexity to Teaching and Learning

1. The Arts Expand Expressive Outlets and Provide a Range of Learning Styles Available to Children.   Integrating the arts as a forum for expression gives students whose learning styles tend toward the visual, kinesthetic, spatial, or auditory more freedom to communicate their understandings. Thus, when a teacher encourages students to work with ideas through the arts, she more fully taps into their varied learning styles and her practice incorporates student-specific pedagogy.

2. The Arts Enable Freedom of Expression for Second Language Learners.   In considering the arts as languages of expression, teachers offer bilingual and limited English students more freedom to work with ideas and express their understandings without having to depend solely on the English language. For example, the first-grader who cannot yet describe in words the motions of the sun and the earth, but who can demonstrate his understanding in drawing or movement, is given an opportunity to participate in learning rather than be hampered by the limitations of a specific language.

3. The Arts Provide a Stage for Building Self-Esteem.   Over and over again, teachers who integrate the arts in learning remark on the positive effect the activities have on self-esteem. Learning becomes more enjoyable, even magical, as students share their works and ideas. Increased use of the arts can raise the self-esteem of struggling students, thereby making them more successful. Teachers also remark on their students' achievements.

4. The Arts Encourage Collaboration and Intergroup Harmony. Working together on art projects can lead to a marked increase in productive teamwork. According to Betsey Mendenhall, a fifth-grade teacher in southern California, "the cooperation that comes out of learning through the arts is great." Often, the arts enable shy students to come out of their shell. They also offer children with emotional problems another venue to not only work with ideas but cooperate with others in the class. The arts allow for greater educational equity, as more students have opportunities to work with and share knowledge. The arts offer opportunites for individuals to work cooperatively with each other, thereby furthering intercultural, interethnic, and intergroup understanding and harmony.

5. The Arts Empower Students and Teachers. The arts are empowering. When sharing art projects with each other, students gain a sense of themselves and their peers as unique individuals with interesting ideas and skills. They also begin to respect and admire others' efforts as they communicate imaginative and original work through the arts. Such experiences potentially enable students to gain confidence as self-directed learners supported in taking responsibility for their own educational growth. The discipline and dedication required in creating artworks provides students with skills for working independently and interdependently to accomplish tasks as well as tackle complex ideas.

6. The Arts Deepen Teachers' Awareness of Children's Abilities and Provide Alternative Methods of Assessment. When observing students engaged in art work, teachers gain a fuller picture of the whole child. For example, the child who often acts as the class bully might suprise the teacher by writing a sensitive love poem to his mother. The child whom the teacher thinks is distracted might draw a picture in science showing that in fact she is completely tuned into the curriculum. In these examples, not only does the teacher see the children in multiple ways but she also has a broader source of information to assess her students' understandings.

7. The Arts Provide Authentic Cultural Voices and Add Complexity to Teaching and Learning. The arts broaden the tools available to students as they study and seek to understand cultures different from their own. Using the artwork of a culture as a core element of a curriculum introduces students to the voices, images, feelings, and ideas of a people in a way that lends it authenticity. It broadens a study while at the same time introducing students to a wider range of experiences documented by individuals through means other than "objective" reporting. Because the arts lend themselves to self-expression, including the arts in, say, the history curriculum, they bring life to people and events studied; it offers dramatic documentation of the struggles, achievements, celebrations, and complexities of living together in our diverse global community.

Principles 1 and 2 speak to the individual child and methods relating to learning and expression. Principles 3 through 5 relate to the building of a community in which members feel confident, respected, and reflective. Principle 6 relates specifically to ways in which the arts broaden a teacher's modes of understanding children in the multicultural classroom. Principle 7 relates to the content of multicultural education and how the arts provide fundamental understanding of world cultures. Together, they provide a landscape of education as it can be strengthened and connected with the integration of the arts.

METHODOLOGY FOR LEARNING

Artists see things in new and often complex ways. When an artist creates, she or he is working with an idea or knowledge base. The work of an artist involves translating an idea into a form such as painting, music, dance, and so on. In education, a test of learning is the ability to translate a notion, concept, or idea from something given to something owned and utilized. For example, in having students read a chapter in a social studies book, the true test of understanding is not their ability to retell the chapter on an essay test. The test of understanding lies in the student's ability to make that information his own—to work with it, to transform it, to be able to apply it.

The work of an artist gives us further insight into teaching and learning. This work involves deep concentration, an exercise of the imagination, sometimes even problem solving. Some artists actually articulate aspects of their work in relation to a methodology for teaching and learning. Arnold Schoenberg, a twentieth-century classical composer, writes in the introduction to his book *Theory of Harmony* (1978), "this book I have learned from my students. In my teaching I never sought merely 'to tell the pupil what I know.'" Schoenberg's chief aim was to engage the students in a search—a search he equated with that of music itself. "I hope my pupils will commit themselves to searching!" he writes. "Because they will know that one searches for the sake of searching. That finding, which is indeed the goal, can easily put an end to striving" (p. 1). Pablo Picasso, on the other hand, in an interview on the activity of painting, exclaims, "Do not seek—find!" He declares that "to search means nothing in painting. To find is the thing" (in Goldwater and Treves, 1972, p. 416).

Both make important points as we relate their ideas to the classroom. The core activity of working with or through the arts, either as a creator or as a participant/observer, puts one on a path of engagement. Whether the path leads toward a discovery, or whether the search is valuable in and of itself, is debatable. For our purposes, we can reconcile the seemingly conflicting opinions of Schoenberg and Picasso by recognizing that both men turn to the arts as a spring of awareness and an opportunity for action.

In the next section, I will outline the three ways in which I feel the arts can be used as an effective methodology for learning in an integrated curriculum. (1) A student may learn *with* the arts; that is, explore subject matter with the aid of an artwork. (2) A student may explore subject matter *through* the arts by creating works of art that express his or her reflections concerning specific subject matter. (3) A student may learn *about* the arts as a subject in and of itself.

Learning *With* the Arts

Learning *with* the arts occurs when they are introduced as a way to study about a particular subject. The Spanish Civilization class at my university learned about Ladino culture *with* the arts. By using the songs and poetry of the Spanish Jews as a basis for class sessions, the students were able to learn about this group of people and their experiences.

Learning *with* the arts may involve various artistic forms. In studying mathematical sets a teacher may introduce her students to the paintings of Georges Seurat, a French impressionist who created paintings with lots and lots of points. To introduce parallel lines she may introduce her students to paintings by Mondrian, an artist who used parallel lines in many of his works. A science teacher may introduce her students to different drums when they are studying sound waves and vibrations. In each case, the students learn *with* the aid of an art form that informs the subject area.

Learning *with* the arts might be an effective method to teach a unit on the civil rights movement to a middle school social studies class. The traditional school textbook describes certain key events and dates that put the civil rights movement in a historical context. Most likely, the text includes speeches by Martin Luther King Jr. and Robert F. Kennedy. The teacher may use the text, but in addition she may introduce the children to the songs of the civil rights movement. In the school library she finds the book *Sing for Freedom: The Civil Rights Movement through Songs* (Carawan and Carawan, 1990), which is perfect for the study; the school library also has recordings of many of the songs included in the book. The teacher plays a number of the songs in class, and the students examine the words and listen to the melodies. The songs provide a text in and of itself, bringing yet another perspective to the civil rights movement. The children are introduced to the voices (literally) of the era in a way that is not only informative but engaging. They are learning *with* art—in this case, the songs of the civil rights movement.

Learning *Through* the Arts

Learning *through* the arts is a method that encourages students to grapple with and express their understandings of subject matter through an art form. Let's return to our middle school social studies class for an example. The students have now read about the civil rights movement in their textbook and listened to many songs from that time. There has been a certain amount of class discussion, but the teacher is not sure the students have a grasp on the events and importance of the movement. She devises a way—through the arts—for her students to work with the knowledge. She invents a number of characters that could have been living at that time, each with a different perspective, and asks her students to form small groups and create a mini-drama depicting the meeting of the characters. Now the students not only have a way to work with the material, but they have a form through which to express their understandings. They are learning *through* the arts and expressing their understandings in a vibrant, creative form.

Learning *through* the arts can be used at any grade level—and probably should be. Over the years I have found an especially effective use of drama in my teacher preparation Learning and Instruction classes. After asking my students to read and study parts of Piaget's *The Child's Conception of the World* and Plato's telling of Socrates' *Meno,* I have them write a mini-drama in which Piaget and Socrates meet each other. With a few guidelines, students are off creating their dramas. The following script came out of one of my classes.

SETTING: Boston Common, 1990s

CHARACTERS: Socrates and Piaget

PLOT: Socrates and Piaget happen to meet on Boston Common by the swan boats—big boats that look like swans powered by a person in the back who pedals (much like the pedaling on a bicycle) as it moves across the pond. One cannot see the person's legs as s/he powers the boat.

SOCRATES: Is it possible that you are Piaget?!

PIAGET: Well, yes—and who are you?

SOCRATES: Well, who do you think I am?

PIAGET: I have heard of you, Socrates, but I have never experienced any of your theories of knowledge.

SOCRATES: You see that boy over there? See him sitting under that tree? What do you think he's thinking?

PIAGET: Well, let's ask him. We'll ask him questions; I know how you and I feel about questioning people, and I myself truly find asking questions exhilarating.

(The two men walk to the boy's side, sitting with him under the tree.)

PIAGET: Excuse me, young man, can you tell me of what you are thinking?

BOY: Well, nothin' really.

SOCRATES: As you sit here, what is it that you are doing?

BOY: I'm watching the swan boats.

PIAGET: How do those things work, do you think?

BOY: I don't know, with the wind I guess.

PIAGET: Oh, so you think the wind makes the swan boats move?

BOY: Yup.

SOCRATES: So, boy, when there's no wind the swan boat doesn't move?

BOY: Oh no, they still move.

SOCRATES: But what makes them move if there is no wind?

BOY: I think that person in the boat?

SOCRATES: And what does that person do?

BOY: Maybe he moves something in the boat and that makes it go?

SOCRATES: What could that something be?

PIAGET: Socrates, he doesn't know!

SOCRATES: Yes, I know he knows; I must ask more questions.

SOCRATES: Son, have you ever been on a bicycle?

BOY: Oh! I get it. The boat moves when the person in the back pedals like I do on my bike.

SOCRATES: Yes, that's exactly right! I was sure you knew how it worked.

SOCRATES: See, Piaget, this young man *did know* how the boat moved. He knew it all along.

PIAGET: Well, Socrates, I truly believe this young man still believes in his first conviction. He was obviously influenced by your mentioning the bicycle and was led by your idea.

SOCRATES: I really feel that this young fellow is aware of his knowledge now that I have asked him these questions.

BOY: Yeah, I know how that boat moves. I always knew the wind made birds move.

After hearing what usually prove to be delightful and insightful mini-dramas, such as this one, I have a sense my students are not only reading the material but are working with it and devising creative metaphors to express their understandings. In this particular case, the students are groping with the nature of knowledge and comparing the notion of knowledge as innate (from souls past)—as Socrates describes in the dialogue of the *Meno*—and constructivism—as Piaget describes in *The Child's Conception of the World,* which we were also examining in class.

It is interesting that in addition to applying their understandings, these students took a stand as to which theory they felt was more convincing. They cleverly took the position of Piaget (constructivism) and showed that even though a child might answer something in the way the questioner would like to hear, it is not necessarily what he or she truly believes. This is evident in the final line of the drama, "Yeah, I know how that boat moves. I always knew the wind made birds move." Another clever twist of dialogue is evident in line three. Rather than answering Piaget's question, Socrates asks a question instead. Here, it is clear that my students were demonstrating their understanding of Socratic questioning.

Learning *through* the arts can take on many forms in addition to drama. The students writing poetry for the science lesson in the beginning of this chapter were learning about ecology through the arts. Another science class might draw from nature as a way to examine and construct an understanding of the phenomenal details of a seashell. Second language learners might write poetry. Second-graders might create a dance to express their understanding of the metamorphosis of pupae to butterflies. In all these cases, the learners are actively engaged in imaginative and creative thinking as they learn through the arts and construct meaning.

Learning *About* the Arts

Throughout the ensuing chapters I will show how learning *with* and learning *through* the arts can lead to a desire to learn *about* the arts. For example, in Chapter 4 I discuss how second language learners become engaged in working with words and language *through* writing poetry. By learning literacy skills through writing their own poetry, children (in a fourth-grade classroom) became interested in poetry itself. After writing poetry almost all students began taking poetry books from the library on their weekly trips to choose reading material. The exercise of learning language skills through the arts led to a genuine interest in reading and interpreting poetry. Because the students were engaged in writing poetry, they had an experiential basis with which to approach poetry as an art form. They became poets, or acted as poets as a way to learn. So their interest in writing poetry evolved into something larger. They began reading and appreciating others' poetry, and sharing what they had read with their friends. As poets themselves, they also developed insights in critiquing poetry. On their own they were engaged in learning *about* poetry!

The same argument may be made for any of the art forms that are employed for the teaching and learning of subject matter. Learning *with* the arts may also lead to learning *about* the arts. After reviewing paintings to study parallel lines and sets, students often are more drawn into (no pun intended) the realm of painting, relating their knowledge of lines to Georgia O'Keeffe, Andy Warhol, or Frida Kahlo. Perhaps they might even be inspired to create their own paintings, having understood something about lines from their mathematical/art study. There is no doubt that learning *with* and *through* the arts can provide a foundation for studying *about* the arts. It can also provide an incentive to students in creating their own artworks.

SUMMARY

The arts serve as a methodology or strategy for learning, expanding traditional teaching methods into a fascinating and imaginative forum for exploration of subject matter. Using the arts as a teaching tool in the classroom broadens their function from the more traditional model of teaching *about* the arts and provides opportunities for students to transform understandings and apply their ideas in a creative form. Using art forms for working with ideas fulfills many of the goals for achieving a multicultural education and provides avenues toward its strategies. As a language of expression, art gives rise to many voices in the classroom and opens many avenues for all students to work with knowledge.

The three ways in which the arts can be effectively used in the classroom are: learning *with,* learning *through,* and learning *about* the arts. In utilizing all three ways, teachers expand the role of the arts in classroom experience. However, this does not necessitate special artistic expertise on the part of the teacher. Rather, the teacher is presenting a method that broadens the acceptable modes of expression in the classroom while offering her students opportunities to engage in reflective, creative, and critical thinking.

QUESTIONS TO PONDER

1. In what ways have the arts been important in your own education?
2. In what ways are the arts important in your life? Do you think that the arts shape your thinking in any way?
3. Can you recall any instances when an experience with the arts caused you to consider something in a new way? What was the art form and experience, and how did it cause you to consider something in a new way?
4. Can you recall specific instance(s) when you learned something in school with or through the arts? Briefly retell the experience(s).
5. What are the ways in which integrating the arts into education meets the challenges of multicultural education?

EXPLORATIONS TO TRY

1. With a partner, listen to three songs by different groups. The groups can be as different as Ice Cube, Aretha Franklin, Culture Clash, Remy Ongala, the Beatles, Miriam Makeba, Elton John, Sting, and so on. What does each song tell you about life? About the songwriter? About culture? About history or an event? About yourself?
2. Write a short essay outlining your philosophy of education. What are the roles of the teacher and learner in education? What is important in education? Facts? Knowledge? Searching? Finding? After you have completed your essay, discuss it with a partner. How does your partner's essay differ from yours? In what ways are your ideas similar?
3. Think about "knowledge." How would you define it? Either write a poem, draw a picture, or create a sculpture, dance, rap, or piece of music that describes your thinking about "knowledge." To get started, see if you can find any artworks that deal with the same subject

matter. For example, the musical group Tower of Power has recorded a song entitled, "A Little Knowledge Is a Dangerous Thing." Listening to the song might give you some ideas.

REFERENCES

Arts Policy for a Multicultural Australia: Towards Cultural Democracy. (1988). "Conference papers." March 1988, sponsored by Office of Multicultural Affairs, Department of Prime Minister and Cabinet; Community Cultural Development Unit of the Australia Council; South Australian Department for the Arts.

Carawan, Guy, and Candie Carawan, eds. (1990). *Sing for Freedom: The Story of the Civil Rights Movement through Its Songs.* Bethlehem, PA: A Sing Out Publication.

Danto, Arthur. (1981). *The Transformation of the Commonplace: A Philosophy of Art.* Cambridge, MA: Harvard University Press.

Davidman, Leonard, and Patricia T. Davidman. (1994). *Teaching with a Multicultural Perspective.* New York: Longman.

Duckworth, Eleanor. (1987). *The Having of Wonderful Ideas and Other Essays on Teaching and Learning.* New York: Teachers College Press.

Ellis, Catherine J. (1985). *Aboriginal Music: Education for Living.* Queensland, Australia: University of Queensland Press.

Gallas, Karen. (1994). *The Languages of Learning: How Children Talk, Write, Dance, Draw, and Sing Their Understanding of the World.* New York: Teachers College Press.

Goldberg, Merryl, and Ann Phillips, eds. (1992). *Arts as Education.* Cambridge, MA: Harvard Educational Review, Reprint Series #24.

Goldwater, Robert, and Marco Treves, eds. (1972). *Artists on Art from XIV to XX Century.* New York: Pantheon.

Greene, Maxine. (1991). "Texts and Margins." *Harvard Educational Review,* Vol. 61, No. 1, February 1991.

Hart, Mickey. (1991). *Planet Drum.* San Francisco: HarperSanFrancisco.

Hoffmann, James. (1991). "Computer-Aided Collaborative Music Instruction." *Harvard Educational Review,* Vol. 61, No. 3, August 1991.

Lewitzky, Bella. (1989). "Why Art?" *University of California, San Diego Regent's Lecture,* May 31, 1989.

Lippard, Lucy. (1990). *Mixed Blessings: New Art in a Multicultural America.* New York: Pantheon.

Nieto, Sonia. (1996). *Affirming Diversity.* New York: Longman.

Okakok, Leona. (1989). "Serving the Purpose of Education." *Harvard Educational Review,* Vol. 59, No. 4, November 1989.

Rich, Adrienne. (1993). *What Is Found There: Notebooks on Poetry and Politics.* New York: W. W. Norton.

Schoenberg, Arnold. (1978). *Theory of Harmony.* Los Angeles: University of California Press.

chapter 2

What Does It Mean to Be a Learner? Intellectual Development Revisited

Open to new ideas, eager for
Knowledge, yearning for experience,
A learner.

Excited by change, looking for
New beginnings,
A learner.

Fulfilled by diversity,
Immersed in expression,
A learner.

Constantly seeking,
Forever evolving,
A learner.

Olivia Friddell, student teacher

THEORIES OF INTELLECTUAL DEVELOPMENT

Intellectual development has been defined in a number of ways and by various people in educational circles. Eleanor Duckworth (1987) writes, "the having of wonderful ideas is what I consider the essence of intellectual development" (p. 1). She continues to say that the having of wonderful ideas is essentially a *creative* affair. "When children are afforded the occasions to be intellectually creative— by being offered matter to be concerned about intellectually and by having their ideas accepted—then not only do they learn about the world, but as a happy side effect their general intellectual ability is stimulated as well" (pp. 12–13).

Howard Gardner (1990) describes intelligence as an *ability* "to solve problems or to fashion a product, to make something that is valued in at least one culture" (p. 16). It is interesting that Gardner's definition of creativity parallels his definition of intelligence: "the ability to solve problems or to make something or to pose questions regularly in a domain; those questions are initially novel but are eventually accepted in one or more cultures" (p. 21). Gardner emphasizes that intelligence as we know it might actually be "intelligences," that there are numerous ways in which human beings can be intelligent.

Gardner (1993) theorizes that intelligence does not relate to a single property or capability of the mind. Instead, he identifies at least seven intelligences: linguistic intelligence, musical intelligence, logico-mathematical intelligence, spatial intelligence, bodily-kinesthetic intelligence, intrapersonal intelligence, and interpersonal intelligence. His theory has been useful to educators who have adapted their teaching styles to match the learning styles and intelligences of their students, thereby broadening the educational opportunities available to many children.

Jean Piaget (1963), known for constructivist theory and developmental stages, writes that "intelligence is an *adaptation*. . . . Life is a continuous creation of increasingly complex forms and a progressive balancing of these forms with the environment" (p. 3). He describes intelligence as an ongoing construction of knowledge, the process being one of continual adaptation. In a somewhat parallel discussion, Lev Vygotsky (1971) defines art in a similar manner. He writes, "from a social viewpoint, art is a complex process of balancing the environment" (p. 294). One wonders what kind of conversation Piaget and Vygotsky might have concerning the relationship between intelligence, art, and environment.

What interests me in comparing these three definitions of intellectual development and Vygotsky's definition of art is that each thinker emphasizes intelligence as an activity, a creative affair, or an evolving process. Whereas Duckworth and Gardner stress a resulting idea or product in relation to the activity or ability, Piaget emphasizes an action: adaptation.

I am particularly drawn to Piaget's characterization of intellectual development because he emphasizes an evolving and ever more complex process rather than a static outcome. Thinking of intellectual development as a continually evolving process enables us to consider learning as an ongoing process with a future rather than the acquisition of a knowledge base as a matter of fact—which is so often the case in education. Although intellectual development is often gauged in terms of answers reported on a test or the retelling of a historical event, these devices leave little room for assessing creative and reflective thinking. Piaget also stresses, along with Vygotsky, that the work is an effort toward balancing, and the balancing is related to one's environment.

In utilizing the arts for intellectual development, my goal is to engage students in thoughtful inquiry and reflective questioning. To that end, the art form provides a method that enables each student to represent and translate an idea. While they work through an art form—perhaps in an effort to find balance—I want the students to be constantly aware and able to perceive aspects of their world from many perspectives. I want them to accept risks in their thinking and be willing to live with confusion. Finally, I want them to accept what they have learned as incomplete. After all, in both teaching and learning there is always somewhere else to go with one's ideas. Like Piaget, I believe that intellectual development is a non-ending, ever-continuous, and life-long process.

In a course I teach on human development, one of the ways I encourage intellectual development is to create activities involving the arts that demand students to go beyond their everyday boundaries. For one activity I ask each student to compose and notate a "kitchen piece." The assignment is to create a short sound composition using objects found in the kitchen. The piece must be performed twice, and it must be accompanied by an invented notation. The notation leads us into a discussion of representation. The activity pushes students beyond their ordinary limits to create something out of an extraordinary situation. Performances make use of pots and pans, occasionally a blender, spoons, glasses filled with water, Tupperware drums, garlic presses, whisks, and so on.

In reflecting on this exercise in her final paper for the class, one of my students, Diane Hunter (1995), wrote, "I have not, nor will I ever, complete my kitchen symphony, or my work symphony, or my bedroom symphony, etc. Everything that once created a 'noise' now has a tonal quality about it and is subject to a Hunter audition. . . . I started to pay more attention to the words of songs, to observe people as they move, and to listen to the sounds of life and the changes of tones." What delights me most about this comment is that the world has somehow changed for Diane. She is open to hearing things in a new way; her awareness of her surroundings is now an "audition" and a source of thoughtfulness rather than an accepted and unquestioned decoration. She is clearly engaged in an intellectual pursuit.

As a teacher, I feel great joy when my students leave class anxious to keep on thinking and open to seeing objects and ideas in new and different ways. I love thinking that my students will continue pursuits started in class, that they perceive the class as opening up a world rather than putting the finishing touches on it. Being open to curiosity and further contemplation is fundamental to intellectual development. A teacher can play an important role in provoking her students intellectually by continually providing occasions that engage and encourage students to be adventurers in learning. The students need not agree with the ways in which teachers pursue any given question; rather, they will critically consider what is offered to them, reflect on it, and decide for them-selves how to proceed. When students accept challenges instead of answers, teachers have accomplished something important. Intellectual development, seen in this light, is not the acquisition of answers but a motivation to learn.

Unfortunately, I believe that many of us—as well as our students—have not been encouraged to think creatively or of ourselves as "creative." Instead, our intellectual development has been relegated to finding and remembering answers. Julie Horton (1995), another student from my human development class, writes, "Throughout my years of schooling, I do not feel that I was challenged to think creatively. As a student, I was seldom asked about my own opinions and ideas. I think this is a sad commentary on the schools I attended. However, I know that teaching strategies can and must be changed."

Julie goes on to propose creating an inviting and secure environment where children feel they can take risks, create, and learn. Another component to this change requires placing children in positions where they can work with ideas rather than accept them. Here the arts lend us a method to do so, and an expanded form of communication to express such learning. In the following section, I will explore the ways in which the arts, through encouraging representational and reflective thinking, provide many opportunities for intellectual growth and development.

THE ROLE OF "TRANSLATION THROUGH REPRESENTATION" IN LEARNING

For some time now I have been documenting the ways in which students translate and represent subject matter content through the arts. This is more than a fascinating journey into how individuals create meaning and work with knowledge; I believe that examining the ways in which children and adults represent emerging understandings can suggest ways in which to approach education and teaching.

When a student listens to a lecture and then writes a paper or takes a test, the instructor has little information that tells her if the student understands the material—although she does know that the student can retell the story of the lecture. If the student actually does connect to the material because she or he has a basis to integrate it into her or his schemas, the student might, in fact, understand and relate to the lecture—it might even be seminal in furthering the student's thinking. In this case, the instructor has had some success.

I would argue, however, that there are relatively few times in learning when lecturing or "telling" is successful. Vito Perrone (1991) points out throughout his book, *A Letter to Teachers,* that learning is a personal matter and varies for different children, proceeds best when children are actively engaged in their own learning, and is enhanced by a supportive atmosphere. John Dewey (1959) wrote of "learning by doing." Jerome Bruner (1962) wrote of "discovery learning." Many educators have argued (and continue to argue) that students relate to information more substantially if they are enabled to work with the material and construct their own understandings (Duckworth, 1991, 1987; Schickedanz, 1990; Watson and Konicek, 1990; Kamii, 1989, 1984; Bissex, 1980; Piaget, 1980; Hawkins, 1978).

When students translate into an artistic expression their emerging understanding of a particular subject, they are actively engaged in their own learning. The act of translating requires the students to work with the ideas as opposed to absorbing them. Often the act of translation leads to the creation of a metaphor. The role of metaphors in learning has been seen as fundamental to intellectual development (Gallas, 1994, 1991; Bowden, 1993; Goldberg, 1992; Belenky et al. 1986; Berthoff, 1981; Lakoff and Johnson, 1980).

Ann Berthoff (1981) argues that metaphors "encourage us to discover relationships and how they might be articulated." (p. 7). She writes, "metaphors are heuristic in function," meaning that they lead to knowledge creation. Similarly, George Lakoff and Mark Johnson (1980) argue that metaphors form a basis for thought and action and are, in fact, pervasive in constructing "how we get around in the world and how we relate to other people" (p. 3). Metaphors are a powerful tool that we all use in conceptualizing our world and our relationships (Bowden, 1993).

Intellectual development requires the ability to translate and represent ideas. Often, this includes the creation of metaphors for understanding. If a student can transform someone else's idea by creating a metaphor, or can integrate his or her own observations of subject matter—nature, for example—by creating a representation in art, then that child is truly engaged in an intellectual journey. This is a far cry from merely mimicking others' knowledge.

Artistic activity naturally encourages representation and the use of metaphors. The artist is steeped in a world of metaphoric representation as she or he begins a process of creating a form that expresses some idea or feeling set to music, put into words (in poetry or literature), or placed in a visual or tactile form. The visual artist translates ideas into visual representations and/or visual metaphors. The musician works with sound to represent ideas, emotions, even events through tones and rhythms. Indeed, the arts provide a natural structure through which students can engage in representational and metaphoric thinking. The arts not only encourage this kind of thinking, they demand it. In addition, artistic activity provides a lens through which students can look at and examine their world as well as expressing it.

I would argue that artistic activity as representational and metaphoric thinking embodies many of the virtues of emancipatory education and could therefore hold a unique key to education. To that end, I offer a quote from James Baldwin (in Simonson and Walker, 1988) that addresses the purpose of education: "The purpose of education is to create in a person the ability to look at the world for himself, to make his own decisions, to say to himself this is black or this is white, to decide for himself whether there is a god in heaven or not. To ask such questions of the universe, and then to live with those questions, is the way he achieves his own identity." Baldwin goes on, however: "But no society is really anxious to have that kind of person around. What societies really, ideally want is a citizenry which will simply obey the rules of the society. If a society succeeds in this, that society is about to perish. The obligation of anyone who thinks himself responsible is to examine society and try to change it and fight it—at no matter what risk. This is the only hope society has. This is the only way that societies change" (p. 4).

Baldwin might have also been addressing an aspect of the artist in society. Let me rephrase his words: "An artist is a person with the ability to look at the world for her- or himself, to make her or his own decisions, to say to her- or himself that this is black or this is white, to ask her- or himself whether there is a god in heaven or not. To ask questions of the universe, and then to live with those questions, is the way the artist achieves her or his own identity." As to when society does not seem terribly eager to have the artist around, we have examples of that as well. Recent reactions against the work of various artists who have received grants through the National Endowment for the Arts attest to this.

The artist can be an autonomous agent, but usually is closely connected to society and reacts to it in some way—through a representational expression. What the artist does through artistic activity is what emancipatory educators encourage: critical, reflective, and creative thinking in the context of society, coupled with expression. That expression might be an attempt to change society or to simply explore its complexities.

When we think of knowledge, as Baldwin does, we must consider *whose* knowledge we are talking about and *who* decides what that knowledge is. There are many ways to perceive the world and many lenses through which to examine it. Is it the school's job to prepare future workers who subscribe to one point of view, or should the school be preparing students to consider multiple points of view and ways to interact as adults within an economically based society? Participatory democracy—or democratic education, in theory— would prepare students to think for themselves and debate critical issues in a process that bears on a society. Through the arts, students may have more opportunities to practice some of the skills necessary to becoming concerned, reflective thinkers and citizens.

Because artists are so steeped in representational transformation, they often see things in unusual ways; they rarely see things as either/or. The following poem by Mitsuye Yamada is a good example.

MIRROR MIRROR

People keep asking where I come from
says my son.
Trouble is   I'm american on the inside
               and oriental on the outside

No Kai
Turn that outside in
THIS is what American looks like.[1]

Mitsuye Yamada, Camp Notes and Other Poems (1976)

---

[1] "Mirror Mirror" By Mitsuye Yamada, In *Camp Notes and Other Poems* by Mitsuye Yamada. Brooklyn, NY: Kitchen Table: Women of Color Press, 1992, p. 56. Reprinted by permission of the author and of Kitchen Table: Women of Color Press, Box 40-4920, Brooklyn, NY 11240.

Here, Yamada implores the reader to examine what it means to be an "American." She surprises us with the lines "Turn that outside in / THIS is what American looks like." She deliberately leads us away from considering that one is Oriental *or* American, and instead urges us to consider the relationships of culture as we think about ourselves or others.

Whereas the artist expresses ideas through a medium such as poetry, music, dance, sculpture, or photography, traditional education has concerned itself with expression via words. However, the notion of expressing understandings solely through the written and spoken word has been challenged by a number of recent initiatives and in a number of publications (theme issue of *Middle School Journal* 1993 devoted to Alternative Assessment, including Stowell, McDaniel, Rios, and Kelly; Wiggins, 1993; Winner, 1991; Gallas, 1994, 1991; Wolf, Bixby, Glenn, and Gardner, 1991; Seidel and Walters, 1990; Prospect Center, 1986). Historically, the notion of art as fundamental to experience and knowledge has been discussed with depth and rigor (Dewey, 1959; Storr, 1988; Coomaraswamy, 1934), although it rarely enters into mainstream educational discussions and practice with equal rigor.

When students (like the ones I mentioned in Chapter 1) create a poem, sculpture, or dance to express their evolving ideas, teachers know at the very least that their students are working with the material. The students are taking ideas, working with them, and translating or transforming them into another medium. The artistic translation and representation involve active participation, thereby enabling students to develop both intellectually and emotionally as they construct greater understandings of subject matter.

WHAT DOES IT MEAN TO BE A LEARNER?

Every fall after about four weeks of working together, I ask my preservice student teachers, "What does it mean to be a learner?" I teach a Learning and Instruction course in which we explore teaching and learning relationships, how knowledge is constructed, and the role of metaphors in understanding, among a number of related topics.

Leading up to this question, I ask the students to do several exercises in which they follow other people's understandings of a simple mathematical problem and a poetry exercise. The exercises are based on clinical interviewing techniques discussed by Eleanor Duckworth in *The Having of Wonderful Ideas* (1987), which is based on her own experiences working with Jean Piaget during the 1960s. Inevitably, the students discover that people think about things in ways that are very different from the way they think—an often surprising and moving discovery.

Once the students have gotten over the shock of discovering that people figure out problems in a variety of ways (ones different from their own, in particular), we begin to explore the multiple ways in which people can express knowledge. To do so, I ask the students to represent ideas concerning metamorphosis through the arts. Most students have not had the opportunity to create artistic representations, and at first they tend to be hesitant. I usually begin by asking the students to describe various metamorphoses and life cycles. To get started, we look at a list of metamorphoses generated by first-graders (Gallas, 1991). The list includes egg-baby-grownup-death-dirt; wind-tornado-cyclone-waterspout; egg-tadpole-frog; and egg-caterpillar-cocoon-moth. We also read about how the first-grade students in Gallas's class dramatized their metamorphoses.

After reviewing the first-graders' list and dramatizations, I ask my university students to break into small groups and brainstorm their own list of meta-morphoses. Ideas bounce into the air with great leaps. "I know," says Sherrie, "the life cycle of a dancer." Laura comes up with the metamorphosis of a salad, from seeds to seedlings, to vegetables, to stores, to homes, to dinner plates, to compost, to dirt, and then the process begins again. Angie asks, "How about the life cycle of a spider? How does that work?" From the other corner I hear Christina ask, "How about the metamorphosis of the women's movement over the last ten years?!"

Soon my students are working in groups to create artistic renditions of their ideas. Later they will present their work to the rest of the class. Sherrie and her group decide to make a mobile of dancers of different ages and the changes they experience. They choose the mobile because of its inherent movement is dance-like. They page through magazines looking for dancers and stumble on pictures of budding flowers. They decide that the buds are a "neat" way to describe the beginning of a dancer's career. One person in the group has the idea of hanging the pictures with different colored ribbon: The colors represent stages in a dancer's life—white signifies purity and newness, the beginning dancer; pink represents the intermediary stage of the dancer's career; and gold represents achievement.

As the activity continues, ideas arise, are discussed, are employed. The students are actively engaged; they are searching for ways to work with their ideas and express them. I sense excitement as a student finds another picture in a magazine. "This is perfect!" Lynn calls out. "We can use it for an older dancer who is now looking back on her life."

From the other side of the room I overhear a conversation about com-posting. Laura is describing to Julie what she knows about the role of worms in compost heaps. Then Ruthanne asks what the worms actually do. The three launch into a very scientific discussion of composting, all the while coming up with questions they would like to know the answers to, sparking their curiosity to understand more about this increasingly complex metamorphosis. From Angie's group I hear lots of laughter. They have decided to dramatize the spider and realize they don't know where the web comes from and how the spider actually can manage such a feat. "Does it come from the spider's mouth? From some-where else? How can it actually do that?!"

The classroom is abuzz with excitement and laughter as the students create their representations. I often stroll around to see what is going on, only to find that my students are so engrossed in what they are doing that my presence remains unnoticed. This is quite different from a more traditional classroom, where the teacher talks or gives instructions and the students figure out how to follow. Being out of the limelight, in fact, took some getting used to in my own case, because being at the center of attention can be fun. Letting go of being the center of attention as the teacher is probably one of the most challenging aspects of giving students the freedom to search for knowledge.

If Sherrie, Laura, Ruthanne, or any other student at any grade level were to simply read a chapter about metamorphosis in a school textbook, or were to listen to a lecture and then answer questions on a test, I would be hard-pressed to know if they really understood the material. On the other hand, when they create a mobile or a dramatic rendition representing a metamorphosis, I sense that they have taken the material and translated it into a different context. I can also assess the degree to which they understand the particular concepts or idea, and then I can proceed from there.

The next week held more surprises. Sue Ann, a student in the "spider group," came to class and said she had had the most incredible experience; she had really observed a spider, and it was unbelievable. She described a web-making event to the entire class from beginning to end (with excitement!). Her appreciation for observing nature was growing and she was invested in learning about spiders. So the conversations continued, the enthusiasm grew, and the students were doing exactly what I had hoped: They were taking learning into their own hands.

The art/metamorphosis exercise gave the students the opportunity to translate their ideas into another medium. The artistic activity opened up many avenues through which they could explore and reflect upon the science topic. In addition, the materials themselves—magazines, paper, scissors, glue, markers—provided tools that inspired critical thinking. For example, as the dance group perused the magazines, different pictures would further their thinking or lead it in a new direction. When one of the students found the picture of flower buds, she began to consider the picture as related to her idea. Without the "tools" (in this case, the magazines), she probably would not have thought of the flower bud in relation to a dancer.

The students were also learning about "being a learner," which is our focus. They were able to use their own experiences in learning as a basis for discussions concerning teaching. In fact, class discussions after the exercise focused on the role of the teacher as a facilitator of learning, as well as the role of the learner as an active being working with ideas and reworking them. Students examined their actions in creating representations and debated their usefulness in the classroom, turning to issues of solitude and collaborative learning. Discussions also addressed assessment. In viewing each other's work, each student was beginning to value what others had come to know. In that way, the students began to discuss how as teachers they can assess what a student knows.

Following the metamorphosis work, I ask my students to reflect on being a learner and to create an artistic "representation for understanding." (Although I do this with university students, the same can be done with children if the teacher is interested in exploring and reflecting with them on the nature of learning.) Now, having introduced the notion that people think and learn in a variety of ways, I ask my students to reflect on their own ways of learning and exploring subject matter.

The students are required to accompany their work with a brief written statement describing their art expression. At this later point in the semester, feeling more confident to apply artistic methods to express their understandings, students willingly agree to the assignment. I present the following examples because they represent a range of the responses and forms that students bring to class. These examples offer only a small slice of the inventiveness and variety found within just one class.

Priscilla came to class with a sculpture: a colorfully painted wooden plank with a broken circle of wires (like the spokes of a wheel), words adhered in different places, and this written accompaniment:

My sculpture represents how I see myself as a learner. I am in the center, as the hub of a partially constructed wheel. The hub is in a state of confusion, continually sorting and processing what the receptors are feeding into it. The hub is also where questions and curiosities are stemming from. Emanating from the hub are feelers that eventually become the spokes of the wheel. The feelers reach out into the world and become receptors for new experiences, information, and knowledge. The world is represented by the painting. The painting is abstract and colorful, implying complexity and intrigue. As knowledge is gained the wheel begins to solidify and take shape. But since there is no end to learning, the wheel is never completely formed. The knowledge transmitted back to the hub sparks new questions, or new feelers that spin out and reach for more. The sculpture evokes movement because learning to me is an active never-ending process.

The following explains the words and phrases chosen:

"Save the world?" "Population's global impact" "Conflict": Represent the very large, difficult issues of our times that through learning we must strive to answer.

"Action/Reaction": In the process of learning, I take action upon or react to new ideas and experiences.

"Balance": As a learner, I seek a balance point where my confusion gives way to comprehension.

"Discover": To learn is to discover new thoughts, ideas, ways of perceiving the world.

"Change is in the wind": Learning is about change. My perceptions change when I learn, and this kind of change is inevitable when true knowledge is attained.

The depth of thought expressed in this work is remarkable. Clearly Priscilla felt engaged, maybe even inspired. Having previously proclaimed herself a "non-artist," Priscilla surprised herself with her sculpture. She also noted how her desire to work and think was nourished by her excitement over her emerging product. I, too, was very impressed with this work. The sculpture appealed to my artistic and aesthetic senses. The theme of the piece and the accompanying explanation delighted me because it was clear that Priscilla was deeply engaged in the issues of our class. Her detailed descriptions indicated her attempt to consider learning from many perspectives (including her own) as a complex and lifelong, evolving process.

Although not all students write so extensively, unique statements and creations emerge in this process—much to the continual amazement of the students and their peers. Working on the same question, Ed came to class with a photo of a young child peering around the corner of an opened door. It was accompanied by his statement (see statement and photo below).

More sparse in words than Priscilla, Ed nonetheless presented a convincing representation of what it means to be a learner. The difference between the two is not so much in the differing form of representation (which in and of itself sparked interesting remarks from the class) but in the level to which each took

"What is it like to be a learner? I like to explore what's behind all the doors in life with the honesty, tenacity, and curiosity of a child."

SOURCE: Ken Heyman.

their translation and worked with it. Priscilla articulated more of the complexities of her representation than did Ed. This does not indicate, however, that Ed put less thought into his work. He thought deeply about his representation and felt it captured the very root of what it means to be a learner. He could take his thinking even further by examining the themes of exploration, honesty, tenacity, and curiosity.

In the following example, Alejandra's representation includes an original metaphor:

> What is it like to be a learner? To me, **learning is like the wings of a bird or a butterfly** [emphasis added]. It gives you the ability to soar to unfamiliar territories and reach inconceivable heights. Yet even though they can be strong and powerful they are also delicate and fragile. A teacher has the power to infringe on the learner's capability or give them the freedom to explore the world. With love and support, the wings of knowledge can take you far beyond your wildest dreams.

I find Alejandra's metaphor a convincing, imaginative, and reflective representation for learning. She has taken information and ideas from class, reflected upon them, and created an original metaphor through which she expresses her understandings. She has gone a step further in expanding on that metaphor by describing the places to which the flyer can go and the strength with which it can maneuver. All in all, a provocative representation.

Carrie took another approach. She chose a familiar object and applied reflections concerning learning to it. Taking everyday objects and examining their connections to another subject is a useful tool, especially if students are having difficulty thinking about the problem. In this case one could ask, "How is learning like an apple? a telephone? a piano? a calendar?" and so on. The exercise can pique the creative thinking of any student who is stuck. In the next example, Carrie related learning to waffle making, an analogy she devised on her own:

> When asked how I view myself as a learner, I thought of waffles. I saw raw materials, each of the ingredients, as the information I receive. Information or ingredients come from a variety of sources. The mixing bowls represent the blending of information as my mind accepts it. The measuring cups show that I get information in varying amounts. The mixer is used to blend the information together, when necessary. The waffle iron is the brain where the information is processed. The waffle is the outcome of this processing. Sometimes the waffles do not come out complete, which represents the concept that learning is never complete. The green light on the iron says it's ready to do more processing. The red light signals overload. The butter and variety of syrups show the many ways I can modify or change the information. The plain waffle is the basic information. The toppings are the ways of changing the basic information for other uses or needs.

Interesting ideas are embedded in this work, and an outcome-based educator or evaluator might even enjoy the recipe! We had, in fact, discussed outcome-based education in class. When Carrie shared this representation with the class, an interesting discussion followed. "How do you know when you're ready to do more processing?" asked a peer. "Who determines what is basic information?" asked another student. Thus, Carrie's representation prompted a considerable amount of important discussion.

In giving this assignment, I am not expecting each student to produce a perfect or even near-perfect representation. To be honest, I am not sure what perfection would look like. The purpose of the exercise is to engage the students in thinking and working with their ideas concerning learning. As such I am expecting that the lesson will give them more to consider about teaching and learning, especially by reviewing each other's ideas. We are also reminded about the complexity of learning; that it is an evolving process within ourselves as teachers and as learners; and that the process will be ongoing with our students as well.

A few more examples highlight the diversity of thinking in the class. Karen brought in a collage made of felt pasted onto a cloth background:

Learning can be as comfortable as an old pair of fuzzy slippers. This happens when the new knowledge fits well with my prior knowledge.

Learning can be as fun as a bright pair of boots. Sometimes the concepts are so exciting that I want to dance with enthusiasm.

Learning can also feel as awkward as a pair of 3-inch heels. The concepts seem so scary that I hesitate to try them out.

Here again, we have an example of a student working with something familiar ito create an analogy to learning. Karen explored how different kinds of shoes are analogous to different learning situations. She applied the notion of prior knowledge and the challenge of newness in learning. Sometimes learning can be fun, sometimes scary. It would be interesting to ask Karen to delve deeper into what makes learning fun or scary, and if she is making a judgment as to the benefit of each feeling.

Sherrie brought in a geometrical art piece. In her discussion she also related the idea of prior knowledge to new knowledge. She then focused on the "bridge" that unites prior and new knowledge:

For me, being a learner means trying to fit pieces of knowledge together—making connections between new information and what I have learned previously—revising and putting all of this new information into a form that makes sense and will be useful.

But learning/understanding does not fit neatly into a particular form. It is uneven. Sometimes it overlaps and makes itself into a daring new form. Sometimes it is out there by itself, no sense about it and not useful until something bridges the gap and makes it comprehensible.

Using my creation to portray these ideas, I have used various shapes to show how the information learned is all over the place. There are pieces that connect to other pieces and form a unit of understanding. There are new items as symbolized by the paper cut-outs as well as established knowledge noted by the marking pens. They are all there, floating around, waiting for an opportunity to hookup in some sort of sensible way.

And finally, Karen's crazy quilt metaphor:

A Learner Is Like a Crazy Quilt

A "crazy quilt" is made of swatches of fabric which are remnants from other homemade garments or crafts. These pieces of fabric are arranged in such a way as to create a beautiful pattern in a quilt block. The quilt blocks are then stitched together to form a completely original finished quilt.

For the learner, knowledge and experience are like the swatches of fabric used in a crazy quilt. This knowledge and experience belongs to the learner and builds upon itself over time just as the pieces of remnant fabric which belong to the quilter are collected and added to over time. The knowledge and experience represented by the fabric combine to make a wholly unique pattern. Quilt blocks are connected to make a beautiful and useful piece of art just as a learner's knowledge and experience connect to make a beautiful and unique human being. The only difference is that the quilt has boundaries, the learner has none.

The variety in response and form is fascinating to me as the teacher and to the other students as they share in each other's thinking. It is especially important to remember that these examples come from an "ordinary" cohort of students who have no special training in the arts. Though I ask students to do this assignment every year, I am continually amazed by the representations and metaphors they create, and by the unique qualities that shine through the individual productions. This says to me that imagination and creativity are blossoming in every student. We are too ready to think that they are not. Simply given the opportunity to work through an understanding in an art form, each student can offer a unique perspective to a class. In this way, we as teachers can tap into our students' imaginative resources; and in turn, with their new-found "imaginative confidence," they can begin to apply artistic methods—or ways of knowing in their own practice—with their own students.

I believe that my students' work in exploring various ways of knowing, including artistic ways of knowing, enables them to achieve complex understandings of learning and subsequently give them much to consider in negotiating their role in a future teaching and learning relationship. In sharing their work they are sharing something of themselves, which I believe benefits all in the learning community we call a classroom. My students were invested in their work and the work of their peers; thus, they invested in the learning and instruction issues of the class. Further, they had an experiential basis in addition to a theoretical basis on which to reflect and question teaching and learning relationships as they prepare to move into their own classrooms.

Maxine Greene (1991) reminds us how fundamental the arts can be to learning: "In truth, I do not see how we can educate young persons if we do not enable them on some level to open up spaces for themselves—spaces for communicating across boundaries, for choosing, for becoming different in the midst of intersubjective relationships. . . . That is one of the reasons I would argue for aware engagements with the arts for everyone, so that in this democracy human beings would be less likely to confine themselves to the main text. . . ." Through encounters with the arts, she continues, students may "become aware of the ways in which certain dominant social practices enclose us in molds or frames, define us in accord with extrinsic demands, discourage us from going beyond ourselves, from acting on possibility" (p. 28).

SUMMARY

By having their students create representations and metaphors for understanding, teachers are not only training children to exercise their minds by thinking but are providing a basis from which children may begin asking their own questions of the world around them. Representational and/or metaphoric thinking is a rigorous task that sets the stage for intellectual and emotional growth. The arts, being a natural structure for representational and metaphoric activity, expand the children's expressive outlets as they proceed on their educational adventures. Intellectual growth begins when the student is participating in learning rather than acting as a recipient of knowledge. In this respect the arts can play a crucial role because they demand participation and awareness. Further, they enable students to pursue questions and understandings by making personal connections to knowledge.

QUESTIONS TO PONDER

1. In fostering intellectual growth among your students, what are your hopes and goals for them?
2. Think of times in your own schooling when you felt intellectually challenged. What were those occasions, and what made them challenging?

EXPLORATIONS TO TRY

1. Create your own metaphor and representation on the topic: "What does it mean to be a learner?"

2. Create another representation addressing the question: "What does it mean to be a teacher?"
3. How do the representations compare?

REFERENCES

Belenky, M. F., et al. (1986). *Women's Ways of Knowing: The Development of Self, Voice, and Mind*. New York: Basic Books.

Berthoff, A. (1981). *The Making of Meaning: Metaphors, Models, and Maxims for Writing Teachers*. Montclair, NJ: Boynton/Cook Publishers.

Bissex, G. (1980). *GNYS AT WRK: A Child Learns to Write and Read*. Cambridge, MA: Harvard University Press.

Bowden, D. (1993). "The Limits of Containment: Text-as-Container in Composition Studies." *College Composition and Communication*, Vol. 44, No. 3, October 1993.

Bruner, Jerome (1962). *On Knowing: Essays for the Left Hand*. Cambridge, MA: Harvard University Press.

Coomaraswamy, Ananda K. (1934/1956). *The Transformation of Nature in Art*. New York: Dover.

———. (1959). *Art as Experience*. New York: Capricorn Books.

Duckworth, Eleanor. (1987). *The Having of Wonderful Ideas and Other Essays on Teaching and Learning*. New York: Teachers College Press.

———. (1991). "Twenty-Four, Forty-Two, and I Love You: Keeping It Complex." *Harvard Educational Review*, Vol 61, No 1.

Gallas, K. (1991). Arts as Epistemology: Enabling Children to Know What They Know, *Harvard Educational Review*, Vol. 61, No. 1, February 1991.

———. (1994). *The Languages of Learning*. New York: Teachers College Press.

Gardner, Howard. (1990). "Multiple Intellegences: Implications for Art and Creativity," in William Moody, ed., *Artistic Intelligences: Implications for Education*. New York: Teachers College Press.

———. (1993). *Frames of Mind: The Theory of Multiple Intelligences*, Tenth Anniversary edition. New York: Basic Books.

Goldberg, M. (1992). "Expressing and Assessing Understandings through the Arts." *Phi Delta Kappan*, April, 1992.

Greene, Maxine. (1991). "Texts and Margins." *Harvard Educational Review*, Vol. 61, No. 1.

Hawkins, D. (1978). "Critical Barriers to Science Learning." *Outlook*, Vol. 29, pp. 3–23.

Horton, Julie. (1995). Unpublished manuscript.

Hunter, Diane. (1995). Unpublished manuscript.

Kamii, C. (1984). *Young Children Reinvent Arithmetic*. New York: Teachers College Press.

———. (1989). *Young Children Continue to Reinvent Arithmetic—2nd Grade*. New York: Teachers College Press.

Lakoff, G., and M. Johnson. (1980). *Metaphors We Live By*. Chicago: University of Chicago Press.

Perrone, V. (1989). *Working Papers: Reflections on Teachers, Schools, and Communities*. New York: Teachers College Press.

Piaget, Jean. (1963). *The Origins of Intelligence in Children*. New York: W. W. Norton.

———. (1980). *To Understand Is to Invent: The Future of Education*. New York: Penguin Books.

Prospect Center. (1986). *The Prospect Center Documentary Processes: In Progress.* North Bennington, VT: Prospect Archive and Center for Education and Research.

Schickedanz, J. (1990). *Adams Righting Revolutions.* Portsmouth, NH: Heinemann.

Seidel, S., and J. Walters. (1990). *The Design of Process-Folios for Authentic Assessment.* Unpublished manuscript.

Simonson, R., and S. Walker. (1988). *Multicultural Literacy.* Saint Paul, MN: Graywolf Press.

Storr, Anthony. (1988). *Solitude: A Return to the Self.* New York: Free Press.

Stowell, L., J. McDaniel, F. Rios, M. G. Kelly. (1993). "Casting Wide the Net: Portfolio Assessment in Teacher Education." *Middle School Journal,* Vol. 25, No. 2.

Vygotsky, Lev. (1971). *The Psychology of Art.* Cambridge, MA: MIT Press.

Watson, B., and R. Konicek. (1990). "Teaching for Conceptual Change: Confronting Children's Experience." *Phi Delta Kappan,* May 1990.

Wiggins, G. (1993). Assessment: Authenticity, Context and Validity. *Phi Delta Kappan,* November 1993.

Winner, E. (1991). *Arts Propel: An Introductory Handbook.* Cambridge, MA: Educational Testing Service and Harvard Graduate School of Education (on behalf of Project Zero).

Wolf, D. P., J. Bixby, J. Glenn III, and H. Gardner. (1991). "To Use Their Minds Well: Investigating New Forms of Student Assessment," in G. Grant, ed., *Review of Research in Education.* Washington, DC: American Educational Research Association.

Yamada, Mitsuye. (1976). *Camp Notes and Other Poems.* New York: Kitchen Table: Women of Color Press.

chapter 3

Piaget, Imitation, and the Blues: Reflections on Imagination and Creativity

THE SWAN

The swan gracefully flies
across the red, purple and orange
sunset. Flapping   its snow white
wings only   once or twice.
Flying   in a circle
searching   for a fish.
It dives   down and
snatches   a fish.
Struggling   to soar up
to the   clouds floating
in the sky. The swan drops the
lifeless fish and soars back
to its home . . . the sky.

Troy Geierman, fifth-grader

Creativity and imagination are probably two of the most important aspects of education and spirited living. Without an ability to imagine and create, cultures would stagnate and the world would be far less interesting. In this chapter I will examine the relationships among creativity, imagination, invention, and originality from the viewpoints of both creators and participants (those who attend to a creation). First, I briefly consider a few ways in which creativity has been defined. A thorough review of creativity would fill numerous volumes and could not adequately be reviewed here. In its place, I focus on a few key elements of creatvity and the creative process.

CREATIVITY

In Western cultures creativity is generally viewed as an attribute that few individuals possess. A person is either creative or not. This is usually determined by something the person has made or invented, some problem solved, or some mystery cracked. Jerome Kagan (1967) is quite clear when he writes, "creativity refers to a product, and if made by [a person], we give him [or her] the honor of the adjective" (p. viii). In essence, creativity has become an elitist notion. Only a select talented few are considered to be among the "creative," and the determination of their creativity is based on the judgment of an outcome or product they have put forth. Unfortunately, this view is considerably limiting.

According to R. G. Collingwood (1958), "to create something means to make it non-technically, but consciously and voluntarily" (p. 128). Jerome Bruner (1962), defines creativity as "an act that produces *effective surprise*," what he calls the "hallmark of a creative enterprise" (p. 18). Howard Gardner (1993), to whom we will return later in this chapter, defines a creative individual as a person "who regularly solves problems, fashions products, or defines new questions in a domain in a way that is initially considered novel but that ultimately becomes accepted in a particular cultural setting" (p. 35).

I would like to explore the following scenario. Creativity is innate. Everyone is creative; we are born not only ready but anxious to act upon the creative proclivity within us. In other words, humans are born creative; and as I will show in this chapter, we act creatively throughout infancy and childhood as a process of natural maturation. Our development is dependent upon creative acts. Our ability to journey through the world and communicate our understandings of it are dependent upon everyday acts of creativity. Unfortunately, once we leave childhood, most of us are effectively taught to think that we are not creative and that creativity is something only a few talented souls possess. What a tragedy this is, especially as we consider the role of creativity in educational settings.

Whereas many people focus on a great painting, work of literature, or piece of music as the defining element of a creative person, we will turn to creative work that may or may not culminate in the achievement of a painting, book, song, computer program, or unique perspective of an everday activity. Assigning a definition to creativity proves challenging in part because of its complexity and multiple manifestations. In its place, some have argued as David Perkins does in *The Mind's Best Work* (1981) that we study the process and ask "how the creative person thinks, not what the creative person is" (p. 5).

Characterizing the work of a creative person in terms of a process or *action* that has a number of associated qualities opens many possibilites. Definitions of creativity that rely on the completion of a product or the solving of a problem require us to judge and develop criteria for the judgment calls. This is limiting. In characterizing creativity as an action, we can focus on the activity of creating rather than the outcome, thereby eliminating some of the problems associated with judging a product. In that light, one might contemplate the notion that it is possible for a person to be "creative" but not "original." In formulating a characterization of creativity, we should consider specific qualities. These include motivation, concentration, the making of connections that enable individuals to transcend previous limitations, and reflection.

From birth, an individual is creative. One has to be in order to begin the process of development. An infant begins life with an awareness and a motivation to develop. *Motivation* is the first quality we will associate with creativity. At its most basic level, this motivation manifests itself through a desire to be nourished—both physically and mentally. Next we see the child motivated to imitate the actions of its caregivers or the actions of things around him such as the movement of a mobile in his crib. The work of an infant is to constantly *make connections* that enable him to transcend the limitations of what he already knows and has integrated into his experience. Thus, in order to imitate the action of a parent, a baby must work hard—and creatively—to transcend previous limitations of their actions. This continues as an active process well into the first year of a child's life. The ability to *transcend previous limitations* while constructing and adding new schemas to one's repertoire is another quality associated with the creative process.

Following infancy, play occupies the bulk of a child's development, physically, intellectually, and emotionally. A huge part of playing involves representation—the ability to use symbols. Play also leads us toward identifying a core quality associated with creativity—making connections. In play children are constantly engaged in creating games, fantasies, dramas, new ways to run on the play-ground, and so on. They are also engaged in trial and error as they try to create skyscrapers with their blocks or figure out ways to keep a kite afloat in the air. Play, viewed as an ongoing process, is essentially a creative activity through which children make connections to what they know and use those connections to explore further. Through play they develop an ability to represent their world.

As children grow older and gain experiences from which to draw in their intellectual and emotional lives, concentration and reflection assume an increasingly important role in the process of development. A creative person considers and even questions the actions he or she performs. The reflective nature of the creative person sets her aside from the person who mechanically carries out an assignment or follows through on a task. *Reflection,* then, is another quality associated with creativity.

Creativity permeates every aspect of living and human development and is not limited to early childhood. As I mentioned in a previous chapter, Eleanor Duckworth (1987) considers the essence of all of intellectual development a "creative affair." She argues that the having of wonderful ideas is fundamental to the intellectual development of both children and adults, and that instead of emerging from some mysterious place in the universe, "wonderful ideas are built upon other wonderful ideas" (p. 7). She writes that there are two aspects to providing occasions for wonderful ideas. "One is being willing to accept children's ideas. The other is providing a setting that suggests wonderful ideas to children—different ideas to different children—as they are caught up in intellectual problems that are real to them" (p. 7). Here the arts play an important role. They can provide a methodology and setting for children to work through problems and questions. Further, they provide multiple forms through which children may express and communicate their wonderful ideas.

To emphasize the point that creativity is an innate quality in all human beings, rather than a special ability of a lucky few, I will turn to language and literacy. Although linguists such as Noam Chomsky (1980) argue that humans are pre-programmed for language (universal grammar theory), our ability to employ it is essentially an aesthetic and creative process. Consider how many words we have access to, and the myriad ways we put them together to communicate with others. It is likely that every time we speak we create a sentence that has never been spoken before. The ability to employ everyday language is a creative ability we all possess. In using language we are constantly making aesthetic choices regarding how to express our thoughts to others. Some of us, however, do it better than others. Some of us also have more or less practice in applying language.

As children learn to read and write, they begin to manipulate letters and symbols. Prior to reading, children first develop ways to write as a form of communication. This activity is known to those who study language as "invented spelling." The phenomenon of invented spelling is well documented as a developmental activity whereby children of 4 or 5 years of age "who do not read, but who know the letters of the alphabet and their sounds, show themselves able to compose words and messages on their own, creating their own spellings as they go along" (Chomsky, 1971, p. 499). Carol Chomsky argues that this aspect of development is essentially a creative affair. She compares the work of the child inventing spelling to the work of a child drawing a picture:

> The spontaneous speller composes words, according to their sounds, figuring out for himself what comes first, next, and so on. He does this for his own purposes, as a means of self-expression. Here spelling appears to share some aspects with the activity of drawing a picture. For example, the child who draws a person is not trying to match an arbitrary pattern or to represent what someone else will deem correct or accurate. He works from his own perceptions and chooses to put down on paper those features which in some sense strike him worthy of representation. As he matures, he represents increasingly many of these features and may organize them somewhat differently. The development from early productions to later ones is clearly visible.
>
> This is much the way it is with spellings. The child spells independently, making his own decisions. He has no preconceptions of how the word ought to be spelled nor any expectation that there is a "right" or a "wrong" way to do it. He spells *creatively,* according to some combination of what he perceives and what he considers worthy of representation. [emphasis added] (1971, p. 500)

In speaking and reading, we tap into our ability to imagine. Words only represent objects, images, stories, ideas, emotions. They are not, in and of themselves, anything more than a representative tool. Our ability to imagine what the words represent is a creative activity that is a natural aspect of human development. Again, when we look at human development, we can make a rather convincing argument that we are, by nature, creative beings who have an innate ability to represent our world.

Now I would like to return to infancy and imitation. Viewing creativity as a process leads us on some interesting paths. One path follows the role of imitation as a creative action. Prior to studying the work of Piaget, specifically his book *Play, Dreams, and Imitation in Childhood* (1962), I thought of imitation as a means toward no good end. After all, imitation couldn't be original or creative; further, the thought of certain "imitations," such as imitation chocolate or imitation cheese, made me cringe. In the classroom I imagined that imitation would teach children to act as parrots and not a whole lot more. Imitation would mean that the students did not need to think. I was wrong. I came to this understanding through an interesting musical journey, which I will briefly relate here.

PIAGET, IMITATION, AND THE BLUES

A few years ago I decided I wanted to learn to play the blues on my saxophone. Although I am an accomplished musician in the realm of classical and folk music by Conservatory standards, I wanted to learn something new—to improvise and play the blues. I also felt that I needed to learn music more by ear than by relying on written music, which I imagined any blues teacher would force me to do.

As I began my lessons, my teacher played notes on the piano that I had to imitate on the saxophone. He would play, then I would try to play; he would play, I would try to play; and this went on for many lessons. I should emphasize "try," because imitating him was not easy. I have to say I was surprised how hard it was in the beginning.

Imitating can demand a great deal of effort. As I listened to my teacher's phrases and melodies, my own thoughts emerged: Is the melody going higher or lower? Where on my saxophone do my fingers need to fall? What is the interval between those two notes? Is it a minor or a major interval? The rhythm, what was that rhythm?! There was a lot to think about, and it wasn't easy.

I had to concentrate to identify the intervals and then translate them to the saxophone. I had to listen with extraordinary care to remember the rhythms and flow of the phrases. I had to struggle. I also felt a determination to "get it right." Away from my lessons I began to consider the job of an infant who is essentially engaged in a similar process. I imagined an infant imitating the various moves of his parent or caregiver. I began to contemplate the complexity of and potential of imitation.

Imitation can be a struggle. It can be a search. Imitation can bring on a will of determination. Later in life, it can lead toward the understanding of a subject. In the case of my blues lessons, I was assigned various pieces to learn. My teacher handed me a tape of Thelonius Monk playing one of his compositions, "Mysterioso," and asked me to learn the melody. It is a wonderful, albeit surprising melody that incorporates interesting melodic twists and turns. His reason for choosing this piece was that it was comprised of many intervals of sixths, a common and recurring interval in the blues tradition. He wanted me to be able to recognize and translate that interval to my saxophone.

I took the tape home, listened to it over and over, and tried to get the melody in my ear. After I thought I had it memorized, I picked up my saxophone and tried to find and match the notes. Again, like the exercises in my lessons, it wasn't easy. I had to break the melody into phrases and go back and back until I could translate them to my saxophone. Then I repeated them over and over until I was confident I had them right. As I was proceeding in this work, I realized I was imitating not only the notes that Monk had recorded but also his style and the manner in which the saxophonist on the recording, Johnny Griffin (Monk was the pianist), was breathing.

I was learning not only the notes but the style and articulations of the piece. I was also learning something related to the mood of the music—something I would never be able to do had I learned the piece from sheet music. I began to consider how each interval fell in relation to the beat and melody. I was learning the blues, and I was learning by imitating my teacher, Thelonius Monk, and Johnny Griffin. Yet still, I struggled until the end. It was a hard piece to learn.

After feeling that I had just about gotten "Mysterioso" under my fingers, I found myself practicing it over and over whenever I took my saxophone out of its case. I'd play it backstage while I was warming up for a concert. A fellow musician would say to me, "Oh yeah, I know that tune, it's 'Mysterioso,' right? By Monk—great tune." Soon, the tune became second nature. I found that I didn't need to think about it in order to play it. What a joy to be able to pull out my saxophone and just be able to play "Mysterioso"! I even began to wonder what exactly had been so hard to learn in the first place.

Then I returned to the infant determined to imitate something new—struggling, practicing, experiencing the joy in getting it to happen and then having it become second nature. The work involved in imitating began to take on a new light, not only for me and the blues but for the infants I was studying in Piaget's book. I realized that imitation can be an intensely creative process whereby one is engaged in the action of making new connections. In my case, it was the process of figuring out a blues standard. In the case of the infant, it is how to re-create what is going on around him, or the ability to make an interesting thing happen over and over.

I should point out that not all imitation involves such a creative process as did my learning "Mysterioso," or every aspect of infancy as it relates to transcending previous limitations. Consider the case of music students in a third-grade classroom. The students are all learning to play the recorder. As the young music teacher with 28 students in front of her begins the lesson, clusters of sound emerge in drifts. I still have a tendency to tremble when I think of that beginning music teacher (how did I ever cope?). The teacher plays a phrase on the recorder; the students watch her fingers and imitate the movements and sounds she creates. Actually, the sounds are secondary; the students are mostly watching her fingers in an effort to re-create what was presented to them. In general, most of the students succeed.

By comparison, the recorder lesson seems a far less demanding exercise than learning the blues. In the case of the blues, I really wanted to learn. This desire provided a motivation to succeed in working at the style and specific notes. Most of the third-graders didn't care much to learn the recorder, just enough to pass the music class and move on to the xylophones! The children were not motivated, nor were they curious. Instead, they were acting mechanically. While studying the blues I reflected on my actions; the third-graders had little need or real opportunity to reflect on their actions. Finally, I made a number of connections that enabled me to transcend my own limitations. The third-graders didn't have that same kind of opportunity.

Drawing some conclusions from these examples, I would argue that imitation can be a creative process, an extremely useful tool in learning if a student is motivated. Sometimes imitation (even as a mechanical act) can be used to simply get a student interested in something—such as the recorder. As a creative act, however, imitation is like a puzzle that requires motivation, concentration, struggle, reflection, and the making of connections. In successfully matching an outcome, the individual transcends previous limitations. It is interesting that imitation as a creative act does not result in an original product, which is usually the judgment of creativity. Thus, an individual can be engaged in a creative process without having to be original. The work involved in imitation is creative, although the end product is not.

IMAGINATION

The relation of imagination to creativity merits attention. It could be argued that imagining is the core of creating. One must imagine in order to create, although one need not create in order to imagine. However, if creativity is viewed as an action or process, the line tends to blur. In that light, imagination could be viewed as a creative process. Perhaps the difference lies in transcending limitations. For example, if I am feeling particularly sad on any given day, I might try to lessen the sadness by imagining myself on a Cape Cod beach—a place I find peaceful. I'm working hard to get to that beach, but I'm not necessarily transcending new boundaries to get there.

Perhaps we can agree that imagination relates to an awareness or consciousness of some sort. R. W. Gerard (in Ghiselin, 1952) writes that "imagination is an action of the mind that produces a new idea or insight" (p. 226). Thus, imagining is a process by which we can perceive things in new or different ways.

Mary Warnock is a scholar who has written extensively on imagination. After critically reviewing the literature on imagination, she comes to the following interpretation. What I find intriguing is her attention to the absent as well as the present in our ability to imagine our world. Further, she posits emotion as a valid arena from which the imagination might emerge.

> There is a power in the human mind which is at work in our everyday perception of the world, and is also at work in our thoughts about what is absent; which enables us to see the world, whether present or absent as significant, and also present this vision to others, for them to share or reject. And this power, though it gives us "thought-imbued" perception (it keeps the thought alive in perception), is not only intellectual. Its impetus comes from the emotions as much from the reason, from the heart as much from the head. (Warnock, 1976, p. 196)

By imagining, a person can detach herself from the ordinary or the everyday and enter a world filled with possibilities. Though artists might be more practiced at imagining, it is an activity that all of us can do. One of the more interesting roles a teacher can play is to place her students in positions where they can actively practice their imagination. This might be in the writing of questions about the life of a raindrop: Does it know where it is falling? Do raindrops go on vacation? Do raindrops miss the ocean? Does the sun move out of the raindrop's way? Or it might be an exercise of juxtaposition, as I have created in the following poem:

Have you ever seen music fly
or listened closely to a painting?
I sang a dance once and
sculptured a poem
in blues and deep grays
as a touch of sandstone lifted
each word to the stars
shooting them outward and
downward encircling planets
until I caught them
back again
in my bare hands

In my poem, I have done at least two things. I have playfully imagined art forms in a new way, and through the poem I have implored readers to stretch their own sensitivity and understandings. I applied my imagination when I created the poem. In so doing, I entered a new arena and was engaged in a creative process. I would characterize this work as meditative. The creative process moves me into another space where I can be lost in contemplation as

I work with images, ideas, and feelings. Often, after having worked in a creative manner, I look back on my work and wonder to myself, "Did I really do that?!"

Children can tap into their natural ability to be creative with ease. That being so, what ignites the creative process? What sets the stage for a child to engage in acting creatively so that the moment of discovery or transcendence occurs? First, the teacher might consider what interests particular children and piques their curiosity. Second, the teacher may be a "creative role model" and practice the activity of creativity with her students. She can do this by providing occasions for them to probe deeply into ideas. She can set up challenges— perhaps playful ones—that inspire them to engage in learning and reflective thinking that become an evolving process, not an outcome.

Here again the arts play a fundamental role in teaching and learning. They provide the challenges and opportunities for children to explore their questions. They provide a medium of expression for working with ideas and feelings. They offer the chance to stretch one's imagination and creativity. In fact, I believe that without the arts, some children would not find a way to tap into their creative potential. The arts also encourage discipline and dedication. From my own experience, that discipline and dedication can be applied to other areas of living as well. As a 10-year-old, I practiced my guitar for hours. This discipline and dedication laid the groundwork for many aspects of my work today. I am convinced that what I learned from my guitar experience enables me to sit for hours and concentrate on writing this book, or to focus at some length on an idea or issue I find intriguing.

HOWARD GARDNER, CREATIVITY, AND THE CLASSROOM

Howard Gardner is a well-known and respected educator who has proposed a theory of multiple intelligences. He has written extensively on creativity, which he links to the theory of multiple intelligences. His definition of a creative individual "as a person who regularly solves problems fashions products, or defines new questions in a domain in a way that is initially considered novel but that ultimately becomes accepted in a particular cultural setting" (1993, p. 35), has interesting implications when applied to multicultural classroom settings.

In his book *Creating Minds* (1993a), Gardner expounds on his theory of multiple intelligences by trying to understand and illuminate the anatomy of creativity. He discusses seven individuals from the modern era that typify the seven intelligences—Sigmund Freud, Albert Einstein, Pablo Picasso, Igor Stravinsky, T. S. Eliot, Martha Graham, and Mahatma Gandhi—and examines them in light of being creative. He devises a framework through which to examine their creativity.

Numerous questions come to mind in considering this work. Is Gardner's definition of creativity adequate? Can it be generalized, as Gardner argues, that his seven predominantly Western and male case studies constitute a "full-blown" research study of the nature of human creativity? How do Gardner's methodology and framework apply to children and women of diverse cultures and linguistic backgrounds? In examining his framework, must the distinction of creativity depend on the judgment of a product (or problem solved?) If so, who does the judging and who has the means to offer their product for such judgment? What is the role of the imagination in creativity? Finally, as I have asked elsewhere (Goldberg, 1991), what distinguishes intelligence from creativity in Gardner's view? The highlighted individuals were originally introduced to readers as intelligent. Now they are also introduced as creative. In what ways are intelligence and creativity different? Alike?

A person who creates is not necessarily consciously engaged in solving a problem or creating a product. The person creating might be the child on the playground, or the child engaged in invented spelling to communicate a message to a friend or parent. The person might have made a mistake or undertaken a playful activity whereby something interesting occurred. George Eliot, the writer, once said in a conversation with Herbert Spencer, "It has never been my way to set before myself a problem and puzzle out an answer. The conclusions at which I have from time of time arrived, have not been arrived at as solutions of questions raised; but have arrived at unaware" (in Ghiselin, 1952, p. 224).

Many people create as a result of play, stress, political urgency, or elation. Often the creative connection is discovered unexpectedly through play. For example, Sir Alexander Fleming, the Scottish bacteriologist (also from the modern era, 1881-1955) known for his discovery of penicillin, was a man who thrived on play. "I play with microbes. . . . It is very pleasant to break the rules" (in Cole, 1988, p. 16). Although it might be argued that Fleming set out to solve a problem when he discovered penicillin, it is also true that play (according to Fleming) was essential to his work in the sciences and, thus, his creative ability. It is not unusual for a child in a class to recognize that he can create something new as a result of spilling paint on a piece of paper. Nor is it unusual for a child in a class to happen upon a new word combination through playing with words, and then to incorporate that word-play into a creative poem or other expression.

As I argued earlier in this chapter, play can be an intensely creative time. It is an opportunity to break the rules, open the door of discovery, and thereby create. Many musicians and composers know this aspect of creating very well—it may lie in one's ability to improvise, that is, to play with sounds. Stephen Nachmanovich (1990) writes, "looking into the moment of improvisation, I was uncovering patterns related to every kind of creativity. . . . I came to see improvisation as the master key to creativity" (p. 6). Creativity as action (in this case, play) is a natural aspect of human development. Imagine two children meeting on the playground for the first time. "Before they have exchanged two words they are running and spinning about, inventing paths and games around the swings and trees. This is the essence of improvisation—play, a kind of freedom that allows spontaneous creative energy" (Goldberg, 1990, p. 381). Surely, this scenario of play has a place in a definition of creativity.

An event might trigger the creative process, enabling one to make new connections or transcend limitations. In Chapter 1 I mentioned the Ladino musical group that visited with a fifth-grade bilingual class. Their visit and their music triggered a powerful and emotional creative action among the children. Adrienne Rich (1993) relays a similar notion in describing a poem composed by Audre Lorde, "Power": "An event may ignite a poem (which may be labeled a 'protest' poem) but not because the poet has 'decided' to address the event" (p. 71). In this case, Rich tells the reader, Lorde did not choose to fashion a poem or solve a problem. She created out of another need. Lorde herself writes of that need, "And that sense of writing at the edge, out of urgency, *not because you chose it but because you have to—that sense of survival*—that's what the poem is out of" [emphasis added] (in Rich, p. 70).

People create out of stress or frustration, as much as they do out of elation or jubilation. In all cases (and all the gray areas in between), the creative act stems from a reflection of or reaction to experience rather than a need to solve a problem or fashion a product. My point is this: A definition of creativity that focuses on a product or problem solved, as Gardner's definition does, fails to take into account a wide range of experiences that promote creativity. It limits the conception of creativity to products judged according to previous experiences and contexts rather than allowing creativity to be related to new actions (judged according to the individual).

Especially from the standpoint of an artist, ultimately focusing on the judgment of a product can be overly simplistic. The creative work of an artist does not lie in the signature on a painting or the performance of a composition; it lies in the mixing of colors on a palette or the juxtaposition of musical notes to form an interesting chord. In further relating this notion of end-product to the work of children, we come up against an interesting dilemma. It is not unusual to encounter children who create and re-create but who may not be original in their finished products. Is a child who re-creates the wheel as creative as the person who first fashioned that product? I would say yes. But the child's product is not original. Many times, we find a child thoroughly engaged in figuring out a unique solution to a problem. Could that process be considered creative even if no product emerges or the solution fails?

Questions of judgment are usually fraught with problems, particularly when the judgments are based on standards created by a club of "great minds" (traditionally, Western male-centered standards). The question of access is immediately an issue. Let me illustrate this point within the realm of Western European culture, just prior to the modern era in the mid-1800s.

George Sand was a prolific and well-known writer at that time. She adopted a male name to gain acceptance in the field. Because of her gender she had little chance of being accepted into the judging arena. She was told by Monsieur de Keratry, a popular writer and critic, "Believe me, don't make books, make babies." This statement came after he expounded on his "theories concerning the inferiority of women and the impossibility for even the most intelligent among them to write a good book" (Sand in Barry, 1979, p. 323). If one doesn't have access to the judging club to begin with, how can one ever be judged as creative? If one is judged by the existing standards, one stands little chance of favorable acceptance. In other words, how can we be sure of a judgment of creativity when the judges are most likely biased owing to their attitudes and positions in society?

Another illustration may be drawn from the life of Muriel Rukeyser, a poet of the modern era. Rukeyser is not well known, although she was recognized late in life by a number of her peers. Her battle was not uncommon for women, then and now. Adrienne Rich (1993) describes her plight:

> in the history of poetry and ideas in the United States—always difficult to grasp because of narrow definitions, cultural ghettos, the politics of canon makers—she [Rukeyser] has not been seriously considered in the way that, say, the group of politically conservative white southern poets known as the Fugitives or the generation of men thought to have shaped "modern poetry"—Ezra Pound, T. S. Eliot, William Carlos Williams, Wallace Stevens—have been considered. . . . Her poetry not only didn't fit the critical labels, she actually defied the going classifications. (pp. 99–100)

George Sand knew how to play the game. Perhaps Rukeyser did not. In the end, Sand might be considered creative because others in her field recognized her position as a writer. But aside from her clever way of entering the playing field, and thus the club of judgment, can we assess if she is creative? She gained acceptance by her peers, but does that acceptance equate with intelligence or creativity?

Let us come back to the present and see if things are different. In my own experience as a woman saxophonist, I have experienced firsthand denial into the "clubs" where male musicians gather. One summer my musical ensemble (an internationally acclaimed performing and recording ensemble) was asked to perform at the Montreal Jazz Festival, an international festival. We were to take center stage (before a crowd of 40,000) in collaboration with a French Canadian ensemble, which was all men. When it came time to practice together, I was politely asked by the men in the brass section of the French Canadian ensemble to "lay out" of the solo sections (i.e., not play) because they had practiced this before and it was a difficult part. However, the trombone player from my band— a man—was not asked to do the same. He was immediately accepted; the French Canadian male performers did not question his ability to play. My feelings at the time were of frustration, knowing that my gender clouded their judgment prior to hearing me play.

In light of Gardner's framework that incorporates judgment by peers, I cannot help but wonder how many people are denied entry into judging arenas not only because of gender but because of color, culture, social status, or political status. I also wonder how many individuals are not deemed "creative" because they have chosen not to share their work with their peers. Gardner does present a response to this question in the conclusion to his book. "I do not insist on the notion of acceptance by the field because I believe that creativity is a popularity contest," he writes, "but rather because I know of no other criterion that is reliable in the long run" (1993, p. 389).

How do we create standards for judging children's work? First, we must recognize that our standards may not apply to the ones set by the children themselves. Second, it is imperative to critique the work of children in a constructive, encouraging, and rigorous manner while at the same time finding ways to train students to critique their own work and understand that there is always room for taking an idea or question further. As children come to rely on their own abilities to reflect critically on their work, they become more self-confident. In this way, they can be autonomous in their ability to forge forward rather than creating work just to please a teacher or critic. In supporting the children, the teacher may adapt her method of grading and assessment so that each child's progress is judged according to his or her previous work rather than on an arbitrary standard that applies to the class as a whole. This can be achieved, for example, through the use of student portfolios.

What are the implications of Gardner's ideas for teaching and learning? Creativity can be conceived as domain-specific, much as Gardner presents intelligences. In this regard, the boundaries of creativity might be expanded to the benefit of individual students. It is true that Gardner's definition and framework apply to some creative people. His emphasis on problem solving is something that most teachers find valuable. Indeed, I find it valuable as well, and some of my most creative moments have stemmed from solving problems. However, problem solving in and of itself needn't be a creative affair. Moreover, one can be creative without solving any particular problem.

Judgment or assessment of creativity presents interesting challenges. It is difficult to cross the boundaries of cultural standards; yet without that effort, certain children might fall through the cracks and be left unrecognized for their work. In addition, it is interesting to consider the relationship of originality to the creative process. Although Gardner's definition speaks to creativity, perhaps it speaks better to the notion of originality. Finally, it is interesting to try to place the role of imagination in Gardner's conceptualization. Although he doesn't address this issue, it can have an important impact on setting up activities that underscore creative moments.

CREATIVITY AND TECHNIQUE

It is important to understand that for a creator or participant, the process of working in the arts encompasses creativity *and* technique. Creativity involves the qualities already mentioned throughout this chapter; it occurs within the context of feelings and a connectedness to or alienation from one's culture. Being creative is essentially a process of awareness that can open new doors and change existing perceptions. Technique is the "how-to" of any art form, ranging from how one holds the brush to how one mixes the paints.

Technique is often given more attention and recognition than creativity in Western culture. It is hard not to be impressed with the violinist who can play skillfully and with gusto. Many people consider technique and creativity as one when thinking about art. But technique is only a vehicle that enables creativity to flow with ease. Let's take an example from music. When most children practice scales and fingerings on their instruments, they are practicing technique—the "how-to" of playing their instrument. The ability to read music is technique. Once a person has some degree of technique, they can let the music happen. Technique provides the vehicle for music to flow through an instrument, and it is definitely fundamental in promoting creativity.[1]

This distinction is particularly important in terms of encouraging children to work artistically. By focusing on the act of creating rather than the judgment of a product, the teacher can encourage students to be imaginative and create an atmosphere in which a desire to create—that is, to see things in new ways and explore complexities—is celebrated. On the other hand, technique enables one to create more easily. As a musician, I am better prepared to create a song or play my instrument if I have mastered some technique. A true artist has a balance of technique and creativity and uses both.

Technique is often aided by an awareness of available tools. Consider water color painting: Having paper that does not repel water is essential; knowing which brush will serve one's purpose enables one to paint with ease. The same is true for learning in general. Providing students with proper tools enables them to work both technically and creatively. In the arts, tools include the implements of the art form. In general education, tools may include microscopes, rulers, dictionaries, source books, and so on. On a more basic level, students need communication tools—spoken, written, artistic, movement, and musical languages—in order to work with and express their understandings.

CREATOR AND PARTICIPANT

At the opening of this chapter I alluded to the idea of creator and participant. Let me briefly expand on that notion as it relates to education. A student can engage with the arts as a creator or as a participant (audience member). Both call for action and attention on the part of the individual involved. When an individual writes a poem, that person is engaging in a creative, reflective act representing in words, phrasing, syntax, and grammar some notion about the world. The process of writing can even clarify those understandings for the individual. When someone else reads the poem and begins to engage with it, poetry happens again. It is in the engagement that the poetry lies, not in the symbols written on the page. Though the words on the page provide the initial

---

[1] If the reader is interested in learning more about technique, especially with regard to music, I recommend Vernon Howard's work (1982, 1991, 1992).

outline of consideration, the poem in fact comes alive only through active engagement on the part of the reader. We therefore have two levels of creation in any artwork that is shared. First is the primary artist whose work might be cathartic, an exercise, or a labor of love. Second, once the art is offered to the public, the engagement with the work takes on many other qualities.[2] A person in Alaska might see something very different in a poem written by Alice Walker than someone reading the same poem in Australia. Both might interpret things that Alice Walker intended or didn't intend, considered or hadn't considered. In either case, what matters is that the poem is pivotal as the genesis of an artistic experience for all—creator and audience.

SUMMARY

Creativity may be characterized as a lifelong and natural process by which individuals journey to new places in their exploration, understanding, and experience of life. Certain qualities can be extracted from the creative process to describe it: motivation, reflection, and the making of connections to transcend previous limitations. Creativity is not a process reserved for artists alone. In fact, when creativity takes center stage in a classroom, members of the learning community can be transformed and inspired to develop many wonderful ideas, inventions, and solutions. The action of creating and the results of engaging in creative processes can be judged according to each individual rather than according to others. In fact, it is important to encourage students to judge themselves and create rigorous criteria by which to reflect on their work. In this way, students can be engaged in creative actions and reflective thinking as they explore all there is to learn.

QUESTIONS TO PONDER

1. Read more about Howard Gardner and his theories of intelligence and creativity. How do you think intelligence and creativity are related? You also might want to consider what others have written about creativity, including David Perkins, Vera John-Steiner, Jerome Bruner, Ananda Coomaraswamy, and Mihaly Csikszentmihalyi.
2. Are notions of imagination and creativity culture-specific? How would you go about answering this question?

---

[2] Roger Sessions (in Morgenstern, 1956) posits a similar notion in discussing the relationship between composers and performers. He describes composers as "primary artists" and performers as "secondary artists." While his analysis lends a hierarchical relationship to composers and performers, I make the argument that artists and audiences are on more equal footing as participants in the arts.

EXPLORATIONS TO TRY

1. Observe preschool children at play with blocks. Make two lists: (1) a list of what they are doing, and (2) a list of the ways in which they are being creative in their actions. Use the "qualities" associated with creativity as your guideline for thinking about creative actions.
2. Think of some moment or time in your life when you felt creative or imaginative. What made it different from other "everyday" events in your experience? Describe your thoughts in an essay.
3. With a partner, develop a list of ways in which to create a learning community/classroom that would support imaginative, creative, and reflective thinking and actions. Be specific.

REFERENCES

Barry, Joseph, ed. (1979). *George Sand in Her Own Words.* New York: Anchor Books.

Bruner, Jerome. (1962). *On Knowing: Essays for the Left Hand.* Cambridge, MA: Harvard University Press.

Chomsky, Carol (1971). "Invented Spelling in the Open Classroom," *WORD,* Vol. 27, 1971, pp. 499–518.

Chomsky, Noam. (1980). In *Language and Learning: The Debate between Jean Piaget and Noam Chomsky.* Edited by Massimo Piattelli-Palmarini. Cambridge, MA: Harvard University Press.

Cole, K. C. (1988). "Play, by Definition, Suspends the Rules," *New York Times,* November 30, Section 3, p. 16, col. 2.

Collingwood, R. G. (1958). *The Principles of Art.* New York: Oxford University Press Paperback.

Duckworth, E. (1987). *The Having of Wonderful Ideas and Other Essays on Teaching and Learning.* New York: Teachers College Press.

Gardner, Howard. (1993). *Creating Minds: An Anatomy of Creativity as Seen through the Lives of Freud, Einstein, Picasso, Stravinsky, Eliot, Graham, and Ghandi.* New York: Basic Books.

Ghiselin, Brewster, ed. (1952). *The Creative Process.* New York: New American Library.

Goldberg, Merryl. (1990). Review of "Free Play: Improvisation in Life and Art," *Harvard Educational Review,* Vol. 60, No. 3.

———. (1991). Review of "Artistic Intelligences: Implications for Education," *Harvard Educational Review,* Vol. 61, No. 3.

Howard, V. A. (1982). *Artistry: The Work of Artists.* Indianapolis: Hackett Publishing Company.

———. (1991). "And Practice Drives Me Mad; Or, the Drudgery of Drill." *Harvard Educational Review,* Vol. 61, No. 1, February 1991.

———. (1992). *Learning by All Means: Lessons from the Arts.* New York: Peter Lang.

Kagan, Jerome, ed. (1967). *Creativity and Learning.* Boston: Beacon Press.

Morgenstern, Sam, ed. (1956). *Composers on Music: An Anthology of Composer's Writings from Palestrina to Copland.* New York: Pantheon Books.

Nachmanovich, Stephen. (1990). *Free Play: Improvisation in Life and Art.* Los Angeles: Jeremy P. Tarcher.

Perkins, D. N. (1981). *The Mind's Best Work.* Cambridge, MA: Harvard University Press.
Piaget, Jean (1962). *Play, Dreams, and Imitation in Childhood.* New York: W. W. Norton.
Rich, Adrienne (1993). *What Is Found There.* New York: W. W. Norton.
Warnock, Mary. (1976). *Imagination.* Berkeley and Los Angeles: University of California Press.

chapter 4

Communication, Expression, and Experience: Literacy and the Arts

Meteors fly like a fly
maybe it's a butterfly
with its wings spread
high in the sky

> *Jaime Padilla,*
> *fourth-grader*

How can the arts be fundamental to becoming literate? How does using the arts provide an effective methodology for acquiring reading, writing, comprehension, and communication skills? These are the questions with which we will begin our journey into the relationships between literacy and the arts. First I will examine ways to set a context in which a rich literary environment is created. Then I will discuss ways to learn with and through the arts. This includes teaching cursive writing through movement, and spelling and vocabulary through drawing (picto-spelling). Finally, I will examine the uses of poetry as it relates to teaching a second language, as well as its potential use in language transitional and bilingual classrooms.

As I argued in Chapter 1, I view the arts as languages (visual, aural, tactile, kinesthetic) that are a part of the everyday communication available to students in a classroom. Although some students have difficulty crossing "word" language barriers, the arts can join students through a common language. This relates directly to Principles 2 and 4 of multicultural education and the arts (see principles on pp. 14–15). Art as language provides freedom of expression for second language learners and in so doing builds bridges among students as they work collaboratively. In a class where some students speak English, others Spanish, and yet others Cambodian, verbal communication can at times be difficult. Yet those students can find common ground in painting, music, drama, movement, sculpture, photography, and so on. The arts can be uniting, providing common languages and fostering intergroup harmony.

Developmentally, the arts provide a means for children as they learn to represent images and ideas. Representation is a major focus of early learning. Through dramatic play, children develop language and communication skills. Dramatic play sets the stage for creative language and symbolic development, especially in an environment that includes a variety of materials (e.g., costumes and props) that support creative play and thinking. Children's speech patterns, which represent early communication attempts, often emerge from a playing with sounds in such environments. According to Nancy Cecil and Phyllis Lauritzen (1994), "Speech play becomes more social as children mature and relate to peers. Joint conversations with creative back-and-forth turns delight participants" (p. 14).

Cecil and Lauritzen recommend providing young students with an environment that encourages literacy development: "A literary-rich dramatic play area would include pencils and papers for waiters and waitresses to write customers' orders in a restaurant that has a printed menu, and alongside the print a matching rebus menu; magazines, newspapers, and books in the playhouse; prescription pads for the doctor's office; signs for stores; notepads for a refrigerator door; stationery, envelopes, and stamps for letters to be written and delivered to the addressee; and any reading and writing materials applicable to the real-life situations being dramatized" (p. 15).

A creative twist on sharing time can provide another entry into developing communication and creative speech skills. Karen Gallas (1994) discusses the use of sharing time to tell "made-up" stories. As she reflected on the different kinds of talk in the classroom, she began to question her role in influencing classroom discourse. After careful consideration, she decided to turn sharing time over to her first-graders. "By removing myself from the teacher's traditional role in sharing time," Gallas writes, "I could explore what happened when the children became the primary audience, or the 'ratifiers' of the discourse" (p. 18). Her turning over of sharing time opened the door for many students not comfortable with the more traditional "show and tell" to contribute in a less formal manner. A child who was homeless with very few possessions could make up a story and travel to the imaginary place where many things are possible. This in fact happened in Gallas's class. In turn, the other children traveled thoughtfully along, asking questions and encouraging the speaker to continue the story.

LITERACY WITH THE ARTS

There are numerous ways to attain literacy skills with the arts. Perhaps the most obvious is to introduce students to quality poetry and literature. Simple, but effective. Like those engaged in Whole Language classroom techniques, utilizing published poetry and literature either instead of or in addition to traditional textbooks enhances learning and at the same time introduces students to great works of art. There are also a number of wonderful children's books that concern themselves with the arts, including biographies of artists. In Chapter 8 we will examine a number of these books and their potential in the classroom.

I have found that students are especially drawn to reading and writing poetry. I believe they are drawn to poetry in part because it is a playful form of writing. Reading poetry can be like figuring out a puzzle; it often has interesting twists and turns, not to mention a concise quality. Not only do children enjoy playing; but as we examined in Chapter 3, it comprises the bulk of their early learning. Consider poems by Shel Silverstein. His poems tend to be humorous, with a twist (puzzle) and to the point. Their compact nature is inviting to beginning readers and second language learners. It is not over-whelming, and its playful quality intrigues young readers.

Storytelling is a natural way to engage students in applying language. Have students examine paintings or sculptures in a museum or reproductions brought into the classroom and create a story to accompany the artwork. I observed a class of second-graders as they did this exercise in a local art museum. The exhibit, entitled "Revisiting Landscape," included a number of paintings about nature. The children sat around one painting and observed it closely, identifying things they noticed such as trees, reflections, water, leaves, and colors. Next the teacher asked them to think of a story to accompany the picture. The results were fascinating and imaginative. One student placed fairies in the story, another invented a game of hide and seek through the trees in the painting, and another student told a tale of a family on a summer picnic.

One could do a similar activity by choosing music for the children to listen to and compose a story. The storytelling may take the form of telling, drama, or writing. You might incorporate writing by asking the children to outline a story and then expand on it by telling it out loud. Children may enjoy composing a story to accompany a movement or dance. Even a dancer who exerts the slightest movement could provide the inspiration for an imaginative tale.

CURSIVE WRITING THROUGH THE ARTS

In a workshop I attended with my student teachers, I was introduced to teaching cursive writing through movement. Dancer and choreographer Bella Lewitzky led this session, which we all found to be an intriguing example of learning through the arts. Lewitzky and her company were given the following problem: A group of young students with whom they were to work were having difficulty grasping cursive writing. Never afraid of a challenge, the dancers devised a way to engage the children in thinking about curves and motion with their bodies.

The dancers asked all the children to stand and begin to make large curving motions with their bodies—figure eights, half circles, and loops. Next the dancers asked the children to do the same motions, but on a slant. No problem. Now the figure eights, half circles, and loops were transformed into giant "L's," "S's,"

rom the giant motions the dancers got the children to make
ler and smaller and smaller until they were so small as to be
iece of paper. Having experienced the movement of the cursive
their bodies, they were far more suited to apply it on a piece
hat workshop, many of my students have tried the exercise in
their classes with great success.

PICTO-SPELLING LEARNING THROUGH THE ARTS

Picto-spelling is an activity that engages children in both spelling and vocabulary
lessons. It involves drawing pictures that incorporate the letters of a specific
word in one of two ways. In the first way, the letters are used to create the
picture or meaning of a word. See Figure 4.1 by a fifth-grader demonstrating
"dinosaur" and "fish." Each picto-spelling is created by using of the letters of
the word.

Another creative way in which students have developed picto-spellings
involves incorporating the word into a descriptive picture. Figure 4.2 shows the

FIGURE 4.1 Picto-spelling of "dinosaur" and "fish."

FIGURE 4.2   Picto-spelling of "round."

word "round." The student clearly demonstrates an understanding of the meaning of the word by displaying its shape through the picto-spelling. Figure 4.3 on p. 64 shows a depiction of the word "dread." In this clever picto-spelling the child draws a plane going down, alluding to an enactment of the word "dread." The "D's" are on the wings, as is the letter "E." The "R" is in the nose of the plane and the "A" is on the tail. "Snap," Figure 4.4 on p. 65, is a picto-spelling that shows the action of the word.

By creating picto-spellings such as the examples shown here, students engage in creative thinking as they learn specific spellings and vocabulary. As a test of their comprehension, the picto-spellings provide a concrete indication of their understanding of specific words.

STORY COMPREHENSION LEARNING
THROUGH THE ARTS

When children dramatize, move to, or create music to represent a story, they become actively involved in working with the ideas in the story. Their engagement with a story through the arts allows them to transform the story ideas

FIGURE 4.3   Picto-spelling of "dread."

from the medium of words to the medium of drama, movement, or dance. Through that translation, the children engage with the ideas, characters, and feelings of the story. As they translate the words to art forms, each story comes to life. Indeed, the act of transforming or translating is fundamental to attaining understanding or comprehension. This next section highlights Principle 1 (p. 14) of multicultural education and the arts by demonstrating how the arts expand the expressive outlets available to children as they engage with reading.

When children actively engage with a book or story through the arts, they have the opportunity to gain ownership of the story rather than merely assimilating the story that is given them. Students move from being listeners to being participants in mediums that encourage the crossing of boundaries and seeing new borders. For small children, dramatizing a story helps to integrate the sequence of events. In so doing, the drama opens the door toward touching one's physical, spiritual, emotional, and intellectual modalities.

If we return to the notion of the arts as languages, we can see the children's potential as they use these languages to work deeply with subject matter and ideas; in this case, a storybook. The teacher introduces a book to children with the expectation that they will engage with its complexities, including the sequence of events, individual characters, and the meaning. In order to do this, the children must make the story their own and move beyond a rote memoriza-

FIGURE 4.4 Picto-spelling of "snap."

tion. By translating the story into drama, movement, or music, the students have a chance to interact with the characters and work with them closely. The students are placed in position whereby they reflect on and evaluate aspects of the story in order to communicate it to others.

A child engaging in these artistic processes of translation becomes a character in the story. This allows the teacher to follow the way in which the child understands and expresses her understanding of the character. When a child moves like the swan in the story, the teacher knows the child has integrated some idea of the swan into her thinking. When a child is able to add music to the story, the teacher knows the child is considering and reflecting on aspects of the action while playing with the book's ideas. Moreover, teaching story comprehension through the arts can add interest and involvement to the study. Approaching character understanding through the arts encourages children to become active thinkers in addition to listeners. In so doing, they begin to work with symbol systems other than written language as a way to communicate their understandings.

Drama (Visual and Auditory)

How is a child's acting out of a story different than reading it or listening to it? When a child acts out a story she has read or heard, she has the opportunity to *become* the story—to internalize the characters, action, emotions. In order to be a character, she must understand something about that character. Therefore, in acting out the story, the child has the chance to actively explore the character and story. This is not to suggest that reading alone is not fundamental or important, for surely it is. Rather, I suggest that drama can be a fundamental tool that enables children to understand the story by way of engaging with it.

Drama is a powerful tool than can open an awareness in children by bringing them to experience something they may have never experienced. Through acting, children can take on roles that make them think critically about the story and about the experiences of characters different from themselves. A bully might take on the character of a meek but kind person; a shy child might take on the role of a powerful king or community leader. These roles enable the children to experience voices different from their own, opening avenues toward thinking more deeply about something, someone, or relationships in a new way.

Movement (Kinesthetic)

Moving or dancing to the story also provides an opportunity to explore it from the inside out through active participation. As the student translates words to movements, he or she is working with the story's ideas. In reading the child is taking information in, such as the wonders of a story. Through movement/dance the child "gives out" by taking the words and bringing them to life, actively interpreting the story. Young children naturally desire to move about. Exploring reading through movement enables children's natural energy to be channeled in a positive and often fun manner.

Music (Auditory)

Adding music to the story, or retelling the story through music, is yet another opportunity for making the story one's own through a process of translating words to sound. Even the addition of sound to words involves an active reflection on the part of the student as he or she decides what sounds are important to certain aspects of the story. Again, the arts open a venue for exploration and active participation. Music can be a magic carpet, transporting children to worlds where they can separate themselves from other characters and events.

POETRY AND LANGUAGE ACQUISITION THROUGH THE ARTS

Writing poetry is akin to play—a playing with words. Poets create puzzles, readers decipher them. Writing poetry gives children the freedom to play as they work with words and language, because in poetry they can play with the rules of grammar and syntax. They can create phrases without worrying about punctuation, complete sentences, or word order. Thus, the writer can concentrate on imagining ways to put words together rather than focusing on the conventions that guide their use in specific circumstances.

Poetry is an art form that bridges representational thinking directly with language. Through poetry, one can often easily see children's personal and emotional connections to knowing and knowledge. It can unlock resources of insight in children. Karen Gallas (1991) writes, "Poetic form is often more suited to thinking and writing of children than prose; it is spare, yet rich with sense impressions. It is a medium in which the images of wonder, curiosity, and analogic thinking which so often characterize children's thinking can flourish" (p. 44).

In the case of student-poets, we see how children can create artistic forms to reveal self-knowledge and make connections to their world. As it relates to second language acquisition, the process might be akin to invented spelling. Given the opportunity to work freely with language, children are encouraged to explore the intricacies of language usage. Not having to worry so much about grammatical rules (or even spellings), students may be willing and eager to invent while they express themselves with language.

In classrooms where multiple languages are spoken, poetry can be a natural bridge in working with words. Every student can benefit from word-play, but it is especially attractive to children who are learning to play with words in a new language. Educators have suggested that writing poetry provides students a forum for exploring the dimensions of their world, expressing ideas and feelings, and working with subject matter (Greene, 1991; Livingston, 1991, 1984; Steinbergh, 1991; Johnson, 1990; Phillips, 1990; Dillard, 1989; Heard, 1989; Koch, 1973; Hopkins, 1972; Tsujimoto, 1964).

There is anecdotal evidence that poetry is particularly well suited to second language acquisition and learning (McKim and Steinbergh, 1992; Steinbergh, 1991; Gallas, 1991). Steinbergh (1991) argues that writing poetry can be particularly comforting to children who come from countries where poetry is an integral part of the culture. "Hispanic, Russian, and Asian students often feel very comfortable with the expressive mode of poetry, even before they have a facility with English" (p. 57). McKim and Steinbergh (1992) notice "children whose first language is not English wanting to find the new words for their poems" (p. 7). Data from my own research over the last few years confirm that poetry can open the door to working with words, language, and ideas. Second language students were documented working with language freely and excitedly when writing poetry.

Research in bilingual and second language acquisition has yielded a number of theories with regard to learning (Krashen, 1981). Two theories the Acquisition-Learning Hypothesis and the Affective Filter Hypothesis—bear directly on this research. The Acquisition-Learning Hypothesis supposes that like first language acquisition, children acquiring a second language learn it for some communicative purpose. The Affective Filter Hypothesis addresses the role of "affect," or personality and motivation, in second language acquisition. The literature describes three variables as related to learners' success: (1) Low anxiety relates to motivation; the less anxiety, the more learning (Stevick, 1976); (2) Motivation is an indicator related to feeling a sense of identity with another group (Gardner and Lambert, 1972); (3) Self-confidence is a factor in learning: "The acquirer with more self-esteem and self-confidence tends to do better in second language acquisition" (Krashen, 1981, p. 62).

In conducting research in fourth and fifth grade classes in southern California, I have found that students tend to be at a low anxiety level when writing poetry. They are motivated to communicate ideas, and they display self-confidence while exploring topics through their poetry. The following list includes observations that I have found significant in researching the role of poetry in language acquisition and the study of subject matter.[1]

- Students are usually eager and excited when the activity involves writing poems. Because one may take liberties with the rules of grammar and syntax when writing poetry, children feel more free to work and play with words and language. This seems especially true for second language learners.

- Students devise strategies in writing and organizing their poems. Thus, they are tapping into a logico-mathematical ability as well as a more creative ability. Forms that emerge in the children's poems are generalizable. For example, many students organize their poems in a "sandwich" form, beginning and ending their poems with the same words or phrases. Others organize according to a written shape on the page, repeating patterns, or employ punctuation in very definite ways.

- Writing poetry clearly serves to further understanding of subject matter in addition to fostering language usage. The writing gives them an opportunity to apply—in words—their understandings of subject matter. Writing poems inspires children to find facts and ideas they wish to include in their writing. Students have shown interest in using reference books as they create poems; others look back into their journals and sketchbooks so as to review ideas they deem worthy to be included in their poem. The poetry-writing process may rekindle a curiosity in the learner and then provide a way to express such curiosities.

- I have found children eager to read poetry after experience with writing it. One student, asked why she was taking poetry books from the library, said, "Poems are better than stories. They make you happy or sad more than stories do." My documentation (over a one-year period) in a fourth-grade class indicated that, on their own, every single child in the class had taken out at least one poetry book from

---

[1] I reported findings concerning poetry and second language acquisition in depth in a paper given at the 1995 AERA meeting in San Francisco, "The Role of Writing Poetry in Second Language Acquisition" (Goldberg, Doyle, and Vega-Casteneda, 1995).

the library. As poets themselves, they have a much stronger entry into the world of other people's poetry.

- I have found that children's ability to read and interpret poetry can be extraordinary. This is an especially important finding, because under traditional testing methods, many of the students with whom I have worked have scored low on reading comprehension. When I asked students to share poems from books they found intriguing, it was not unusual to hear poems by any number of poets. I was especially heartened on a day that a child who was a non-reader in September read to me a poem by Longfellow in March. What is especially important about this example is her comprehension of the poem. It would have been easy to assume that her comprehension level was on par with her ability to read, when actually her ability to make sense of the complex poetic puzzle indicated she had abstract thinking skills and a certain depth of thought.

- I have found that a teacher's view of individual children is continually enhanced (and perhaps changed) as she sees sides to children she had never seen before through their poetry. A teacher may acquire a more complex picture of her students as she reads their poems and is introduced to the ways in which they see and express their world. Poetry projects always manage to bring surprises into the classroom with regard to perceptions of individual children: their emerging knowledge and personalities. This point relates directly to Principle 6 of multicultural education and the arts in that the arts deepen the teacher's awareness of children's abilities (see principle on p. 15).

- It is not unusual for the children's views of themselves to be changed as a result of writing their own and listening to others' poetry. Many children show confidence in sharing their written work. In my research I have noticed that this is especially true among children who were identified by their teacher as having low self-esteem. This point also speaks to Principle 3 of multicultural education and the arts in that the poetry activity sets the stage for building self-esteem (see principle on p. 14).

PLAYING WITH WORDS

I would like to take the reader through a series of lessons concerning poetry writing for language acquisition. The examples used here are taken from a language transition fourth-grade class in San Marcos, California. For two years I have been working in this school with a classroom teacher, Michelle Doyle, studying the role of poetry in language acquisition. Fully 96 percent of the children at San Marcos Elementary school are "minority"; 92 percent of these are labeled "Hispanic" and are of Mexican or Mexican-American descent. In this particular case, with the school being only 45 miles north of the Mexican–U.S.

border, most of the students are transitioning from Spanish to English. There are a few other languages interspersed, including Filipino and Chinese. Most of the students are in their first or second year of transitioning into an English-speaking class. There are a few students who speak English only.

In introducing poetry to the children, we first began by engaging them in a discussion about poetry. We asked them to describe their ideas concerning poetry, asked if any of them had written, read, or remembered any poetry, and so on. Michelle and I also read one of our favorite poems to the class. Following that, we got into the activity of writing. Prior to the session we had decided to focus on the topic of "family" for the first poem. We wanted a topic that was familiar (in one form or another) to everyone in the class.

First we had the students do a group brainstorm of words in English relating to family. As the students thought of words, Michelle and I wrote them on the board. We then asked the students to create their own list of family words on a separate piece of paper, using the words on the board as a starting point. The next step was to take the words from their list and organize them into a "word poem." Admittedly, we were not sure what we would get from this exercise. Our goal, however, was to get the class working or playing with words—to find ways to manipulate or put the words together. Much to our surprise, the children unhesitatingly went about their word organizing and created word poems that astonished both them and us.

Here are a few examples:

Topic: Family
Lesson One: Word Poems
Brainstorm: grandma, mom, dad, sister, brother, uncle, aunt, cousin, baby, niece, nephew, grandpa, caring

Poem
Caring grandma, grandpa,
mom, dad, aunt, uncle, cousin, niece, nephew,
sister, brother, baby

Comments: There are many noteworthy aspects to this poem. The student has organized the words from oldest to youngest. The gender is consistent: male/female in pairs (with the exception of "cousin," which does not have a gender pairing). "Caring," which is qualitatively different from all the other words, is placed in the beginning—separate from the people words. The organizational technique is remarkably consistent and identifiable, giving us insight into this child's ability to organize and categorize while employing language.

Brainstorm: sister, brother, baby sister, baby brother, mom, dad, reunited, relatives, cousin, grandma, grandpa, aunt, uncle, shop owner, household chores, cooking, cleaning, shop, manager, mother

Poem
Relatives, mother, father,
brother, sister, babybrother,
babysister, grandma, grandpa,
cousin, aunt, uncle, relatives

Comments: Note the "sandwich effect." By using the word "relatives" to begin and end the poem, this child has created a definite form. Also note the sets of relatives in generational pairs by gender: mother, father; grandma, grandpa—though the gender order is not completely consistent.

Brainstorm: family, love, friends, aunt, cousin, baby brother, baby sister, mom, dad, grandpa, grandma, uncle, niece, pictures, babysitter, caring

Poem
Caring, grandpa,
grandmother uncle
niece, aunt, mom
dad, babysitter,
babysister, baby
brother, friends
picture, love

Comments: Here is another example of "sandwich" organization using descriptive words instead of words for people (relatives), as the child in the first example used.

What surprised Michelle and me in addition to the children's willingness to compose word poems was the inventiveness with which they devised ways to organize their words. Interesting and consistent patterns emerged, such as the gender, age, and sandwich forms. The children were genuinely interested in inventing a form for their words. Having this success, we forged onward to similes.

The children were asked to create similes based on a particular family member. To introduce this notion we offered some initial models. For example, I wrote, "My grandfather is like a gift to me that I opened long ago and never forgot." We asked each child to choose one family member and create a simile based on that family member. Following that activity, we shared the similes as a class. That night the teacher and I took home all the similes and circled one word in each child's phrase. We brought them back the next day and asked the children to brainstorm and then generate more words based on the circled words. The object was to create a word bank to write a poem

Michelle Doyle and her fourth-graders in San Marcos,
California, work on their family poems.

based on that family member. Following are a few examples of the children's
initial similes, their subsequent brainstorm list, and then a draft of the poem
that emerged from the work. I have underlined the word we circled on the
child's paper.

Topic: Family
Lessons Two and Three: Similes
Simile: My brothers are like <u>spider webs</u>
Brainstorm: spider webs
spider, tarantula, cockroach, webs, sticky, dracula

First Draft:

My brothers are like spider webs walking up
and down the house. they look like
spiders when they walk, they look like
draculas with their two front teeth
they are sticky when they eat. they
look like tarantulas when they crawl.

Second Draft:

MY BROTHERS

My brothers are like
   spider webs walking up
      and down the
         house.

They look like spiders
   when they walk.

They look like draculas
   with their two
      front teeth

They are sticky when
   they eat.

They look like tarantulas
   when they crawl.

They are cockroaches eating
   everything.

They are webs when
   they are asleep.

              Raquel

Note the careful placement of Raquel's phrases and the spacing of the lines. This showed that she was employing organizational skills in addition to her creative use of language.

Simile: My mom is like a beautiful <u>flower</u> blooming in the spring

Brainstorm: flower

beautiful, smell good, bloom, rose, spring, red, bouquet, pollen, bees, garden

Poem

MY MOM

My mom is like a beautiful flower blooming in the spring
she is like the beautiful red rose in a bouquet
you could plant her in your garden and
she smells so good!
Anybody would like to plant her in your garden
she is beautiful!

Heather Mendez

Simile: My mom is like the queen of my <u>heart</u>

Brainstorm: heart

pretty, beautiful, red, lovely, pumping, desire, love

Poem

My mom is like the queen of my heart
When she crowned me I never forgot the day and
now she is the queen of my heart
As beautiful and sweet as a flower.
I desire my mom's lovely heart and,
she is the queen of my heart

Kekoa Villanuevo

Note that in addition to his original simile, Kekoa goes on to create and employ another simile in his poem: "As beautiful and sweet as a flower." In the next poem, Elizabeth not only creates one simile but strings together several.

Similes: My mom is like a gift to me; she is like cotton candy; she is like the moon in the night

MY MOM

My mom is like a
gift to me and she
is like cotton candy.
She is like the moon
in the night.

Elizabeth Cerros

Garret creates a wonderfully descriptive simile in the next example. His brainstorm includes many related words, some of which he includes in the final poem. If we devoted more time to the family poems, I would ask him if he could incorporate even more of his brainstormed words into his poem.

Simile: My dad is like a friendly <u>bull</u>
Brainstorm: bull
nice, brown, big, mean, white, strong, spots, runs fast, hates red, big strong horns, sharp horns, blue eyes
Poem

MY DAD

My dad is like a friendly bull
but sometimes he's not a friendly bull
sometimes he's a mad bull
but I'll like him and love him
as long as I will live.

Garret Ingram

In the last example, we find another poem concerning the most popular relative chosen by the children for this assignment: mom.

Simile: My mom is like a <u>flower</u>
Brainstorm: flower
beautiful, color-red-yellow-white, little, cute, special, picking, roses-black red, loolie pines, outside, garden, mom, me

FLOWERS

Flowers are cute   there color
are red, yellow, white   there
color are special for me
Roses for mothers and
colors for me
beautiful gardens and
green plants
you see flowers outside
you see flowers everywhere
and remember when you pick a
flower up that's your mom.

Adan Gonsalves

Each of these poems is representative of something known to the student-poet. The known—or the knowledge—is a perception of each one's world woven together and expressed in the words and phrasing of the poem. Each student-poet created similes to reveal and express his or her understandings. For example, Raquel created an original way to describe her twin baby brothers as spiders. Her description moves beyond the ordinary as she continues to create phrases that portray their actions, such as being "tarantulas when they crawl" or "cockroaches eating everything." Adan surprised us with his last line, "remember, when you pick a flower up, that's your mom" (commas added). The line shows an extraordinary understanding and use of language, especially for a 10-year-old whose first language is not English. In addition, for Adan it shows a depth of feeling otherwise usually hidden, perhaps for lack of an outlet.

Though many of the poems may have a magical quality, there is nothing magical about the process through which each child began to write. The brainstorm activity was adapted from strategies described by McKim and Steinbergh in their book *Beyond Words: Writing Poems with Children* (1992). We introduced the class to published children's poems and specific poetic devices such as the simile. It was important that the teacher and I could write and share our own poems along with the children as a way of modeling poetic forms.

As mentioned earlier, my own "family" poem began with the line, "My grandfather is like a gift to me that I opened long ago and never forgot." One can see from comparing the beginning of my poem to Elizabeth's where she might have gotten the idea to start her poem. She modeled the idea of the gift as a simile, and then she used it as a springboard for two other similes that

Fourth-graders with the author sharing a light moment after writing and reading original similes.

were clearly of her own device. Other students created their own similes right away. Throughout the sessions on "family" the students invented similes, "word-stormed" on key words (a "wordstorm" is a brainstorm—coming up with related words to key words), applied the words to their poems to include words from the wordstorm, edited, and re-edited their poems.

Poetry as a writing tool can be used to explore subject matter. In Chapter 6, we will revisit some of these same students as they practice literacy skills while applying their writing to topics in science. Although our work with the students was specifically designed to help with their language skills, we found that we could naturally combine language skills with subject matter exploration. The same principles applied: The children were playing with and applying words, but the topics could be drawn from other subjects throughout the day.

JOURNALS: WORKING WITH IDEAS
OVER A PERIOD OF TIME

From the very beginning, we created poetry journals out of folded colored paper with white lined paper inside. Each child decorated his or her journal and kept all in-class work there as well as any other poems they found or composed. Students were given the option of writing in their journal during the morning silent reading time. Many students took advantage of this offer. Two things emerged. Children began writing poems in addition to the class assignments, and children began copying poems from books—and each other—into their journals. By periodically collecting the children's journals, I was able to document their work over time. The following was written by a second language student who, over a period of six months, played with the notion of "flying."

Meteors fly like a fly
maybe it's a butterfly
with its wings spread
high in the sky

Jaime wrote this poem in October during a class assignment in which the students were to write a "science poem." I was first struck by the imagery in Jaime's poem. What a lovely picture of a meteor as a butterfly. I was especially delighted because Jaime could be described as one of the class "bad boys" (written affectionately, of course). Here was another awakening for me into the reality of what was possible by a child whom I had labeled in a way that didn't match my expectations. In looking at the poem closely I was interested in his ability to manipulate the word "fly" in three different ways. Jaime shows a sophisticated understanding of various uses of the word "fly" through his applications of the word in the poem. What becomes more evident is his desire to follow through—in writing poetry—on the idea of flying in general. In his journal, his next related poem was as follows:

Butterfly fly like a fly
with its wings spread high in the sky
I don't know why
but it can fly

Here Jaime begins to wonder about the nature of flying. He employs some of the language and phrases from his original poem, including the lines, "with its wings spread / high in the sky." The meteor is now gone, and in its place is a butterfly. In his next poem, Jaime continues to work on the flying butterfly notion but relates it more to himself, as he expresses a wish to be a butterfly:

I like a fly cause it flys
like a butterfly
with its wings spread high in the sky
I'd like to be a butterfly

The following poem was written in February around Valentine's day. Jaime is so into contemplating flying that the Valentine cupids retell his flying theme, this time, with love:

Valentine's day
cupids are flying with love
and people are caring and sharing

Finally, we see where Jaime's writing and thinking is taking him: to his wish to fly freely and be able to see things from a different perspective. Here Jaime offers a view into his inner life that does not ordinarily emerge in discussions or other ways in which we interact together.

IF I COULD FLY

If I could fly where would I go?
I would go across the sea and the desert
I'd fly with the hawks, the falcons
I'd like to fly

Another student, Anna, was interested in what I would describe as word-play. She wrote the following poem and entered it into her journal. She centered it in her journal as is shown here:

Flowers are colors
like purple murple
red reddy blue lue
yellow mellow
orange growange

> I like colors
> especially
> the color
> of you

I was interested in the playfulness with which Anna employs and invents language. In addition, her final line brings forth the depth to which she is able to apply metaphorical thinking through language. Again, I believe this is an example of how the poetic form can provide an opportunity for students who are willing and eager to play with words, language, and, of course, ideas.

Each student's poem documents an organizational process of thought and reflection. Each one's willingness and ability to think metaphorically amazed us. We found that the poetic form seemed to encourage and even inspire the students to work with language. Reflecting on writing poems, a few students wrote the following in their journals: "I like writing poetry because it ryms [sic] and it has interesting words." "I do like writing poems, thats [sic] one of my best things I do." "I like writing poems becuase [sic] it could tells [sic] how people feel or how people would feel happy, sad, mad, confuse [sic] and puzzled." "I like [writing poems] because it captures the heart in you."

Copied Poems

In our work with the fourth graders we encouraged them to copy poems they had read into their journals. Students whose English skills were fairly new tended to copy more poems into their journals than those more skilled, who included more original poems. A number of interesting aspects of the copying should be put forth for consideration. In order to copy poems, students must read poems and make decisions about which ones are interesting. From this we can learn about each child's ability to comprehend a poem—or at least their interest in the poem, and also their interest in reading poetry. I have found that it is not unusual for students to copy lengthy poems. Nikki, a fourth-grader, copied the following poem from another student's journal:

> If ever there's a moment
> when you need a friend to listen,
> if ever someone can reach out
> to dry the tears that glisten,
> I'll be there.
> If ever you have special needs
> and hope someone will see them
> If ever you have secrets and would like a friend
> to free them, I'll be there.
> If you just need encouragement
> to help you on the way,
> if you need a cheerful voice

to pull you through the day,
I'll be there.
If you need one who cares a lot
and thinks about you often
If you need one who shares your hopes, your worries
strives to soften,
I'll be there.
If you would like to be yourself
with someone who respects you,
if you need one who understands how all of life
affects you,
I'll be there.

A lot of work went into copying this poem. Nikki not only copied a lengthy poem but paid attention to spelling and grammar as well. Her choice of poem may also indicate something to us about her thinking. What we know for sure is something about her willingness to enter poems into her journal on her own, and her attention to careful copying with regard to spelling, punctuation, phrasing. Nikki then became interested in a poem shared by a classmate. This child's sister composed the poem. For her next entry, Nikki chose to copy the poem into her journal:

NIGHT COMES

Night comes
leaking
out of the sky
stars come
peeking
moon comes
sneaking
silvery
Who is
a king?
Who is afraid
of the night?
not I.

Copying poems also serves as a bridge for students who are not comfortable with their writing ability. Ladianni had a truly difficult time writing a science poem. In her journal she wrote "Science—Aluminum." She just could not—or was not willing to—go beyond those two words. Finally she asked if instead of composing a poem she could find and copy a science poem from a book. She proceeded to copy a number of poems from the *Random House Book of Poetry for Children* (Prelutsky, 1983). The first poem was "The Universe" by Mary Britton Miller, concerning itself with the cycles of the moon, stars, and seasons.

THE UNIVERSE

There is a moon, there is a sun
Round which we circle every year,
And there are all the stars we see
On starry nights when skies are clear,
And all the countless stars that lie
Beyond the reach of the human eye.
If every bud on every tree,
All birds and fireflies and bees
And all the flowers that bloom and die
Upon the earth were counted up,
The number of stars would be
Greater, they say, than all of these.[2]

Ladianni's next copied poem was Michael Flanders's poem about the activities of a hummingbird. Her third entry was this one by Ogden Nash:

THE CANARY

The song of canaries
never varies
and when they're molting
they're pretty revolting[3]

The poems clearly indicate Ladianni's understanding of the poetry as it relates to science. We also glimpse Ladianni's sense of humor as we read "The Canary" by Ogden Nash. The Nash poem is an interesting choice in that the vocabulary is advanced, using the words "molting" and "revolting." One sumises that Ladianni understands these words; otherwise, why would she bother to include it in her journal? In fact, when we asked her about the poem she described its humor and restated its meaning, proving her comprehension. After copying these poems into her journal, which she enjoyed doing, she surprised us with this entry:

SCIENCE

Science is magic
sometimes it's fun
Magic is wonder
wonder is fun

---

[2] From ALL ABOARD by Mary Britton Miller. Copyright © 1958 and renewed 1986 by Pantheon Books, Inc. Reprinted by permission of Patheon Books, a division of Random House, Inc.

[3] From VERSES FROM 1929 ON by Ogden Nash. Copyright 1940 by Ogden Nash. Copyright © renewed. First appeared in THE SATURDAY EVENING POST. By permission of Little, Brown and Company.

fun is making experiments
experiment is thinking
thinking is smart
smart is you

What a breakthrough! Although she did not write an original poem when her classmates did, she eventually went on to write the poem "Science." In this case, Ladianni needed the time—and perhaps the models—before she could compose her own poem. It was certainly worth the wait.

A fourth-grader carefully considers her word choice as she begins a new poem.

KEY ELEMENTS TOWARD WRITING POETRY

In researching the role of poetry in language acquisition, I have developed a list of key elements that the reader might find useful. These few elements were constructed with Michelle Doyle, the students' classroom teacher and my partner in the poetry research project.

Wordstorming: Every time the children were to write a poem (in the class setting), they would brainstorm words as a way to get started.

Modeling: We presented the students with poems written by other children, especially in the beginning of the project. Throughout the work we always modeled brainstorming, editing, and other elements of the writing process. We often did this with overheads, being careful to clear away the poem-models quickly to avoid copying or dependence.

Editing and Revising: We encouraged the children to constantly edit and revise. Often we would spend several weeks on the same poem.

Publishing: The children's poems were "published"—either put up on a bulletin board, displayed at the local university, or given away to a friend or parent. At the end of the year each student chose a poem to contribute to a class poetry book.

Journals: The children each had a poetry journal of their own—a simple construction-paper book they made and decorated, with plain lined paper inside. They kept all their poems in their journal and could add to it at any time.

Finding the Interests of the Students: We tried to find engaging topics based on the students' interests and the curriculum.

Timing: Guided poetry writing occurred at a specific time during the week—in our case, every Friday morning. It gave the students something to look forward to and gave the project importance. The students could also write on their own at any other free time. In addition, their teacher gave them the option of writing during silent reading time.

Sharing: Enabling the students to share their work was empowering. Sharing also took the form of reading poems they had found in books from the library or poetry center.

SUMMARY

The arts provide many methods for gaining literacy skills while also fostering imaginative, creative, and critical thinking skills. The arts can support reading and writing skills while also reaching individual children's interests and abilities. Picto-spellings and cursive writing through movement give insight into the many creative ways through which students learn and apply their emerging literacy skills.

Poetry has an especially important function with regard to literacy. Through writing poetry, students may explore a world of words while taking liberties with the rules of grammar and syntax that might otherwise impede their willingness to compose. Other insights can be gained when children learn literacy skills through the arts. In working with fourth- and fifth-grade teachers, I continually hear expressions of surprise over how much teachers learn about their students. Teachers began to view their students in new ways as they observe their arts-related activities and read their poems. Students themselves seem to view themselves differently. Mostly they exude a sense of confidence and fulfillment in their ability to create and be creative. Children with low self-esteem come out from behind their own walls, delighting in their work.

QUESTIONS TO PONDER

1. What is a language? Consider communication and expression in your reflections.
2. How are art forms a kind of language? What makes them a language, or not a language?
3. What is the role of arts as a language of "literacy"?
4. Do you think "literacy" would be defined in the same way universally (in all cultures)?
5. What is the role of literacy in technology?

EXPLORATIONS TO TRY

1. Brainstorm as many ways as you can to learn literacy *with* the arts. See how many ideas you come up with.
2. Brainstorm three specific ways to learn literacy *through* the arts. Choose curriculum ideas/topics/mandates that come from your school.
3. Take a weekly spelling list or vocabulary list that you will use in your class. Create a picto-spelling using one or more of the words.
4. Using the same spelling list, choose two words and brainstorm related words. Then compose a poem. Reflect on your experience: How did you brainstorm and think of new words? Did you look up any words? How did you start applying the words to a poem? Did the words give you an idea, or did an idea come to you and then you added words? Did you add words to your poem *other* than those you originally brainstormed?

REFERENCES

Cecil, Nancy Lee, and Phyllis Lauritzen. (1994). *Literacy and the Arts for the Integrated Classroom.* New York: Longman.
Dillard, A. (1989). *The Writing Life.* New York: Harper and Row.

Gallas, K. (1991). "Arts as Epistemology: Enabling Children to Know What They Know." *Harvard Educational Review,* Vol. 61, No. 1.

———. (1994). *The Languages of Learning: How Children Talk, Write, Dance, Draw, and Sing Their Understanding of the World.* New York: Teachers College Press.

Gardner, R. C., and W. E. Lambert. (1972). *Attitudes and Motivation in Second Language Learning.* Rowley, MA: Newbury House.

Goldberg, Merryl, Michelle Doyle, and Lillian Vega-Casteneda. (1995). "The Role of Writing Poetry in Second Language Acquisition." Paper presented at the 1995 American Educational Research Association meeting, San Francisco, April.

Greene, M. (1991). "Texts and Margins." *Harvard Educational Review,* Vol. 61, No. 1.

Heard, G. (1989). *For the Good of the Earth and the Sun: Teaching Poetry.* Portsmouth, NH: Heinemann.

Hopkins, L. B. (1972). *Pass the Poetry Please!* New York: Harper and Row.

Johnson, D. M. (1990). *Word Weaving: A Creative Approach to Teaching and Writing Poetry.* Urbana, IL: National Council of Teachers of English.

Koch, K. (1973). *Rose, Where Did You Get That Red?* New York: Random House.

Krashen, S. D. (1981). *Schooling and Language Minority Students: A Theoretical Framework.* Los Angeles: Evaluation, Dissemination and Assessment Center, California State University.

Livingston, M. C. (1984). *The Child as Poet: Myth or Reality.* Boston: Horn Book.

———. (1991). *Poem-Making: Ways to Begin Writing Poetry.* New York: HarperCollins.

McKim, E., and J. Steinbergh. (1992). *Beyond Words: Writing Poems with Children,* 2nd ed. Brookline, MA: Talking Stone Press.

Phillips, A. (1990). "Thinking on the Inside: Children's Poetry and Inner Speech." Cambridge, MA: Harvard Graduate School of Education, unpublished.

Prelutsky, Jack, ed. (1983). *The Random House Book of Poetry for Children.* New York: Random House.

Steinbergh, J. W. (1991). "To Arrive in Another World: Poetry, Language Development and Culture." *Harvard Educational Review,* Vol. 61, No. 1.

Stevick, E. W. (1976). *Memory, Meaning and Method.* Rowley, MA: Newbury House.

Tsujimoto, J. (1964). *Teaching Poetry Writing to Adolescents.* Urbana, IL: National Council of Teachers of English.

chapter 5

The Voices of Humanity: History, Social Studies, Geography, and the Arts

VOICE OF THE TURTLE

Beauty arrives on
the wings of your song
as our hearts dance
to the beat of
our collective pasts

We dream up memories of
ancient wisdom,
wrinkled hands that
reach out to us across the
eons of time,
touch our tender souls
and speak the language of
pulsating rhythms,
melancholy words,
undeniable passion.

Praise to the enduring
spirit that allows us
young and old
to gather here to share
the cries of our ancestors
the voice of the turtle
within all of us.

Judy Leff, fifth-grade teacher

"In ancient Mexico the wise man was called *tlamatini,* or 'he who knows,'" writes Bradley Smith (1968); "he was the repository of the collected knowledge, oral and graphic, of a rich culture. The visual records in his keeping took the form of sequential picture-symbol drawings illustrating, among other themes prosaic and profound, the creation of man, the histories of dynasties, and the laws and customs of the times" (p. 7).

"His story," or history is a documentation and retelling of the past in some manner or form. For the *tlamatini* it took the form of pictures and symbols. For the Australian Aboriginal, it is through song. For many school children, the traditional textbook does the trick. In this chapter we will explore the relationship between the arts and social studies, and the ways in which the arts can be integrated into social studies subject matter.

In documenting and retelling our pasts, we consider, interpret, analyze, and question events and actions. We then consider the study as it relates to the present and our own lives, and we include "her stories" as well as "our stories." The arts are, and have always been, a major force in history, documenting and reflecting times and changes in our lives. Judy Leff's poem at the beginning of this chapter is representative of the power of the arts in social studies. Through her poem Judy reflects on the impact of a history lesson carried out in her classroom, a bilingual (Spanish-English) performance/workshop presented by the Ladino group Voice of the Turtle, which I mentioned in Chapter 1. Presenting songs of Spain's Jewish population in the Diaspora from 1492 to the present, Voice of the Turtle not only entertains but communicates source materials documenting the events, dreams, frustrations, passions, and hopes of a people.

The poems written that day by both Judy and the students in her class were in response to the workshop, but they hold a deeper meaning. Each poem reflects a serious attempt at integrating that day's history lesson with the everyday lives of the members of the class. Not only did students and teacher consider history as subject matter in and of itself, but through their writing they contemplated the connections of the history lesson to their present-day experiences.

The arts serve various functions with regard to history and social science. First, they are documents to the past through which we are introduced to individuals in every corner of the world and the ways they have expressed their perception of some part of their life. The arts serve as voices of a people and images of their lives. As far back as rock art and cave painting, the arts have provided a venue through which people have documented their experiences and provided a tremendous source of information for interpretation to later inquiries.

The arts serve another function beyond a rich documentation of culture. They are a powerful tool for social change. Victor Cockburn is a folksong writer and singer who as a teenager attended a concert that changed his way of thinking. Pete Seeger, Odetta, and Reverend Gary Davis provided his first introduction to the power of music for social change. Cockburn (1991) writes, "the simple beauty of the music and power of the lyrics inspired me to become more deeply involved with this universal form of expression. The effect it had on the audience—bringing a large roomful of people together in song—and the information and history I learned through music motivated me to learn more about folk music" (p. 71).

While deliberating history and social studies in relation to the arts, I would like to ask the reader to consider a few critical issues and questions. These are meant to guide your thinking rather than dictate a certain point of view. I take the stand that social studies is both a subject and a methodology. We can study events in our lives as subject matter, but at the same time the manner in which we consider the events is equally important. In that light, I believe social studies must be a course of action in addition to a course of study. I suggest that the focus of a social studies course is to create historians and social scientists rather than able "tellers" of the past.

If we accept that history is, in part, stories from the past, then from whose perspective will the stories be told? How will they be told? How is it decided which stories will be told and subsequently included in the curriculum? Is history more than stories? Is history a chronicle of events? If so, how to choose which events are noteworthy? Does history ever change? If so, what changes it? Finally, perhaps most critical, what is the point to studying and understanding history?

According to the *It's Elementary!* (1992), a California task force report with regard to the state's educational framework, "a strong history–social science program at the elementary level helps all students to develop their full potential for personal, civic and professional life" (p. 9). In California, the elementary curriculum is centered on historical and geographical knowledge, "integrating the social sciences and humanities, with an emphasis on ethics and democratic values" (p. 9). Philip Cohen (1995) writes that "proponents of new history curriculums and methods say a more inclusive approach to history is inherently more accurate than the traditional, one-sided presentation" (p. 1).

Teachers moving away from a presentation of history as a list of events are using historical context as a stepping-stone toward an integrated curriculum. Stories of the past are contextualized in the interrelationships among geography, economics, politics, culture, and so on. Events of the past are used as a methodology for understanding current events. Contexts and multiple perspectives are derived from primary sources including diaries, journalism, songs, poetry, and artwork.

LEARNING WITH THE ARTS

Studying history and social change *with* the arts offers students a number of interesting issues. Art examples drawn from music, visual art, poetry, sculpture, drama, photography, and so on provide the history student with primary sources to examine. Among the benefits of using artworks as primary sources is that they provide an extra bonus in their depiction of the life of a community, person, or event. Ruth Rubin (1979) discusses this bonus in her book on the history of the Jewish people through Yiddish folksong: "In the songs, we catch the manner of speech and phrase, the wit and humor, the dreams and aspirations, the nonsense, jollity, the pathos and struggle of an entire people. . . . These are the songs that served the needs, moods, creative impulses, and purposes of a particular environment at particular periods in the history of [Jewish communities]" (p. 9).

I might argue that the songs Rubin presents are more "authentic" than an "objective" accounting by a person documenting important events. Songs and other artworks reflect human complexities in their most personal form. They remind us that there is no such thing as a standard history of a people, because events and life are experienced in multiple ways and through multiple lenses. Through their melodies, harmonies, and phrasing, songs give insight into the feelings and nuances of people and cultures that cannot be found in a more journalistic report. They contain the world's repertoire of personal accounts of life experiences, including children's songs, songs about love, courtship, marriage, customs, beliefs, events, religion, struggles, survival, and so on.

On another level, songs or other artworks can be inviting. For some students, studying an art form may be more to their liking than a history text and therefore engage them in serious contemplation. Utilizing art forms in a historical context opens the door to many students who are interested in artistic forms and/or whose learning styles are visual or auditory.

Let me highlight a few resources to get you thinking about the possibilities of integrating the arts into history lessons. By no means should my examples be taken as the best or only sources. Rather, they are a sampling of the kinds of material available to you. We will begin with poetry.

Poetry

There are many historically based poetry books. One that is used in classrooms I have visited is *Hand in Hand: An American History through Poetry*, collected by Lee Bennett Hopkins (1994). This particular book is based on subject matter rather than a strict chronological framework. Poems represent aspects of experiences from multiple perspectives and with multiple voices. Some were written by people living at the moment in history, and others were written by poets who have reflected on the experiences of a time or life.

In the section of the book dedicated to the social changes of the 1960s–1990s, poems concerning the civil rights movement, homelessness, Kennedy's assassination, Vietnam, and social injustice are included. The poems serve to get students thinking about the time period, but they also act as an impetus to involve the students in questioning. The poem "en-vi-RON-ment" on p. 91, written by Lee Bennett Hopkins, is an example. It opens up a stream of consideration. It includes facts about what homeless people do. But the magic of the art form adds another dimension: It gives the reader things to think about. The poet presents a complicated image that prompts the reader to think about homelessness in many ways, including the relationship of homelessness to the environment. For me, one of the major impacts of art as history is its ability to put a face on the subject. In this case, Hopkins puts a face on homelessness and invites his readers to examine it up close.

en-vi-RON-ment

Homeless People
line up at 8:00 a.m.
sharp
in front of D'Agostino's
on Bethune Street
in Greenwich Village
waiting patiently
for
Automatic Door
to swing open.

They have empty cans.
Sorted.
Placed neatly in rows
in discarded
cardboard flats
or layered in
past-used plastic bags.

A good firm Pepsi is best.
A dented Bud needs
a crack of the fingers
to straighten it back
to its original shape.

A foot-flattened
Orange Crush
is no good to anyone.
(it gets carefully tossed
into the city-trash-can
on the corner.)

Empty cans are coins.

Coins add up
    to a cup of coffee
    to a bowl of soup
    to a tuna on rye.

Empty cans
are important
to
Homeless People.

They need them
to
feed Them.

And
they help Them
do their conscience-bit
to
protect
the
en-vi-RON-ment.[1]

Visual Arts

Let's now move into the realm of visual arts. Paintings can lend greatly to historical contexts and understandings. *Mine Eyes Have Seen the Glory: The Civil War in Art,* edited by Harold Holzer and Mark Neely Jr. (1993), is not, according to the editors, "an illustrated history of the Civil War, or perhaps one should say *another* history of the Civil War" (p. x). "Rather," the editors suggest, "we considered [the paintings] as a part of a great effort to comprehend the Civil War, and the opportunity for comparison offered by this approach revealed meanings in the works about which we had never read before" (p. xi). These meanings lie within emotions the paintings evoke, information the details of the images provide, and sentiments the faces in the paintings portray.

Especially for students who enjoy visual images, but apropos for any student, paintings provide the images to which texts can only allude. In examining paintings from the Civil War, for example, I can see the clothes the soldiers wore, the manner in which they marched, the look and size of the guns they carried, the vastness of the fields through which they traveled, the tents they constructed for sleeping, the size of the cannons and the way they loaded them for battle, the look of the camp along the Potomac, and even specific details of events—such as the "Presentation of the Colors to the First Colored Regiment of New York by the Ladies of the City in Front of the Old Union League Club, Union Square, New York City, in 1864" in a painting by Edward Lamson Henry (1841–1919).

Music

In the same way, music can provide auditory understanding and connection when used critically. There are numerous songs written in response to historical events or relating to periods and characters in history. Returning to the theme of the Civil War, Jeanette Allen, a high school teacher in Sparks, Nevada, used the following songs to introduce her students to the origins of the Civil War and the personal struggles of individuals of the time: "Battle Cry of Freedom," "All Quiet on the Potomac," "Battle Hymn of the Republic," "John Brown's Body," and many more.

In using the songs, Jeanette went beyond critical listening. She had the students compile a journal of responses. She then asked groups of students to present to the class their responses to stories of the Civil War as represented

---

[1] Reprinted by permission of Curtis Brown Ltd. Copyright © 1994 by Lee Bennett Hopkins. First appeared in *HAND IN HAND: An American History Through Poetry.* Published by Simon & Schuster.

through the songs and artworks. Students also used textbooks to gather information to support their opinions in their stories. One student reported to Jeanette that he felt "more connected" to the time period, the people and their struggles, and the enormous toll the war took on this country because of the personal flavor the arts brought to the topic.

One of my favorite collections of music for teaching about a time in history is *Sing for Freedom: The Story of the Civil Rights Movement through Its Songs,* edited and complied by Guy and Candie Carawan (1990). In addition to the songs (complete with musical notation) and accompanying commentary, the books includes a bibliography, discography, and suggested films and videos.

Drama

Considering drama, dances, and literature from various periods in a historical perspective can be a unique opportunity to understand history and social change while also giving a "feel" for the time. Many teachers have even *become* a historical character as they present information to students. This is always an enjoyable and engaging activity.

I once became Jean Piaget for a conference on teaching and learning. A few educators—myself among them—were asked to become characters rather than discuss them. So, I (as Piaget) along with Maria Montessori and John Dewey spent an afternoon talking with each other in front of an attentive audience. We even took questions from the audience about our theories and answered them in character. It was a wonderful afternoon, and the participants had a joyful time learning about the various theories and people. They were clearly intrigued and subsequently involved as they asked question after question. We as participants also delighted in our discussions among ourselves when we disagreed on a topic or answer. It was fun for me to take on the character and arguments of Piaget rather than to present them as I usually do. I wore a beret and carried a knapsack like Piaget did. I even learned a little French to be more convincing. But more important, the role playing forced me to consider the thoughts and words of Piaget in a meaningful and diligent manner. After all, I wouldn't want people to go away from the session with a false idea of Piaget the person and Piaget the thinker.

LEARNING THROUGH THE ARTS

Learning social studies and history through the arts prepares students to be social scientists and historians. As students become engaged in art-related activities, they are likely to become interested in the subject matter itself. Their authentic experiences may lead to curiosity and the asking of important questions. A historian or social scientist who merely documents events is missing out on the true value of the documentation—to better understand the human condition and the contexts in which we negotiate our lives together in a community, city, country, or even on our shared earth.

In conceptualizing a language arts/social studies unit for her students, Lynne Ogren, a second-grade teacher in Reno, Nevada, decided on biography as a theme. This nicely integrates reading and history. The students could choose a biography from several in their reading book, or they could select a biography from the library or home as long as it was at the appropriate reading level. Students were asked to read through the biography at least three times and take notes under the following topic headings: Family, Childhood, School, Talent, Job, Interesting or Important Facts. Students were given class time to look through other source materials to find other facts about their subject.

When the students had completed this work, they were asked to present something to the class that represented their character. Suggestions included wearing a costume; creating a picture, poem, diorama, or song relating to the person; or re-creating the art form of that person. Students chose for their presentations Harriet Tubman, known for her work with the Underground Railroad; Chief Standing Bear, a Lakota Indian chief; Robert Goddard, a rocket scientist; and Maria Martinez, a Pueblo potter. The child who presented Harriet Tubman came to class wearing clothes based on pictures she had seen of Tubman, and she presented a poster she had created. She told the class she knew the Railroad was not a "real railroad" and instead was a code for the path to freedom, but she wanted to make the poster "anyway." The poster was of a train representing the Underground Railroad with a quote from Harriet Tubman: "I will never run my train off the track and I will never lose a passenger." Another student, a girl, gave a talk on Robert Goddard in first person, and dressed as a man! She also made a 3-foot-tall posterboard rocket.

The teacher felt that the students became more in touch with the subject as a result of the artwork. For several, "I know it was the carrot at the end of the stick in motivating them to put together a biography," she wrote in a journal entry. In addition, she commented, "the artwork also made the presentations much more interesting for the rest of the class to listen to." This is a point less considered, but important. If presentations are engaging, as they often are when the arts are involved, they have that much more power to keep the attention of the audience. The more attention toward the subject matter, the more likely the children will remember details of the class and be interested in following up on the subject. The arts can keep not only the work interesting but the class time spent in presenting it magical as well.

Presidential Puppetry

The next story illustrates how students and teachers can be empowered through arts-based activities. It relates to Principle 5 of multicultural education and the arts (p. 15). Betsey Mendenhall, an experienced fifth-grade teacher in Escondido, California, took another approach to history in her classroom. As part of the SUAVE project (a cultural partnership program that will be highlighted in Chapter 10), Betsey had an artist-educator, Mindy Donner, as a coach in her class working to find ways to integrate subject matter and the arts. Betsey was teaching a unit about U.S. presidents. As part of the SUAVE partnership, Betsey and Mindy decided to have the students create president puppets. Hesitant at first, Betsey was worried there wouldn't be enough time for this kind of project. She also was not convinced that her students would be interested in such a project.

Mindy, drawing on her skills as a puppeteer, had the students bring in as many plastic grocery bags as they could find. Using only plastic bags, rubber bands, and masking tape, the children, Betsey, and Mindy began to form shapes that resembled people. Having completed the basic shapes, students added papier mâché to form the skin and then created clothes for each puppet to wear. The students loved creating the puppets and seeing them come to life from such simple materials. Each puppet would eventually become one of the U.S. presidents.

Betsey's goal was that upon completion the puppets would talk with each other, thereby enabling the students to get into their "historical characters." Her plan was to have groups of students create scripts of the various presidents talking to one another. What actually happened was even more interesting.

To get the students started, she held up two of the puppets and asked the students, "What kinds of things would you like these two to talk about?" She thought the students would ask questions about politics. Much to her surprise, the questions revolved around these three themes: environment, violence, and family. Some of the questions the puppets would ask included: "What did you do with your trash?" "Who took care of it if there were no trash collectors?" "Where did you go to the bathroom?" "If you didn't have a hose, how did you water the plants?" "Are you afraid of dying?" "Who does the president ask if he has a problem?"

Every question created another question, and Betsey was fascinated by the enthusiasm that was growing in her classroom. She sensed that the students felt much freer to ask questions when it was the puppet asking the question and not them. Since the other puppet didn't have to answer the question, students became interested in the challenge of coming up with interesting questions. Some of the questions raised interesting avenues to explore as they revealed what could be labeled as erroneous assumptions. One such question was, "How did you deal with the drug problem in 1870?"

Not having an answer to this question readily available in the textbook, students were mystified about how to find the answer. They turned to Betsey. She told them she wasn't sure there even was a drug problem in 1870—certainly she didn't know if the problem existed in the same manner that the students had it framed in the present, and she told them as much. Though she didn't have an answer for them, she said she had an idea about how to begin finding out. '

Betsey soon realized that her goal of creating scripts might be put off a bit, for the students had their own agenda, and it included becoming historians. Because they had raised many probing questions, Betsey started them thinking about ways to pursue answers. She asked them to consider what their sources of information concerning various questions might be—and the students started with the drug problem of 1870. Students generated the following list of places to look for information: the library, the art museum to find paintings of the period, and grandma. One student said she had noticed that the history text contained pictures from the Civil War. If the Civil War took place in 1860, she decided there were probably pictures from the 1870s that they could draw upon. Another student wondered if they could get helpful information from hospitals.

Betsey Mendenhall and Zulma Acosta with their president puppets.

From there, students began to ask related questions, including, "Did they have band-Aids then?"

This "tangent" led into a wonderful discussion of inventions in history and what contexts led to certain inventions. Students looked around the room and became curious about their immediate environment. Who thought of the rubber band and how come? Kleenex? What did they use before Kleenex? The more obvious, such as the light bulb, was skipped over; it seemed as if Thomas Edison was old hat. "Been there, done that," they declared. Betsey then told them there was an inventor among them in the class. "Who?!" the students wanted to know. "Zulma," answered Betsey. Zulma looked confused and probably thought to herself, "What is the teacher talking about?"

Betsey then pulled Zulma's president puppet from the back of the room and showed it to the class. "How did you sew the president's clothes, Zulma?" asked Betsey. Zulma answered, "I didn't; I stapled them." Zulma had invented a new way of sewing. "But that's not an invention," declared a classmate. "But she invented a new way to sew," called out another student. As Betsey had hoped, a fruitful discussion emerged. Then one of the students asked about the Happy Face logo that Betsey used when she signed her name. "Did someone invent that?" one of the students asked. This led into a discussion concerning patents and how to find out if something is patented.

The class was animated. Students were engaged and having fun. Rather than learning *about* history, students were learning to be critical thinkers and how to be historians. They were engaging in the activities critical to the field of history and were finding ways to pursue their questions. Rather than have them create scripts at this time, Betsey shifted her focus to match the students' interest in pursuing questions. In partners, she asked the students to choose three questions they would really like to have answered. Knowing that the students would likely think they would then have to find the answers, she devised a twist. After each pair came with their questions, Betsey had them switch questions with another pair.

Having experienced success, Betsey has considered having a monthly "jam session of questions." She thinks she might start with volunteers in pursuing answers, and then eventually include all students. She also has not given up the idea of the presidents discussing politics with one another. What was of particular interest to her in reflecting on all this work was the enthusiasm and dedication exhibited by the students. Because the "puppets" had nothing to lose, they could ask all sorts of questions—perhaps questions that a "student" might be too shy or self-conscious to ask. Though the students' direction in the puppet activity went in a way completely unexpected to Betsey, she found that the journey was thoroughly productive, worthwhile, and engaging.

Mural Making and History

Mural making can provide an opportunity for students to develop and carry through on a time line. Murals also relate well to math lessons concerning proportion and graphing. This works for both younger and older students. The time line in and of itself presents interesting challenges with regard to decision making. What time period should the mural cover? What dates should be used? What events should be highlighted? How to decide which events should be depicted?

An interesting mural/history idea comes from a project in San Yisidro, a border town in southern California. By reproducing photographs from the San Diego Historical Society, artists working with children created twelve murals expressing the cultural vitality and evolution of the town. In this case, not only did the students learn about local history, but in doing so they interacted with local artists and applied what they were learning to a community project.

Another example is the red clay brick project in Birmingham, Alabama, where students learn to make and decorate bricks. Started as an education program through the Birmingham Museum of Art, the project involved 150 inner-city school children. After learning about how the red clay in the ground surrounding their community was used to make bricks to line steel ovens, the students were introduced to decorative uses of red clay such as eighteenth-century Wedgewood pots. Students learned about "the scientific background of clay, glazes and firing techniques, and much about Josiah Wedgewood himself, including his role as an early opponent to slavery" (Frame, 1994, p. 22). According to Anne Arrasmith (quoted by Frame), a co-director of the project, "Now the students know more about Wedgewood and the Industrial Revolution than most adults and can relate that knowledge back to Birmingham and its history as a steel town" (p. 22). As a follow-up to the project, 2,000 bricks have now been commissioned by the city for a mural project.

Geography and Papier Mâché

To conclude this chapter I would like to return to Betsey Mendenhall's class, where the geography lesson centered on making a globe. This activity turned out to be a rich forum that informed the teacher about what the students knew (or didn't know) about geography. The globes were created from balloons covered with papier mâché. This gave the students the base structure. Because they had seen many flat maps, Betsey assumed the fifth-graders could transfer that knowledge onto a globe. Much to her surprise, she discovered that the majority of the children had never made the leap from flat map to globe. Therefore, it was the class consensus that the points furthest from each other on the map were the two outer edges of the paper. The thought of rounding the paper to meet the ends was not a part of their conception.

East and west for the students was based on their conception of California being the "West Coast." Therefore, the idea that the Appalachian Mountains were west of the East Coast was difficult to grasp. When they started looking carefully at the maps, they discovered that the United States was not the largest country in the world—a big surprise! "When they made the globes, they created their own experiences," reported Betsey. "It was their lesson to learn, and they needed to do it themselves."

Unfinished president puppets seem to take a rest next to the papier mâché globe.

While creating their globes through the arts, the students were finding ways to think about geography. They were working with knowledge and confronting assumptions, rather than taking in information given to them. The exercise not only got them directly involved with the subject matter but provided their teacher with information concerning their understandings and interests. The children were participants in the geography lessons and were given the opportunity to make decisions. After creating the continents and oceans, students decided to add other features such as rivers, mountains, states, and capitals.

SUMMARY

In addition to enhancing a social studies/history curriculum, the arts can be a core element of a program in two ways. First, the arts set a historical context for any study through their documentation of events, eras, cultures, landscapes, and people. In and of themselves, the arts are a rich historical text that offers the student of history authentic voices from which to study (see Principle 7 of multicultural education and the arts on p. 15). In their authenticity, often the works of artists communicate much more than a typical text because embedded in the words, images, or movements of an artist are questions as well as answers, contemplation as well as fact.

Second, the arts lend a framework for the action of being a historian or social scientist. The effort involved in creating an artwork lays the groundwork for the effort in which the social scientist engages. As the students in Betsey Mendenhall's class started contemplating what the president puppets would say to each other, they began to engage in the core activities of social scientists and asked the kind of questions historians pose. Moreover, for several reasons the making of artwork opens possibilities through which students may be more willing to travel. In the first place, arts are engaging and can speak to the interests of many children. Second, as we saw with the puppet example, students felt more comfortable dreaming up and asking questions when it was the puppet asking and not them directly, giving the children a greater opportunity to explore a broad range of issues.

Returning to the California framework, which states that "a strong history-social science program at the elementary level helps all students to develop their full potential for personal, civic and professional life," we can see how the arts—through their engaging and hands-on learning qualities—can prepare such individuals.

QUESTIONS TO PONDER

1. In considering events and ideas in history, how do you know what is the "truth"? Is there any one truth in history? If there is truth, how do you determine it? If there isn't, how do you approach history?
2. What are the reporting tools of a historian or social scientist? Do the tools vary according to cultures?
3. Are you familiar with your own family's past? What are the ways in which it is told?

EXPLORATIONS TO TRY

1. Brainstorm a list of social studies topics. Now, brainstorm ways to learn about three of the topics *with* the arts.
2. Using the same topics, brainstorm three ways to learn about the topic *through* the arts.
3. Identify three songs and/or poems that reflect any period in history. They may be three different periods. What aspects of history does each relate? What makes these particular pieces different from history texts with which you are familiar?
4. If you could be any character in history, who would you be? With whom would you like to interact? With a partner, create a script focusing on a specific theme whereby the two characters interact and

converse with each other. They may be from different time periods. Reflect on your script. What are all the things you learned from this experience?

5. Create a "sound" map whereby people in your classroom can navigate from one point to another using only sounds, not a visual map. What other kinds of "maps" could be created? What use might they have?

REFERENCES

Carawan, Guy, and Candie Carawan. (1990). *Sing for Freedom: The Story of the Civil Rights Movement through Its Songs.* Bethlehem, PA: A Sing Out Publication.

Cockburn, Victor. (1991). "The Uses of Folk Music and Songwriting in the Classroom." *Harvard Educational Review,* Vol. 61, No. 1, February 1991.

Cohen, Philip. (1995). "Challenging History." *Curriculum Update,* ASCD, Winter 1995.

Frame, Allen. (1994). "Building Arts Programs, Brick by Brick." *New York Times,* Education Life, August 7, 1994.

Holzer, Harold, and Mark E. Neely Jr. (1993). *Mine Eyes Have Seen the Glory: The Civil War in Art.* New York: Orion Books.

Hopkins, Lee Bennett. (1994). *Hand in Hand: An American History through Poetry.* New York: Simon and Schuster.

It's Elementary! (1992). Sacramento: California Department of Education.

Rubin, Ruth. (1990, 4th printing). *Voices of a People: The Story of Yiddish Folksong.* Philadelphia: Jewish Publication Society.

Smith, Bradley. (1968). *Mexico: A History in Art.* New York: Harper and Row.

chapter 6

The Wonder of Discovery: Science and the Arts

THE LIFE OF A WAVE

I envy the life of ever-pounding waves.
The huge steep hill of water coming
steadily, surely towards me at an alarming rate
Seeming like they are swallowing me, though never brushing my skin.
my human friends, a mere ten feet away
seems like infinite space impossible to travel,
getting longer every whole second, while the waves seem to be getting closer
bigger every half
the sensation of getting crushed,
alone yet contentful and cool.
cold and bleak
but together
together with others the same
I wish my life was one of a wave.
the mere secret of the truth and meaning of life.
overall the purpose of wishing and wondering
excitement,
fun and
survival.

Michael Sieble, fifth-grader

The work of scientists and artists could be seen as very closely aligned. Each is engaged in a process of discovery as they experiment and search for new connections in and to their world. Each experiences a sense of urgency, wonderment, and perhaps magic as a new connection is pondered or an intriguing questioned is pursued. "All of us are born with an interest in the world around us," writes Gerald Durrell (1983). He continues:

> Watch a human baby or any other young animal crawling about. It is investigating and learning things with all its senses of sight, hearing, taste, touch, and smell. From the moment we are born we are explorers in a complex and fascinating world. With some people this may fade with time or with the pressures of life, but others are lucky enough to keep this interest stimulated throughout their lives. (p. 9)

If we accept Durrell's notion of the human as explorer, then we can say that scientists and artists live parallel lives, although they express themselves through different media. They share a curiosity about the world, a desire to reflect upon it, and a need to express or communicate their understandings. They are investigators on a mission to explore or answer questions; in so doing, both tend to create new questions in addition to uncovering "findings." According to Kimberly Tolley (1993), the differences between scientists and artists are evident in how each reflects upon their relationship to their environment. "The scientist asks questions about the working of the natural world. The artist asks questions about the ways in which the world can be interpreted and re-created" (p. v.). Though both are essentially concerned with questioning the world and its inhabitants—be they animate or inanimate—each relies on a distinct way of thinking about and reflecting upon their "findings."

Now let's examine the methods of the scientist and artist and their differences. In seeking answers, "the scientist uses the processes of observing, communicating, comparing, ordering, categorizing, relating, inferring," writes Tolley. The artist, in seeking answers, "uses the processes of perception, creation, and evaluation" (1993, p. v.). From this description, one might infer that the scientist's method of thinking is the more stereotypical "objective" manner and the artist's is a more "aesthetic" view of the world. This characterization, although popular, does not reflect in its entirety the work of either the scientist or the artist.

Consider the example of a visual artist and a naturalist as they study a seashell. In order to create a painting of the seashell, the artist observes it closely looking for colors, shapes, lines, inconsistencies. The artist takes the context and environment into account. The scientist looks at the shell from a different perspective. She seeks an understanding of the object, but utilizes a different form of observation through which she documents the lines, colors, and context of the shell. Her representation might be in the form of field notes rather than a pictorial representation. To illustrate this point further, let's compare the attributes of a naturalist and an artist.[1]

---

[1] The attributes are adapted from the writing of Durrell (1983).

A naturalist could be described as someone who:

- Questions his/her world and the things in it
- Learns to be silent and patient
- Uses all the senses to develop her/his power of observation
- Keeps an open mind
- Has an inquiring mind and poses questions
- Takes copious, detailed notes and sketches
- Develops a deep reverence for the world around him/her
- Is disciplined and reflective of his/her findings
- Interprets findings in relation to other scientific findings
- Expresses his/her findings in words and drawings

An artist could be described as someone who:

- Questions his/her world and seeks to explore it
- Learns to utilize solitude
- Uses many senses in observing the world around him/her
- Sees things in new and often interesting ways
- Poses questions and ponders
- Carefully records and interprets the world in sounds, colors, shapes, words, and movement
- Develops an understanding of the world around him/her
- Is disciplined and reflective of his/her work
- Expresses her/his understandings through a variety of media

The characteristics associated with the naturalist and the artist can be remarkably similar. A fundamental difference between their work and thinking lies in (1) the expression and communication of their "findings," and (2) the objects (or issues) of their questioning upon reflection. Their reflections are what take them on different journeys. The artist reflects upon nature, considering its relation to the everyday and human experience. Moreover, the artist generally has a broader range of expressive media than does the scientist who relies heavily on the written word. The scientist usually reflects upon the findings in order to place the work in the realm of other scientific data and to further uncover mysteries of the natural world.

Alhough the ways in which the scientist and artist consider the natural world can differ, each offers the other an opportunity to expand the exploration. As well, each shares a fundamental curiosity and desire to understand the wonders of nature. The remainder of this chapter is devoted to science/art connections in teaching and learning. Beginning with ways in which science can be introduced *with* the arts, the reader will find examples of activities and exercises that serve as an idea bank.

A fifth-grader sketches plants at the Bataquitos
Lagoon in Carlsbad, California.

LEARNING WITH THE ARTS

Painting

If you and your students have access to an art museum, you might find this an
interesting exercise. Choose a gallery that includes landscapes. Examine the
paintings, using the following questions as a springboard for a discussion about
the natural world: How would you describe the weather in the different paintings?
Can you predict the weather? What are your clues? What kind of clouds are
depicted? What elements of nature are shown in each painting? How authentic
is an animal in a drawing? How would you describe the light and shadows in

the work? (If you do not have access to a gallery or museum, you might replicate this activity by introducing posters of paintings to your class.)

Another use of paintings involves the study of colors. What is a color? How does the artist create colors? Looking at specific paintings, what combinations of colors might the artist have used in order to create the scene? You might even move into mathematics by estimating the proportions of colors mixed to achieve an effect.

Music

Many people have introduced the study of acoustics through musical instrument demonstrations. For example, study the sounds of drums as they vibrate. Perhaps a more familiar activity that involves music and science has to do with listening. I have often gone on "musical" listening field trips, where the students and I document the songs and sounds of nature. After completing this exercise, I draw upon the works of musicians who have incorporated or imitated the sounds of nature in their compositions. When we listen as a class to a selection, we discuss the ways in which the music expresses an aspect of nature—what instruments are played; tempos, feelings, or moods created; and so on.

There are endless possibilities of musicians and composers who have recorded pieces on the theme of nature. There are many American Indian song collections, such as *Songs of Earth, Water, Fire and Sky* (New World Records), that relate specifically to earth and nature. Likewise, there are many songs in popular song collections about nature and science. To get you thinking further on this topic, I include a brief sampling of composers and their music as they relate to issues in science:

- Kronos Quartet: Cadenza on the Night Plain
- John McLaughlin: The Mediterranean
- Steve Reich: The Desert Music
- Claude Debussy: La Mer
- Ferde Grofe: Grand Canyon Suite: "On the Trail"
- Gustav Holst: The Planets
- Rimsky-Korsakov: Flight of the Bumblebee
- Igor Stravinsky: The Rite of Spring
- Antonio Vivaldi: The Four Seasons
- Paul Winter: recordings on Whales and the Grand Canyon

Poetry

Poems on the topic of nature and science can be integrated as a way to generate interest in science topics. *The Random House Book of Poetry for Children* (Prelutsky, 1983) contains many appropriate poems, including "Nature Is . . .," "The Four Seasons," and "The Ways of Living Things." A poem might be as simple as the one shown below. Although it is not particularly profound or informative, this anonymous poem has stirred many a young child's imagination during scientific investigation of the life of a bug:

> Curious fly,
> Vinegar jug,
> Slippery edge,
> Pickled bug.

Perspectives related through poetry provide opportunities to view science in an expanded manner. This particular poem might give the child insight into the world from the bug's perspective. Students might be inclined to consider the "inner life" of a bug in addition to the more objective description of what it does, how it moves, what it eats, and so on.

LEARNING THROUGH THE ARTS

There are numerous ways to learn about science through the arts. In this discussion, I will highlight the activities of drawing and poetry. But first, a few ideas drawing from movement and drama.

Dance

Dance can enhance lessons in anatomy and physics. Looking at the movements of a dancer, perhaps a student in your class, what muscles are being utilized? How does the dancer relate to and create motion and energy? How can the dancer defy motion by being still? What is the dancer's relation to gravity? Momentum? Centrifugal force? Time? Space? Contraction? Expansion?

To explore chaos, a teacher might have the students move throughout a room without touching each other. Make the space bigger or smaller, the tempo faster or slower. To explore the motion of atoms, centipedes, or blood moving through a vein, have the students re-create the motion through movement. To explore life cycles, have them dramatize the events of a metamorphosis. Have them act out the life of a butterfly from pupa to full-grown butterfly, or the life cycle of a tornado.

Ecology: Drawing from Nature

Drawing and sketching are the tools of the naturalist. They are also tools for students as they begin to explore and understand their surroundings. Especially for second language learners, learners who are more visual, and learners who enjoy the visual arts, drawing can be a fantastic tool for science understanding. In this manner, the activity addresses Principles 1 and 2 of multicultural education and the arts (see p. 14), which speak to expanding the expressive outlets available to learners and enabling freedom of expression for second language learners. Karen Gallas (1994) relates a conversation to this effect between Juan and David, first-graders who were sketching their way toward understandings in science:

> DAVID: I'd heard people talk about this thing. I think it was a praying mantis, but I didn't know what it was. So I looked at a book, and then I drew it, and then I knew what it was.
>
> JUAN: Or if you don't know what a wing is and how it's made, you can draw it and then you know. (p. 134)

In teaching a unit on ecology, most teachers want their students to become familiar with objects in nature and make connections to the larger context of their environment. An effective use of the arts in studying nature is to draw nature: sketch leaves, shells, flowers, seaweed, and so on. As a student carefully sketches nature, she becomes an active observer of an object and may become interested in asking questions about the object she is drawing. Margot Grallert, an arts specialist in Massachusetts, works closely with classroom teachers. She sets up "graphic observation centers" where children can illustrate "something they were looking at, or ideas they had that had no concrete form, such as the abstract quality of a weather condition, or of motion" (Grallert, 1991, p. 263).

An interesting technique that Grallert employs is to work from the "inside out." This is both a philosophy about learning and an actual artistic technique. The artistic technique is simple: Pick a place in the middle of the object, and sketch from the inside out. Do not begin with a border; do not outline the object as you draw. For example, if you were on a beach, you might choose a seashell and observe it closely. Then choose a place somewhere in the middle of the shell. Begin your drawing from that middle spot. Draw continuously outward from that spot. You will be surprised with the difference between beginning in the middle and beginning with an outline. As you are drawing you will be observing the shell carefully. You must observe it closely in order to draw it—and re-create its image on paper.

As you are drawing you might become curious about its makeup and history. Most children become curious as they sketch. I often ask students to create two lists while drawing: a list of the things they notice, and a list of their questions that arise. They often note interesting things about their shell such as the amount of lines in its curved shape, the detail in the patterns, and shapes on the shell. They may begin to wonder: What is the shell made of? Does it grow? Did anything live in this shell? Where is it now? How did it get out? How did the shell end up on the beach? Was it out very far in the ocean? Did it travel from somewhere else to get here? Did the waves push it? How far? These and other questions that arise from the graphic exercise form the basis for the science lessons.

Not only does the art exercise provide the motivation to form scientific questions, but it also provides a method through which the students translate a

Students sketching from the "inside-out"
and writing intently on a path at the Bataquitos
Lagoon.

three-dimensional world into a two-dimensional picture. This translation, as I have mentioned previously, is one of the keys to unlocking and stimulating intellectual development. Curiosity inspired through the exercise, coupled with attentive guidance from the teacher, will set the students searching for answers to their questions.

Tara deArrieta, a kindergarten teacher in the Reno, Nevada, area, tried a plant drawing and question activity with her students. "After introducing the unit with a garden story," writes Tara, "I had the students draw a fresh chrysanthemum flower with the leaves intact using the [inside out] method. The pictures were remarkable and the questions very sophisticated." Following are examples from the students' list of questions:

- Why are leaves in different shapes?
- Why do flowers have leaves?
- What kind of flower did we draw?
- Why are stems green?
- Why do flowers smell?
- What do plants make for us?
- How do plants make their food?
- Why do some plants have thorns?
- Why are there so many different plants?
- Why are they all colors?
- Who names flowers?
- How do you know what flower it is?
- Why do they need soil, water, and air?

Tara reports that in order to answer some of the questions, her class is continuing to learn through the arts:

We started a movement activity demonstrating the metamorphosis of a seed. We are using art to make paper models of our plants as they grow under grow lights to record the changes from seeds to roots, etc. We are writing a poem about the life cycle of a plant that we are putting into a pop-up book. And, we are using metaphors to connect the needs of plants to our own needs.

The children remained engaged for the better part of the year, following through on their study. Tara also encouraged their explorations through the arts in other areas of the curriculum.

In considering "working from the inside out" as a philosophy as well as a practice, Grallert writes, "[it] is an individually directed thought process, an unpremeditated search for an unknown reality. It is a way of figuring out something that is your own" (1991, p. 260). According to Grallert, working from the inside out can be characterized by the following three conditions:

- a belief that every person has an inner sense of self that can and must provide direction for learning;
- an environment that encourages and stimulates the individual to find his or her personal direction;
- a conviction that there are no final answers. (p. 260)

The third condition might interest readers who consider science a field that is in search of final answers. Unfortunately, there exist very few (if any) truths or final answers. Instead, there are webs of complexities. If we examine the history of science, we find that "truths" or "theories" change as more is discovered about the world. There was a time, for example, when it was common "knowledge" that the world was flat. As scientists sought to understand more about the world and developed tools to interpret it, their theories and knowledge of science evolved and changed. The same is true for geocentric theory, plate tectonics, and the ongoing search to understand the extinction of the dinosaurs. Science is a study of complexities. Our search for understanding never ends; it only evolves as we gather more and more experience.

The Nature of Poetry: Working with Ideas

The first time I approached the study of science through poetry was with a fourth-grade transitional language (Spanish-English) class in southern California. Because of a time-sharing arrangement, a teacher other than the regular classroom teacher taught science. This science teacher worried that the children were not retaining the science lessons, and she asked us if there was a way to explore science topics at another point in the day. Thus the science-poetry project began. Our first strategy was to engage the students in brainstorming words related to science while we wrote the words on the blackboard. Within minutes the board filled up, yet the children were still offering words and phrases.

As they were brainstorming, another interesting phenomenon occurred. Different students began revisiting the ideas related to certain words. They started asking questions dealing with concepts they had studied; their curiosity about science topics was rekindled. One example that I especially remember involved "nickel." The class was studying the elements, and many element names appeared on the brainstorm list on the blackboard. When one child said "nickel" another child questioned, "Do you remember how much nickel is in a nickel?" Others thought, then they decided to look it up—without suggestion from their teacher. The brainstorming alone gave them inspiration to revisit the properties of a five-cent piece.

Following the brainstorm, we asked the children to choose words from the board and apply them to a poem. We encouraged them over a two-session period to edit and revise their poems. Here are a few examples that evolved from the activity.

Kevin is a special needs student who is in this class for language arts. He is reticent about writing, although excited about the poetry class. He surprised us with this wonderfully descriptive and imaginative science poem:

There was a night
I thought I had a dream
but I woke up
I looked outside and I looked up in the sky
but there was nothing there
but, I saw a star
but, I saw another star
It was a shooting star

Kevin

The next poem, by Alicia Finley, incorporates a number of science topics. Not only does she use science vocabulary, but it is clear to the teacher and me that she knows something about the concept of "chaos." She employs the concept in a way many of us can relate to—our chaotic rooms, or desks, and so on. The poem reminds me of my own room when I was 10 years old!

Alicia finishes her poem and is ready to read it out loud.

My room is like science because there is
volume,
liquids,
mass,
experiments,
products,
and different kinds of chaos
and, maybe my sister too.

Alicia Finley

I find the next poem particularly intriguing because Adriana Rosales Rosales not only writes a "science" poem, but she incorporates one of the most fundamental aspects of science into her poem: the notion of asking questions. How better to capture science in a poem than to ask questions?

Why is the sky
so blue tell me
why
oh why
do I have
brown hair
Why do I
see with
my eyes
Oh please tell me
why

Adriana Rosales Rosales

An interesting way to build on the children's "question poems" might be to write another poem that includes some "answers" to their questions. Students could exchange poems during the questioning and answering.

For the last example from this initial brainstorm and editing activity, I have included the first, second, and final drafts of Susanne Chea's poem about the ocean. Susanne was in an after-school science group that focused on oceanography; one can see through her poem and illustration (Figure 6.1) how much of the topic was integrated into her thinking.

FIRST DRAFT:

Science
Science Under the Sea!
Sea hair [sic], wet rocky places.
Coral reefs, Deep in water,
Kelp forest, swaying in water!

SECOND DRAFT:

Science

Science under the sea!
Sea hair, wet rocky places.
Coral reefs Deep in water.
Kelp forest swaying in water
muscles, stuck to rocks where hard waves are
I love science under the sea!

Susanne Chea

FIGURE 6.1   Susanne's final poem and illustration

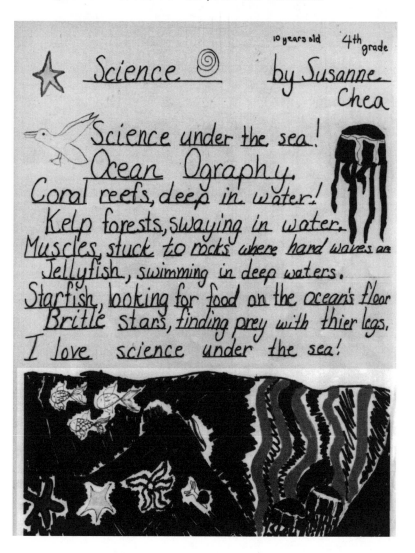

Susanne, working on her final draft of "Science."

In addition to working with children, I often have my college students write poems and raps about science. Inspired by a child's poem about photosynthesis, one of my graduate students composed the following poem about the food chain. It was written by Paul Montell, a science teacher in the Las Vegas, Nevada, area. I have "rapped" this poem to my fourth- and fifth-graders to great applause and appreciation.

I see you twitch
You caught my eye
You freeze with fear
Now prepare to die
Your mousy scent
so sweet to smell
your slender body
slides down so well
I'm part of the food chain
and you're next in line
It is upon you
which I must dine
Symbol of evil
or so you say
Hey, I'm just a predator
in search of prey
So sorry to kill
But it's just me
It's my makeup
genetically
So there's my tale
for all to see
I've left nothing back
quite honestly
At least I admit
Everything I do
Can the same be said
for all of you?
So now don't bother to flinch
because my aim is true
Now I must do
what snakes just do.

Paul Montell

Lagoon Poems.   In keeping with the theme of ecology, we will next look at the role poetry can play in studying nature. The first group of poems below were written after a session at a local lagoon that is currently under restoration. The restoration project is a huge undertaking involving dredging and pumping in order to re-open the lagoon to the ocean. To do so, a large waterway must be dredged and a tremendous amount of sand displaced. While they were at the lagoon, each student took notes or made sketches in a sketchbook. At the start of the exercise, the teacher had them look in all directions, up, down, left, and right. The students then observed, in silence, as they wandered along the perimeter of the lagoon, that was open to school groups. Prior to the trip the teacher had engaged the children in extensive discussions about the lagoon and nature;

they also had practiced observation sessions. Since the lagoon is located very close to the school and the children's homes, it is something with which each child had some familiarity.

Once back in the classroom, the children were asked to take their notes and organize them into poems. In the first poetry session we asked them to simply write a poem based on their notes and sketches. In the second session we asked them to compose a poem from the perspective of the lagoon. What was the lagoon's perspective on the restoration process? If it could speak, what would it say? By asking the students to go this extra step, we hoped they would delve more deeply into the issues concerning restoration. At the same time we

FIGURE 6.2 Carson's lagoon poem

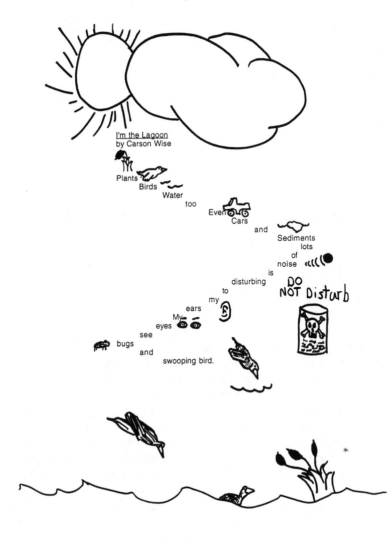

were conscious of placing the students in a position where they could exercise their imaginations. Both sessions are reflected in the following poems.

This poem in Figure 6.2 was written by Carson Wise, who wrote in his journal, "I can't write what I'm thinking." It is remarkable to see what he created in light of (or despite) this statement. Note the careful visual design of his words and all the symbols that accompany them.

"I'm the Lagoon (after)" is Carson's poem from the perspective of the lagoon. It is quite different from his first poem. Many children, including Carson, found writing from the lagoon's perspective easier. It was as if the freedom to write from a perspective other than one's own was an inspiring source.

I'M THE LAGOON (AFTER)

I have eyes all around
I listen quietly
there is no sound
out of nowhere
a brown pelican
dives into my water
breaking the silence
that was there before.

Carson Wise

The next poem is by Casey Dandeneau, a student who likes to write poetry but is challenged in many other academic areas throughout the day. Like most of us, when he is interested he becomes engaged. When he is not interested, however, he can be a challenge. Fortunately, with expanded avenues of expression and work available to him, Casey has many moments throughout the day when he is actively engaged in learning and even enjoying himself. His poem addresses a number of aspects of the lagoon project. He refers to the sand displacement, the algae, and how once the lagoon is restored its life will return.

JUDGING THE LAGOON

When the pumps first start it starts my heart
To hear the sound of leaving sand
it's like the greatest music band.
When the algae is gone and the fish are near
it makes even more life come near
Life's so great
it's something no one can hate
to help me survive
That's a life so great
it's something no one can hate
No matter what it did
not even if you tried.

When they're all done
and the trouble is gone
that life will return again.

Casey Dandeneau

"I See I Feel" was written by the class-identified poet-in-residence, Emily Birnbaum. This child is constantly writing poems, joyful in sharing them with her classmates and teachers. She composed this particular poem for two voices. The lines in the center are meant to be read simultaneously by both readers. Other than that, each reader recites his or her lines according to the alternating order in which they fall. One could also imagine that the spacing of the words on the page looks like the pistons, simulating the dredging action! It is a poem written from the perspective of the lagoon.

I SEE I FEEL
(a poem for two voices)

YES ME THE LAGOON

Dredging

Pumping

Dredging

Pumping

Take all this sediment off my face
Once again make me a part of your human race

Oh yes, oh yes let this water flow, sediment algae, bacteria go
Life from the rivers, mountains, and seas

Oh yes bring this all to me

My face feels refreshed

But oh no, am I doomed?

I don't want to end up a

shriveled prune

Emily Birnbaum

Finally, another poem written from the perspective of the lagoon. What interested me about this poem was its questioning and wonder. Through the science exercise, Jenna Timinsky has captured the wonderment of science. Her questions, set within the context of an imaginative poem, reveal much of her understanding of the lagoon and the issues surrounding the restoration process.

INSIDE OF ME

What is this I hear?
help? scared cries of fleeing birds?

a change? monsters roaring on my surface?
fresh start? what did I do?
What is this I feel?
my skin ripping into painful wounds?
weights holding me in? a breath?
the rush of incoming water? churning and tossing?
stealing my bottom dwellers?
What is this I taste?
salt? danger? future happiness? fresh body?
renewal?

Finding a solitary spot at the lagoon, this fifth-grader composes her poem.

What is this I smell?
rusty lead? no birds? dying plants? algae?
my deathbed? cleanliness? a war?
Will I die or will I live?
Fogginess invades my mind
I express my feelings to a wise blue heron.

Jenna Timinsky

Ocean and Beach Poems.   The next set of poems were written after students
did a similar observation exercise on a local beach within walking distance of
their school. Again, the students were asked to look in all directions as they
began their observations. Each sat on the beach in solitude for 10 minutes as
they observed, made notes, and sketched (if they chose to sketch) something
around them in the environment.

THE BEACH TODAY

The waves crumbling outside
and the shorebreak pounding
on the smooth surface
and exploding like a volcano.
A pelican gliding across the waves
seagulls eating scraps. That's the beach today!

Darrell Goodrum

Note Darrell Goodrum's attention to motion. He has focused on the action
of the waves. In applying his observations, he chooses interesting descriptive
words and metaphors. While Darrell mainly focused on the breaking of the waves
and the seabirds in the vicinity, Jenna Timinsky, his classmate, honed in on one
rock she found intriguing. It was a speckled little rock broken in texture by a
line of another rock or sediment. In addition to documenting the rock's qualities,
she goes a step further and adds an imaginative mystery to the rock.

ROCK

I've found a rock
a light gray rock
a plain rock—with something special
it had a heart—a cracked heart
How did it break? Who was the lad?
Was it the pounding sea and its raging waves?
or was it a beloved companion, a long lost companion?
Who was it who cracked the speckled heart?
as speckled as a bird's egg
The heart is now only a tattered stone.

Jenna Timinsky

The next poem was written by Anain Matias, a Spanish-speaking student who is focusing on developing English skills throughout the day. She generally writes and speaks in her first (and at this time, most comfortable) language—Spanish. It was very interesting to the teacher and me not only that (1) she chose to apply her observations in the poem in the manner that she did, but that (2) she chose to write the poem in English, thereby pushing herself in a language direction where she seldom ventured. This might illustrate how poetry can be a useful and manageable tool for second language learners as they explore subject matter.

why the water is blue clean
water is blue the water is blue
because we take care of it
the water needs to be blue
for the fish could swim
and the birds could eat fish
that are not poisoned

Anain Matias

In the following poem, Megan Riel-Mehan applies her observations of the motion of a red-tailed hawk. In addition to capturing and expressing the image of a red-tailed hawk, Megan communicates that it has "well trained eyes," indicating that she has retained information about the hawk's ability to search for prey.

RED TAILED HAWK

Soaring
Swiftly through the blanket of a sky
Swooping
Diving
Looking with its well trained eyes
Gliding
Gracefully through the enchanted and brilliant
Sky

Megan Riel-Mehan

To conclude this section, I can't help but return to our poet-in-residence, Emily, as she applies her observations and reflections about the ocean.

THE EXPLOSION

The waves glide on a blazing hot day
The seaweed rolls through water as a wave forms
turning and turning until it becomes a white
explosion running over the enchanted water

filtered with light because of the sun spreading its
glistening shadow
the explosion gets smaller and smaller until it's
just a salty shadow gliding along
the soggy shore as it approaches the ancient and face filled
cliffs of insanity
it shines as it disappears leaving only a foam

Emily Birnbaum

Through these poems, we can document students' attention to detail in their observations—a critical scientific skill that is reinforced through the writing exercise. We also see how the students have reflected upon their observations and asked new questions—also critical scientific skills. As teachers we are not only involving the students in an interesting study of nature but are giving them the opportunity to apply and reflect upon the study as it relates to their lives and the things that are important to them. Throughout the poetry projects, I have found that most students become actively engaged in creating imaginative poems. This is in part because they are continually practicing their observation, reflection, and imaginative skills. As in any course of study, some students are more interested in the subject and process than others. I have found that this kind of exercise tends to engage most of the children because they have freedom in choosing an object to observe and freedom in the manner through which they apply their work in the poetry.

Question Poems.   The last set of science-related poems were written after an exercise of guided wonderment. The first part of the exercise involved asking questions about nature. I brought a piece of sea glass to the classroom and asked the children to brainstorm questions concerning its origin, its travels, and so on. The children were encouraged to be imaginative in their questioning. Among their questions were: How did it get to the beach? What was it a part of originally? Did someone drink from it? Who held it? How did it get smooth? Is it smooth on the inside? How far has it traveled? How does the water carry it to different places? Has a seagull looked at it? After this brainstorming session, the children could choose any object and form their own questions. The teacher then introduced them to a number of poems by Pablo Neruda, who has written and complied a book of question poems. For our purposes, because this is a bilingual class, Neruda was a wonderful choice: His poems are written in Spanish and translated into English, giving both Spanish and English speakers examples and models for consideration. Students could read, and then write, in either Spanish or English.

QUESTIONS

What do raindrops do after they hit the ground?
Do raindrops have a life?
Why do raindrops go only one way?

Do raindrops miss the ocean?
Does the sun make water disappear?
Why are rocks hard?

Matt Motter

QUESTIONS

What does the ocean laugh about?
Does a tornado ever get dizzy?
Why do the waves slap the sand?
Does the ocean ever sleep?
Does the sun ever drown?
Is the night afraid of the dark?
How cold is death's hand?
Does death fly or does it walk?
Does solitude talk with silence?
Does solitude ever get lonely?

Megan Riel-Mehan

CLOUDS

Are you friends with the wind?
Why are your tears so wet?
Do you and the sun have fights?
Why do you make your home so high in the sky?
What do you observe about mankind?
If you could talk, what would you say?
How big is the sky?
Do you and the sky understand each other?
Does the wind control you?
Are you and the birds friends, and do you talk with them?
How big are you?
Why do you hide the sun?
How long is your life-span?
How old are you?

Nicole Laperdon

SUMMARY

Combining science and the arts creates an exciting and explosive arena for understanding the natural world. The possibilities for exploring science with and through the arts is just about as limitless as science itself. When used as a methodology for learning about science concepts and gaining scientific skills, the arts can lend complexity and inspire further questioning. When children begin to draw an object in nature, they begin to observe it closely—a fundamental skill for any scientist. When children begin to reflect on their experiences through writing (such as poetry), they participate in the work of a scientist seriously contemplating the mystery of the natural world. Thus, the natural bridge between the arts and science engages not only the child's mind but his or her imagination as well.

QUESTIONS TO PONDER

1. Think about a person who makes pottery. What relationships to science are involved in creating a bowl, cup, or other object?
2. Would you consider the potter to be a "scientist"? If yes, how? If no, why not?
3. Can you think of instances when a scientist might also be considered an "artist"?
4. Debates in the art world revolve around whether or not nature is "art." What do you think, and why?

EXPLORATIONS TO TRY

1. What are three ways in which you can explore some topic in science *with* the arts?
2. What are three ways in which you can explore the same topic *through* the arts?
   To help you with Explorations 1 and 2, consider the following topics (or choose one of your own topics): oceanography, chaos, mammals, energy, astronomy, magnetism, light and prisms, botany, insects, food chains, photosynthesis, the planets.
3. Try drawing a flower or seashell from the inside out. Keep a list of (1) what you notice, and (2) your questions about the object.

REFERENCES

Durrell, Gerald. (1983). *The Amateur Naturalist.* New York: Knopf.

Gallas, Karen. (1994). *The Languages of Learning: How Children Talk, Write, Dance, Draw, and Sing Their Understanding of the World.* New York: Teachers College Press.

Grallert, Margot (1991). "Working from the Inside Out: A Practical Approach to Expression," *Harvard Educational Review*, Vol. 61, No. 3, August 1991.

Prelutsky, Jack, ed. (1983). *The Random House Book of Poetry for Children.* New York: Random House.

Tolley, Kimberly. (1993). *The Art and Science Connection: Hands-on Activities for Primary Students.* Menlo Park, CA: Addison-Wesley.

chapter 7

Puzzles of the Mind and Soul: Mathematics and the Arts

Nature is relationships in space.
Geometry defines relationships in space.
Art creates relationships in space.
            Newman and Boles (1992a)

ANSWERS COME TO ME

Soaring high overhead
I become that bird up there,
flowing through the silent roads of nature,
I realize what life really is
it is me
what I like to do,
it is nature

those silent paths I've walked are the paths of life
I feel it, and slowly become myself again
I climb, into the sturdy branches of the tree
opening itself up for any being to sit in, or live in
and I know these are the real virtues of living,
the real reasons that I'm here.

            Katrina White, fifth-grader

Mathematics and the arts. At first glance they might appear to be distant cousins. But on closer examination we will see that there are so many connections between the two, describing them as fraternal twins might be more apropos. In almost every way the two are interrelated yet have their own lives. At times they can even be dependent on each other. Consider the painter who at the moment of conceiving a watercolor is also dealing with lines, points, shapes, and space; or the musician who acts as a mathematician working in patterns, time, and rhythms. A dancer is a geometrist moving within the dimensions of a stage or performance area while exploring the possibilities of space.

A common misconception is that mathematics is dedicated to finding answers. This is only a small part of the work. The mathematician is an inventor creating and finding ways to understand relationships among time, space, plane, point, and line. Like an artist, the mathematician seeks the adventure of solving or creating problems. Each does work that demands imagination. Each follows a language of action and reflection moving toward greater understanding.

Consider what each might bring to the understanding of nature. Nature is continually inventing new and complex patterns for the mathematician and the artist: the branching of a river after a great winter melt, or the cumulus clouds flowing steadily with a forceful wind. While nature gives the mathematician infinite patterns and shapes to consider, at the same time it gives the artist beauty and natural wonder to contemplate. Put together, a greater—or one might argue, more balanced—perception of nature is possible. "Despite the essential difficulties in understanding the whole of Nature," write Rochelle Newman and Martha Boles (1992a), "both Mathematics and Art reflect a human desire to comprehend [nature] . . . each never fully explains her, but in their complementarity they work to give wholeness" (p. xiii).

Cathy Bullock, a fifth-grade teacher in Encinitas, California, regularly has her students explore mathematical concepts in nature. She brings her students into nature, both around the school and at a local botanical garden where they sketch flowers and leaves. The students apply their mathematical knowledge to the sketching by describing aspects of nature in mathematical terms. The following examples taken from one child's sketchbook illustrate this point. For the first sketch in Figure 7.1, the child has considered a Daylily. She has identified Fibonacci numbers ("13 lines" and "three petals"), something that can be found throughout structures created by nature such as the petals on a sunflower or the scales on a pine cone.

For the second sketch in Figure 7.1, the student has drawn a Scarlet Pimpernel. The mathematical relationships she identified included the number of petals on each flower, the numbers of flowers in a group, and the number of groups on the stem. For the last sketch in Figure 7.1, the student has drawn Millet. She recognized that the "plant is not a Fibonacci, it is a fractal." The student is on to an important discovery as she learns that nature offers infinite fractal and Fibonacci patterns to consider, observe, and understand.

Another relationship between art and mathematics articulated by Newman and Boles relates to games, or constructs of the mind. Games or constructs of the mind are basic to each discipline, and "both disciplines look for the relationships among the game pieces" (p. xiii). In each case the game pieces, or constructs, build on each other and are related to each other. In music there is often a development of themes, recapitulations, even improvisations. No single

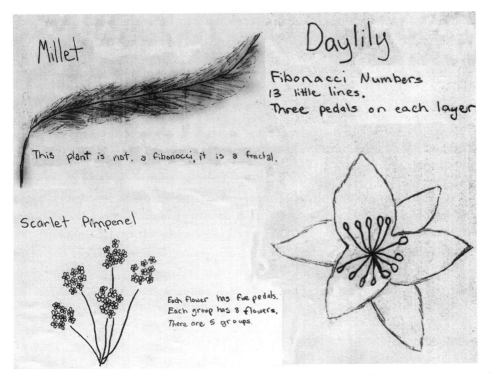

FIGURE 7.1 Nature sketches

note or timbre is enough to create a melody. Even after a melody is established, it is often brought to life with the addition of rhythm, harmonies, counter-melodies and the like. In algebra we find formulas, properties, and proofs. Concepts and/or numbers come to life as they are connected in relationships with other concepts, numbers, measurements, perceptions. In both cases the "game" pieces work in harmony toward a greater end, or solution. In both cases there are endless avenues to explore.

One could argue that the arts are in the realm of metaphor, whereas mathematics is in the realm of logic. If this is true, then the combination of the two provides a unique balance. I would argue that on the surface, this characterization might have some validity. On closer examination we may find even greater complexities in this relationship. For example, the visual artist is concerned with mathematical relationships among points, lines, and spaces. The concepts are fundamental to the artist's ability to depict a scene or create a design. The mathematician must be able to think beyond the concrete level, as the artist does—in other words, stretch his or her imagination to solve mathematical problems. In this way the mathematician works on a level usually associated with the artist.

Take another example, the geometrist who seeks to understand relationships among shapes reacts to something interesting or worthy of reflection. More often than not, the reaction is an aesthetic awareness. In response to that awareness, the individual seeks greater understanding. As with the artist, the geometrist is guided by a creative force. He or she engages in the same creative process as the artist in seeking to interpret relationships found in the natural world. Thus, when the worlds of the mathematician and the artist meet (as opposed to co-existing in parallel universes), a unique and evolving understanding has the opportunity to emerge.

Before reading on, brainstorm a list of ways in which mathematics and the arts (visual art, music, sculpture, dance, poetry, etc.) intersect. Here are some ideas to get you going:

- repetition, patterns: *reggae music:* recurring rhythms and beats
- points and sets: *pointillism:* impressionist paintings
- symmetry, geometry: *origami:* the Japanese art of paper folding
- counting, shapes: *square dance:* patterns in time and space
- time: *photography:* shutter speeds, and exposure
- addition: *recipes:* the ingredients in a culinary delight, *oil painting:* the mixing of colors on a palette, *songs:* the additive song "Old MacDonald"
- subtraction: *songs:* the song "BINGO"
- equivalents: *rounds:* each section of a round ("Kookaburra," "Frère Jacques," "Row, Row, Row Your Boat")
- equilateral triangle: *round* in three parts
- balance: *pottery:* throwing a pot on a wheel

Now, can you brainstorm a list of professions in which mathematics and the arts meet? Consider the work of architects, engineers, sculptors, muralists, quilters, tailors. All deal with angles, art, and aesthetics. What other professions connect mathematics and the arts?

LEARNING WITH THE ARTS

In this section we will explore the many ways in which the arts relate to areas of mathematics. We will begin in the realm of visual arts.

Visual Arts

Paintings provide a rich source of material for the emerging mathematician. According to Richard Millman and Ramona Speranza (1991), "art can be used to present early concepts of geometry, including the notion of the infinite" (p. 133). To illustrate their point the authors focus on the work of many artists, including Georges Seurat (1859-1891), a French painter who developed a technique involving lots and lots of points—dots—applied very closely together to create images. This technique was quite innovative in comparison to the more traditional technique of employing brush strokes. Seurat's technique, also utilized by other impressionist artists including Manet and Monet, became known as *pointillism.*

In considering works of the impressionist painters, students learn how points are used as "building blocks" to make sets. A tree can be seen as a set of points as well as a tree; the monkey in Seurat's *A Sunday Afternoon on the Island of La Grande Jatte* can be seen as yet another set. The addition of sets to sets creates a whole.

The works of other well-known artists such as Paul Klee, Pablo Picasso, Wassily Kandinsky, Jasper Johns, and M. C. Escher can offer students a lesson in geometry as well. Moreover, no doubt there are local artists within your community who could provide works for your class consideration. (Not only is it a chance to incorporate works of art, but it gives your students a chance to meet and interact with local artists.) Observe the sketch in Figure 7.2. This is a

FIGURE 7.2 Original artwork by Deb Stern: geometrical house

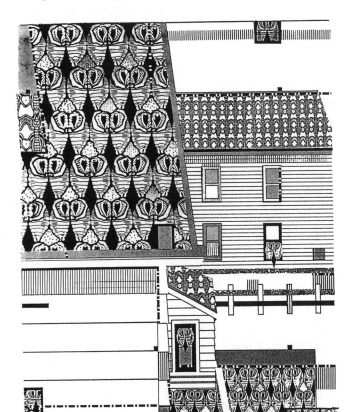

work by Deb Stern, a local artist in my community. Notice all the mathematical relationships and concepts in her sketch. Make your own list before reading mine.

I notice rectangles, squares, and many lines. There is a perimeter. There are lots of parallel lines. There are many angles throughout: right angles in corners, and angles of varying degrees. Note the triangles. What kind of triangles are there? Is there a line of symmetry? Are there symmetrical patterns? Looking more closely, I identify polygons throughout the painting. Is there any part of the sketch that gives you a feeling of infinity? This is an important concept in Euclidean geometry, "where lines are assumed to be 'straight' and never ending" (Millman and Speranza, 1991, p. 136).

In looking through one of the art books in my school library, I was struck by its organization. The art concepts and math concepts are nearly interchangeable! The book is *Latin American Art: An Introduction to the Works of the 20th Century* (Chaplik, 1989). Most of the chapters are organized around a mathematical theme. The first three chapters focus on line, shape, and space. Other chapters focus on pattern, rhythm, contrast, balance, and unity. This is a good source and model for discussing visual art in a mathematical language. Although intended as a structure for the study of twentieth-century Latin American art, the author's format is perfect for the math teacher. If you cannot find other books organized in a similar way, Chaplik's thematic approach to discussing works of art can be easily applied to other paintings or sculptures as well.

The teacher does not need an in-depth knowledge of art in order to carry out any of the explorations mentioned so far. In fact, this work might inspire you and your students to become more interested in artists and their works. A good place to start might be your school or community library. Most collections have art books and slides. A nearby art museum or an art teacher in your school might be willing to serve as a consultant. No doubt, with a little help you can begin to discover the rich resources within your own community.

After studying various artists' paintings, you might have the students create original works of art that incorporate mathematical elements they have uncovered. "The insights that students get from this approach," conclude Millman and Speranza, "range from, at the minimum, becoming exposed to some magnificent works of art to getting a visualization of various concepts from both mathematics and art" (1991, p. 138). Students can begin to understand that seemingly different fields are really quite connected.

Dance

In Chapter 6 I mentioned a few relationships between science and dance. Now consider the mathematical possibilities as well. If you have a chance to attend a dance performance, observe the dancers and note the lines and shapes involved in the choreography. In southern California, many schools have their own folklorico ballet ensembles. The students learn and perform folk dances from the various regions of Mexico. In watching the performances, one can discern mathematical concepts including shape, lines, parallel lines, symmetry, sequence, patterns—both in groups of dancers, and in the repetition of individual steps.  Counting is important as well. Are the dancers moving consistently to a certain number of beats? What are the counts? How often do they repeat? Can you detect the concept of odd and even by observing the dancers? What else do you notice?

If you are unable to attend a dance performance, find out if any student in your class takes or has taken ballet lessons. Perhaps the student would be willing to demonstrate the various positions, such as those illustrated in Figure 7.3, and go into pliés and grand pliés in each position. What shapes and angles does the body create in each position?

Do any of your students take tap dance lessons? How is a tap dancer different in mathematical terms from a ballet dancer? Consider the sounds as well. Are there regular patterns? Are there additive steps? Are there any shapes in various steps? What other forms of dance do the students know? In what ways do they relate to mathematical concepts?

Of course, one dance genre that is usually part of a physical education program is square dancing. Work with the physical education teacher and relate the mathematical concepts to the dances. Square dancing affords an enjoyable opportunity for mathematical discussion and action.

FIGURE 7.3 Ballet positions

Literature

There is a world of literature concerned with mathematical concepts. And there is another world of literature that I might label "math ready." Donna Burk and her colleagues, in *Math Excursions 1* (1992), present many wonderful examples of an integrated curriculum. One example begins with the book *Where the Wild Things Are,* by Maurice Sendak. The book has been selected as source reading book, yet its potential for investigating math concepts is great. Burk et al. suggest that the teacher ask of the children, "How many different ways can you think of to sort this group of wild things?" (p. 1). Take a second look at the literature you are using in your classroom. What potential does it have for math lessons?

Literally hundreds of books relate directly to concepts in mathematics with themes including algebra, mathematicians, discrete mathematics, problem solving, geometry and patterns, logic and language, measurement and mass, capacity, volume, length, temperature, money, size, and time. There are also numerous books relating to numbers and counting, number concepts, number relationships, place value, addition and subtraction, multiplication and division, estimation, fractions, probability, statistics, and graphing. Many can be used in the integrated classroom as an example of great literature as well as a "math book." What do you already have in your classroom that fits this category?

Music

You might begin to think about the relationships between music and math by listening to some music. Take reggae music, for example. Notice the recurring patterns on the part of the instruments. Are the patterns of equal length? Or, sing a familiar folk song such as "O, Susanna," and discuss the mathematical relationship between the verse and the chorus. Are they the same length? If not, how would you describe the difference? Is the chorus the same as, or longer or shorter than, the verse? Is it half as long as the verse? A third longer?[1] How does "Old MacDonald" convey addition and the song "BINGO" convey subtraction? Can you think of any other songs that fall into the same categories? Can you make up different categories?

All the activities just described provide students with real-life (and familiar) applications of particular mathematical concepts. Students begin to associate numbers, lines, shapes, patterns, and the like to real situations. They also see how the study of mathematics is interrelated with many other subjects.

LEARNING THROUGH THE ARTS

There are a myriad art-based activities though which the teacher can introduce and reflect upon mathematical concepts. I hope the following ideas will inspire you to create your own activities. Most of the examples can be adapted to upper or lower grade levels.

---

[1] In this particular song, "O Susanna," the chorus is half as long as the verse.

Distance Estimation

To get his class of third-graders interested in estimating distances, Eduardo Parra, an artist-educator in California, brought in a conch shell and blew into it to produce a sound. He proposed this question to the children: If you were on a deserted beach, how far do you think you could travel and still be able to hear the sound of the shell? The students came up with various answers, mostly in the range of 1 mile to 10 miles. The actual answer is closer to 40. After hearing the true estimate, the students were challenged to consider other angles and questions. They began by considering what might cause the sound to travel a lesser distance. They also began to wonder what the distance might be in a city versus along the beach, or if nighttime might make a difference.

Because the students became interested in the idea of estimation, the classroom teacher developed related activities. He brought out his collection of tempura paints and showed the students an array of unmixed colors. Into each of three cupcake holders he poured 3 tablespoons of red paint. Then, behind a cardboard screen, he measured different amounts of yellow (using the tablespoon as his guide) and added a different amount to each cupcake holder. The students then estimated the amount of yellow added to each holder. Later that same day, the students mixed their own colors and painted sunset scenes.

Permutations

On another occasion when the children were studying permutations, Eduardo brought in his hand flute made of pottery. The flute has four holes altogether, all on the top section of the instrument. He posed this question: How many different sounds can I make with this flute by changing the combinations I make with my fingers? (This is an interesting twist on permutations because in addition to all the combinations, the flute can sound without any fingers covering any holes.) Although the students did not arrive at any definitive answers in this case, they thought deeply about the question and—perhaps more important—were interested in pursuing the answer.

Fractions

Music is a terrific source for exploring fractions. If there is a music teacher in your school, consider joining forces with that person in this endeavor. The following examples, however, are easy enough to get you and your students going. Begin with simple "sound fractions" or "sound ratios." In the example that follows, each "x" is a symbol for a beat. The beat may be on a drum or a tabletop; it could be a hand clap or a stomp. You need two players (or divide the class in half—another fraction!) to play this piece, which highlights the fraction $1/3$ or the ratio 1:3. Together, one person or group plays the top line while the other person or group plays the bottom line. The vertical lines in between the "x's" serve to guide us visually but have no sound attached to them. In musical terms, they signify measures. In mathematical terms, they indicate the base of the fraction.

```
x         | x       | x         |
x   x   x | x   x   x | x   x   x |
```

Test yourself. Can you identify the next sound fractions?

```
x     | x     | x     | x     | x     |
x   x | x   x | x   x | x   x | x   x |
```

```
x   x     | x   x     | x   x     |
x   x   x | x   x   x | x   x   x |
```

The first one signifies ¹/₂. The second one signifies ²/₃. Have your students create their own sound fractions. This may serve as an assessment tool as well as a learning tool. The more confident the students become, the more inclined they might be to create intricate pieces that mix fractions. As long as the students can identify them, they are onto something important.

Another approach to the fraction idea comes from Marni Respicio, a dancer and artist-educator who integrates movement and fractions. Keeping a steady beat, she has the children create movement patterns to ²/₄, ³/₄, or ⁴/₄ time. In this case "o" indicates hands up in the sky and "x" indicates hand clapping. Here are three patterns. Try them yourself and see if they make sense to you:

1. o   x   o   x   o   x

2. o   x   x   o   x   x   o   x   x

3. o   x   x   x   o   x   x   x   o   x   x   x

In all these examples of sound and movement fractions, not only are the students exploring fractions but they are also learning about the fundamentals of musical composition. By creating their fractions they are putting sound or movement to symbols, creating original compositions, and arranging the "instrumentation." These are the same tools used by the composer and arranger. The composer places sounds together to form musical pieces. The arranger decides which instruments should work together and when. For example, when blues singer Bonnie Raitt plays with the Boston Pops, an arrangement has to be created so that her songs—originally written only for guitar, bass, and drums—can be played by violins, trumpets, trombones, and so on. The arranger takes the original material and re-arranges it for a full orchestra. Sometimes a composer and arranger are the same person; sometimes arrangers take the compositions of others and arrange them in another way. Our "fraction composers and arrangers" are beginning musical composers and arrangers.

Should some of your students prefer a more visual exercise, consider one presented by Cathy Bullock: "fraction collage." Students are given six rectangles of equal size but different colors. The first one is a whole. The second one must be cut in two halves; the third one in thirds; the fourth in fourths; the fifth in fifths; and the sixth in sixths. The students then create a collage using all or some of their pieces. What was interesting about one student's picture was her attention to symmetry and design. She cut the rectangles in such a way that she created interesting shapes, including polygons.

Shapes, Symmetry, Angles, and Geometry

Students can create shapes with their bodies. In small groups, students might be challenged to create parallel lines, right angles, perpendicular lines, squares, triangles, circles. Have students move around the perimeter of a figure, or walk in a diagonal line through a square. Individually, can they form shapes with their arms, fingers, or legs only? Can they form symmetrical shapes with their two hands? Can they create symmetrical figures with a partner? How about an asymmetrical shape? Have the students choreograph a short movement piece that includes three shapes (various triangles, square, circle, rectangle, polygon, etc.) and/or concepts (parallel lines, symmetry, perpendicular, etc.) to present to the class. The class must identify the shapes/concepts.

More advanced students might even add sounds to their performance. In addition to presenting the shapes, they might present them in time that can be described in terms of fractions. For example, student one taps the desk once to every three claps of student two ($1/3$), who moves into various positions. The positions/shapes change at specific times, or last for specific times. Give your students this challenge and see how many mathematical concepts any given group can incorporate into their "performance piece."

Origami, the ancient Japanese art of paper folding can provide students with magical lessons in line, symmetry, angles, and function. Students apply concepts of geometry as they create swans, fish, or the wings of a dragonfly. Because many of the shapes come from nature, this can also be part of an integrated unit on nature. According to Peter Engel in *Folding the Universe: Origami from Angelfish to Zen* (1989), one of the wonders of both nature and origami is that "simple elements make complex patterns" (p. 46).

Cathy Bullock and Karen Burke (another teacher in the San Diego area) both use art extensively to teach geometric concepts. In exploring bilateral symmetry each teacher gives her students half a photograph, which the students must complete by mirroring the image. Burke indicates that she has the greatest success when she asks them to work on the images upside down. This forces them to carefully mirror the lines and shapes; otherwise some students tend to draw to make it "look good." Below are examples from the fifth grade and second grade. Can you tell which side was the original photograph in Figure 7.4?

Of course, the students can create their own original symmetrical paintings as well. Karen Burke has used an exercise she adapted from a workshop to create symmetrical castles. Students begin by folding a paper in half to create and

FIGURE 7.4 An example of bilateral
symmetry by a second-grader

identify a symmetrical reference line. Then, by carefully measuring the shapes
they place on one half of the paper, they create a symmetrical castle. The teacher
may want to place an example on an overhead for reference. Both teachers
expand on this concept by adding the notion of positive and negative space.
This concept can be easily introduced through symmetrical cutouts. In
the examples in Figure 7.5, students have explored positive and negative space
and symmetry.

FIGURE 7.5 Symmetrical cutouts

Single-Digit Addition and Subtraction

I have had young students create "secret codes" in addition and subtraction through sound. An easy way to begin is with hand clapping simple problems such as 2 + 3. Student one claps twice, and student two claps three times. Another student must clap the answer:

$$/ \, / + / \, / \, / = / \, / \, / \, / \, /$$
$$/ \, / \, / - / = / \, /$$

The secret codes can become more complex for older students as they invent sounds to represent things other than single digits. One group of students working collaboratively presented the class with the following problem. (The / represents a handclap. The * represents a foot stomp.)

/ * / + / * = 7   Can you guess what number * represents?

A group of fifth-graders working with Eduardo Garcia invented another twist in the secret code game. They wanted to do multiplication problems in sound but realized it was too difficult to clap the answer to 8 × 7. Rather than clap all 56 beats, they substituted a stomp for units of ten. So the answer was: stomp stomp stomp stomp stomp clap clap clap clap clap clap. When they got into even bigger numbers, they decided to do a twist for units of 100. For example, twist stomp stomp clap clap clap represents the number 123. In doing this, the students were inventing a decimal system!

I have challenged my student teachers to create these kinds of problems to present to each other. Admittedly it can be a stretch for many students, but a stretch that has them truly *thinking* about mathematics and representation. I usually provide students with instruments that have multiple tones, such as xylophones and glockenspiels, and set them on their way. I never know what they will come up with, which is part of the fun. Many students have created addition, subtraction, multiplication, and division problems by adding or taking away tones played simultaneously. Students have also found ways to represent permutations, and concepts such as sequence and patterning, through sound.

Points and Coordinates, Parallel Lines

Visual arts lend themselves to mathematical concepts such as graphing. Murals, for example, provide the math student with an opportunity to make use of graphing skills, study proportion and measurement, and apply those skills to a real life setting. In an integrated study the mural can reflect a curriculum theme in addition to being a mathematical focus for learning. With the help of an art teacher or local artist, you can obtain appropriate paint materials.

In considering this undertaking for the first time, I recommend collaborating with an artist who can guide the students in design and implementation. You can take charge in terms of theme and mathematical connections. If you are unable to collaborate with an art teacher or artist, start small and work yourself up to larger murals. Schools often have ample wall spaces for this kind of project. Some classes have even created murals on moveable walls and large boards so they could be displayed rather than remaining permanently in the classroom.

As an entry into the world of mural making, you might consider the option of drawing to scale. Take a cartoon, such as Calvin from "Calvin and Hobbes," and place it on a graph with coordinates. Then, on larger paper, have the students re-create the cartoon using the coordinates as their reference. Another idea is to cut up one or more greeting cards into squares or rectangles and hand them out to students without letting them see the whole. Each student enlarges his or her square or rectangle using the same predetermined scale. When the students have completed the task, put both cards back together and see the finished products!

To work with parallel lines, consider the following exercise. Students in Cathy Bullock's class were asked to create a visual art piece using parallel lines. Their tools included a pencil, ruler, and—later on—colored markers, pencils, or pens. Students created a design and completed it by using parallel lines only. Figure 7.6 is an example of one student's work. In reflecting on this math-art project, Anabel Contreras, a fifth-grader, incorporates mathematical language, indicating not only that she can apply her understanding to a project, but that she can also discuss it in mathematical terminology: "If you draw two parallel lines, then you would be using math by making the lines equidistant from each other. For instance, if you drew a road, the two lines for the sides of the road will never meet."

Drama, Story Problems

Students might enjoy the following challenge. Create a story or drama to illustrate 4 + 3 = 7, or 3 - 2 = 1. "As students dramatize, tell, write, share, and solve story problems over an extended period of time," write Burk et al. (1992), "they begin to learn about processes, language, and symbols associated with addition

FIGURE 7.6 Parallel line drawings

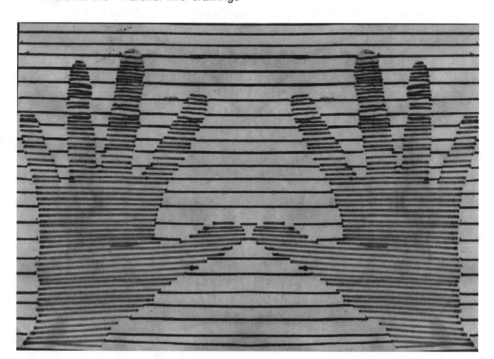

and subtraction" (p. 15). Cathy Bullock integrates story problems with language arts. She gives groups of students a newspaper headline: for example, "3 - 2 = 1." Students then write a story to go along with it, paying attention to who, what, where, when, and why.

SUMMARY

The possibilities of integrating art and mathematics are numerous, if not infinite. Interrelationships among the two offer creative and enjoyable activities that will no doubt interest your students and inspire them to work seriously with mathematical concepts. As I have shown throughout this chapter, the art activities can offer many avenues to students as they become open to the wonders of the natural world and the connections to mathematics within their own world. As students begin to comprehend that much of their world revolves directly or indirectly around mathematical concepts, they may also become interested in the application of those concepts.

QUESTIONS TO PONDER

1. What math/art connections can you find in the poem by Katrina White, fifth-grade student, at the very opening of this chapter? Can you identify any other connections between this poem and the chapter (philosophical, theoretical)?
2. What connections not mentioned in this chapter can you think of between math and arts in your own life?
3. Brainstorm a list of professions. Now consider the ways in which math and the arts relate to each profession. Is one more important than the other? Is it different in other cultures?
4. Consider quilting and weaving. In what ways do they directly relate to mathematical concepts? How could you infuse them into your curriculum, both learning *with* and learning *through*?
5. Consider the work of M. C. Escher and its relationship to mathematics. How about tessellations?

EXPLORATIONS TO TRY

1. With a friend, create three sound pieces that represent a mathematical problem or concept. Now add movement to make it even more complex. In what ways does the movement add to the original concept? What new mathematical ideas can be derived from the *addition* (hint) of the movement?

2. Create three projects that demonstrate ways in which you can learn specific mathematical concepts *with* music.

3. Brainstorm a way to learn multiplication *through* visual art.

4. Create a way to represent subtraction *through* movement.

5. Go into your kitchen. What are all the connections you can make to math with things found in the kitchen? What are all the connections you can make to art with things found in the kitchen? How many of the connections incorporate both math and art? Can any of them exist without one or another?

6. Look at a painting in your house or local museum. How many shapes, patterns, concepts can you identify? Do you think that all paintings would be good for this exercise? How would you begin to differentiate?

REFERENCES

Burk, Donna, et al. (1992). *Math Excursions 1: Project-Based Mathematics for First Graders.* Portsmouth, NH: Heinemann.

Chaplik, Dorothy. (1989). *Latin American Art: An Introduction to the Works of the 20th Century.* Jefferson, NC: McFarland & Company.

Engel, Peter. (1989). *Folding the Universe: Origami from Angelfish to Zen.* New York: Vintage Books.

Millman, Richard S., and Ramona R. Speranza. (1991). "The Artist's View of Points and Lines." *Mathematics Teacher,* February 1991.

Newman, Rochelle, and Martha Boles. (1992a). *The Golden Relationship: Art, Math & Nature.* Book 1, 2d rev. ed., Universal Patterns. Bradford, MA: Pythagorean Press.

———. (1992b). *The Golden Relationship: Art, Math & Nature,* Book 2, The Surface Plane. Bradford, MA: Pythagorean Press.

chapter 8

Setting the Stage for a Turn of Events: Subject Matter Informs the Arts

ODE TO A CLUSTER OF VIOLETS

Crisp cluster
plunged in a shadow.
Drops of violet water
and raw sunlight
floated up with your scent.
A fresh
subterranean beauty
climbed up from your buds,
thrilling my eyes and my life.

One at a time, flowers
that stretched forward
silvery stalks,
creeping closer to an obscure light
shoot by shoot in the shadows,
till they crowned
the mysterious mass
with an intense weight of perfume
and together
formed a single star
with a far-off scent and purple center.

Poignant cluster,
intimate
scent

ODA A UN RAMO DE VIOLETAS

Crespo ramo en la sombra
sumergido:
gotas de agua violeta
y luz salvaje
subieron con tu aroma:
una fresca hermosura
subterránea
trepó con tus capullos
y estremeció mis ojos y mi vida.

Una por una, flores
que alargaron
metálicos pedúnculos,
acercando en la sombra
rayo tras rayo de una luz oscura
hasta que coronaron
el misterio
con su masa profunda de perfume,
y unidas
fueron una sola estrilla
de olor remoto y corazón morado.

Ramo profundo,
intimo
olor

of nature,
you resemble
a wave, or a head of hair,
or the gaze
of a ruined water nymph
sunk in the depths.
But up close,
in your fragrance's
blue brazenness,
you exhale the earth,
an earthly flower, an earthen
smell and your ultraviolet
gleam
is volcanoes' faraway fires.

Into your loveliness I sink
a weathered face,
a face that dust has often abused.
You deliver
something out of the soil.
It isn't simply perfume,
nor simply the perfect cry
of your entire color, no: it's
a word sprinkled with dew,
a flowering wetness with roots.

Fragile cluster of starry
violets,
tiny, mysterious
planet
of marine phosphorescence,
nocturnal bouquet nestled in green leaves:
the truth is
there is no blue word to express you.

Better than any word
is the pulse of your scent.[1]

de la naturaleza,
pareces
la ouda, la cabellera,
la mirada
de una náyade rota
y submarina,
pero de cerca,
en plena
temeridad azul de tu fragancia,
tierra, flor de la tierra,
olor terrestre
desprendes, y tu rayo
ultravioleta
es combustión lejana de volcanes.

Sumerjo en tu hermosura
mi viejo rostro tantas
veces hostilizado por el polvo
y algo desde la tierra
me transmites,
y no es sólo un perfume,
no es sólo el grito puro
de tu color total, es más bien
una palabra con rocio,
una humedad florida con raices.

Frágil haz de violetas
estrelladas,
pegueño, misterioso
planetario
de fósforo marino,
nocturno ramo entre las hojas verdes,
la verdad es
que no hay polabra azul para expresarte:

más que toda palabra
te describe un latido de tu aroma.

Pablo Neruda, Odes to Common Things (1994)

Imagine! Pablo Neruda could have been out in the field with us using poetry to describe his observations of the violet. His scientific and aesthetic descriptions are not dissimilar to the fifth-graders' in Chapter 6, though admittedly he has had a bit more practice in expressing himself through poetry.

---

[1] From ODES TO COMMON THINGS by Pablo Neruda, selected and illustrated by Ferris Cook. Odes (English translation) copyright © 1994 by Ken Krabbencroft. By permission Little, Brown and Company.

Although the bulk of this book focuses on using the arts to teach subject matter, this chapter takes a slightly different viewpoint. Here we will explore four related topics: (1) the aesthetic experience and how it is related to arts in education, (2) how the arts can set the stage for learning, (3) how subject matter informs the arts, and (4) how the arts, in and of themselves, are intrinsically valuable in the school curriculum.

By nature, human beings have an aesthetic sense. We see the world in many colors. We react to sights, smells, sounds, nature, and just about everything and everyone with whom we come into daily contact; and our reactions are integrated according to previous experiences. In other words, each of us does more than merely *exist* in a world; we *perceive* our world. That perception is, in part, an aesthetic perception. Pablo Neruda's poem is an aesthetic expression of his observation of a cluster of common violets. It also includes what one could consider scientific description. It is likely that any of us, upon viewing a cluster of violets, might have an aesthetic reaction. The difference between Pablo Neruda and the rest of us is that he is a practiced poet; he applies his perception to a poem and shares his perception with a public.

There is a tension in Western life, as well as in schools, that pits "aesthetic" experience against "practical" experience. Daily life is seen as a series of practical exercises, including waking up on time, planning for dinner, reporting to work, finishing the report, taking tests (or administering them), and so on. Aesthetic response, on the other hand, "comes when we stop, even briefly, to look, to listen, to *savor* the qualities of experience beyond what is required for fulfilling our practical needs" (Hospers, 1982, p. 335). Everyone has an aesthetic sense. You might exhibit this sense in the way you arrange the furniture in your living room or by the choices you make when you create a bulletin board display in your classroom. Unfortunately, because of the rapid pace of our lives, we risk losing a sense of the aesthetic, even to the point of forgetting it altogether. One could argue that as a result, many of us lead lives that are out of balance.

What is the importance of balance and aesthetics to teaching and learning? At first glance, one could argue for its intrinsic value. We live in a world that is not only objective but rich in experiences. Even practical applications have some element of the aesthetic. One need only look to the most simple and common objects to understand that design is an important element. Consider telephones. Compare the phones in your home, school, and/or office. You will note that they come in many colors, sizes, even shapes. Some phones may be more practical, some may be more aesthetically pleasing. Every object falls somewhere on a continuum of practical/aesthetic. However, understanding this dualism is not the most important function that aesthetic awareness plays in the classroom.

Using our aesthetic sense means that we are aware. We stop to look, to listen, to feel, to reflect. By participating in an activity that involves our aesthetic senses, we are in a position to think more deeply about something and reflect upon it. Many would describe this as a goal of teaching and learning: to be intensely engaged in considering subject matter. In this manner the arts, by definition, enable students to stop and reflect deeply upon what they are learning. For some people, acts of awareness are not so separated from the everyday. Instead, they are fundamental to culture and daily life. Consider the words of Tewa Vickie Downey, of the Tesque Pueblo:

> Most people look to the elders as teachers. They are. But we also look at the children, look at them as teachers. We study life. Our life is studying. We study everything, everybody, even the tiniest insect. Like the other day, we noticed that the ants went into the house early. So what does this mean? We study that. We watch the ants or the bees or the trees. Every second of our life we're studying everything around us. The sounds. The music. Outside our culture people don't have that awareness. We have to bring that awareness back. It's just being in tune with the spirit. So what people have to do now is be in that awareness.[2] (in Wall, 1993, p. 20)

In an earlier chapter I mentioned how practicing my guitar in childhood helped prepare me to be a disciplined and dedicated writer and thinker. It prepared me to take on other areas with the rigor and self-discipline needed to follow through in my studies. When practicing my guitar I was able to experience varying states of awareness: I was aware of my own abilities, the sounds I could create, the quality of sounds I created. Through my practicing, I was being trained with an aesthetic awareness. That awareness potentially transfers to all other areas of learning, promoting deep reflection and a wholeness of experience.

As teachers, we are in positions to reach students so they may begin to tap into the action of being aesthetically aware. An important distinction to make at this point brings us back to the realm of judgment and personal taste. When I talk of the aesthetic experience, I mean an action that requires each individual to stop and consider aspects of his or her world. This is outside the realm of personal taste. For example, as someone who is not a fish eater, I will never like the taste of fish. Yet I can appreciate its preparation and presentation despite my distaste for it. Therefore, one can be aesthetically aware regardless of personal likes and dislikes.

The arts provide a means and form to express our understanding of the world in an aesthetic as well as objective manner. Just as we can learn subject matter through the arts, the arts can teach us about the world in which we live. Recently, I attended a dance performance that included a piece on homelessness. Through the dancers' movements, expressions, and contact with each other I felt I was introduced to the emotions and stresses of homelessness. Although I didn't learn facts or figures relating to numbers of people who are homeless, I did walk away with a deeper compassion for what it could feel like to be homeless. That feeling no doubt informs my overall understanding of homelessness.

Even though the arts might not provide an answer to questions of AIDS research, how to curb pollution, or as Denis Donoghue remarks (in Greene,

---

[2] Quote from WISDOM'S DAUGHTERS: CONVERSATIONS WITH WOMEN ELDERS OF NATIVE AMERICA by Steve Wall. Copyright © 1993 by Steve Wall. Reprinted by permission of HarperCollins Publishers, Inc.

Katrina White, a fifth-grader, finds a moment of awareness as she writes a poem reflecting on the sturdy branches of a tree and the virtues of living.

1991), "cure a toothache," they do provide the tools needed to imagine the solutions and the dedication needed to follow through in pursuing answers. The student who is practiced in seeing things from an aesthetic point of view and in using his or her imagination is more likely to come up with solutions to problems. The more practice one has in working imaginatively and reflectively, the more likely one will be able to apply those skills while discovering, say, cures in medical research or solutions for promoting a clean environment.

I do not mean to imply that a student who thinks aesthetically is necessarily going to think with clarity. In contemplating things deeply, confusion often arises before clarity. However, confusion is as normal a state of being (in learning) as is clarity. Confusion implies thinking—if I am confused about something, I am certainly thinking about it. When my thinking becomes clear, I can then move on to an even deeper understanding. Confusion often leads to curiosity, and curiosity paves the way to learning. When I stop to contemplate the design of the chair in my kitchen, or the colors of a flower in my patio garden, I usually come up with questions in addition to logging an observation. Why doesn't the weight from the back of the chair knock it over? Where do the colors come from to make such vibrant flower petals? These questions may emerge from an ability to stop and ponder objects in an aesthetic manner, forming the genesis of what could evolve to be more objective, or scientific, pursuits.

Aesthetic experiences lend themselves to teaching and learning in at least five ways: (1) *perception:* an awareness of one's surroundings and actions; (2) *concentration:* a tool for exploration through actively stopping, listening, seeing, feeling; (3) i*magination:* a journey of the mind to new places; (4) *contemplation:* an opportunity to question and search; (5) *action:* our questions and searches are pursued.

ARTS SETTING THE STAGE FOR LEARNING

One use of the arts that we have not addressed so far is in setting the stage for learning. In the next section we will explore ways in which a teacher can utilize art forms to create a learning atmosphere and prepare students for serious reflection. Drawing on our discussion of the aesthetic, the arts can promote or awaken perceptions and imagination while at the same time providing a tool for concentration and contemplation as students begin a study.

An example can be drawn from one of the elementary classes I visit weekly. Once I showed up on a cloudy spring day. The children had been on the verge of acting up for a few weeks now, and it seemed like a lot of class time was spent dealing with discipline issues. On the spot, the teacher and I decided to try something new. I always carry my penny whistle in my backpack and have played it for the class on numerous occasions. The penny whistle is a small Irish flute, familiar to those who listen to Irish folk music. It has a high and delicate sound, and the kids love to listen to me play. When I arrive it is not unusual to hear, "Do you have your penny whistle today?!"

We sat the children in the front of the room where we usually sit for class discussions. I explained to them that we would try an experiment today, and that I wasn't sure if it would work or not but wanted their participation nonetheless. The experiment was that I would play the penny whistle and the students would write poetry at the same time—on the subject of nature. The students readily agreed and went back to their seats, where they pulled out their poetry journals. I began to play an improvisation on an Irish tune, the "Swallowtail Jig."

As I played, each student began to write. The only sound in the class was of my penny whistle. When I stopped to rest for a moment the silence seemed almost strange, unwanted. The children were extremely engaged, writing with ease; so I continued my improvisation. After a few moments I would stop, but the children wanted me to continue. Before all was said and done, I improvised for half an hour as the class composed their poems. Even the most boisterous students seemed calmed by the magic of the flute and engaged in reflective writing. We stopped only because the art teacher arrived, ready to continue her lesson from the previous week—a watercolor work to accompany the nature poetry. As we shifted into the art lesson, we were surprised at the concentration and attention the students continued to exhibit. What was going on?

It was clear to me that the music had set the stage for the students. For many it was a calming mechanism, and for others it was an inspiration as well. The students were concentrating on their writing and were serious in their contemplation of nature. Their imaginations were freed and their ability to perceive—their awareness—was heightened. Although I have experienced the effects of music in other circumstances, this experience was a reminder of the power such a simple musical melody can have in a teaching and learning situation. Others have noticed this as well. Recent research has shown that music can reduce anxiety and increase attentiveness in classroom settings (Blanchard, 1979; Russell, 1992). Listening to music can even improve test scores (Giles, 1991; Black, 1993).

Creating illustrations and artwork may improve a child's ability to write, according to Beth Olshansky (1994). "When art becomes truly integrated through-out every stage of the writing process, both children's creative processes and their finished products share a quality of richness previously unequaled" (p. 351). Olshansky argues that when children have the opportunity to express themselves both visually and verbally, they are in a better position to work with ideas and unleash their creative juices. Illustrations give rise to words as words give rise to illustrations, offering students pathways to understandings. This speaks to learning styles as well. For the student who likes to draw pictures first, the pictures help with describing words for a poem or story. For the student who prefers to start with words, the words lend shape to pictures.

In both cases, we have examples of how enabling children through the arts serves many purposes. Music might calm and center students as they return from recess or lunch. It might re-focus them as the teacher prepares to switch lesson gears. Further, it might inspire students to visualize images or stories, formulas or methods, as they work seriously on the subject matter at hand. Similarly, having the opportunity to draw while working on subject matter such as writing can further thinking and inspire original thoughts. Of course, other art forms can do the same. Photographs might inspire a historical essay, and movement might clear up a mathematical problem. In sum, use of the arts in the curriculum may set the stage for reflective, creative, and serious contemplation.

SUBJECT MATTER INFORMING ART

In this section we will consider how subject matter knowledge informs art, rather than how art informs subject matter. It is a bit of a twist, but an interesting twist nonetheless. This brings me back to balance in learning. If the arts inform subject matter, then subject matter should inform the arts. We will begin by thinking about mathematical knowledge. I learned how important mathematical skills were to a group of university students as they prepared to paint a mural on one of the walls outside our school. Like all muralists, the students were faced with re-creating a design on a wall that was much larger than their original design on construction paper. The math majors began graphing and calculating, creating grids to facilitate the painting. Without a math background the students may have labored long and hard and might have ended up with a lopsided, or out of proportion product.

Now let's imagine that we are visiting a museum with a mathematician. We are in a gallery hosting a special exhibition of Braque and Picasso. Imagine the perspectives that you and the mathematician bring to your viewing of the paintings. Whereas you might be interested in the colors and representational figures, the mathematician is drawn to the geometry, symmetry, and patterns in various paintings. Knowing something of mathematics, in this case, informs our viewing of the painting. Indeed, knowing something of mathematics informed Braque and Picasso as they created their works. Walking through the gallery with the mathematician, you might be more likely to pay attention to aspects of artwork you would not notice otherwise. The mathematical perspective opens routes to understanding something more about the painting. Mathematical knowledge informs our viewing of the painting.

Now, in addition to looking at the hidden figures in the Picasso painting, we are looking at the geometric shapes creating it and surrounding it. As we follow the rectangular figure, we notice other shapes in the painting and how they connect. Our initial reaction to a painting begins to change as we notice the intricate and detailed lines and points and how they work to highlight a representational figure similar to a guitar. As we look even closer, we notice the figure is composed of a series of polygons; the "guitar" begins to appeal to our math sense as well our aesthetic sense. Our viewing of the painting is now more complex. We have a greater appreciation of the mathematical knowledge communicated through the painting, as well as the aesthetic appeal.

It is time to leave the mathematician with the Braque and Picasso works and move next door into the natural history museum, where we will view a gallery dedicated to prehistoric rock art. Here we will be joined by Juanita, an archeologist in town on a grant spending a year at the local university. Juanita's expertise happens to be in the area of animal rock art. Lucky for us, much of the exhibit is dedicated to exactly that!

I enter into the gallery and am confronted with an exhibit entitled "Roadrunner Tracks in Southwestern Petroglyphs." What I notice immediately is the rawness of the shapes embedded in rock: tracks, bird shapes, faces, and interesting geometrical patterns. Admittedly, I haven't a clue as to what they represent. I walk around in wonder, contemplating the figures created by the Mongollon peoples of the lower desert of southern New Mexico between roughly A.D. 1050 and 1400. The figures, I read on the exhibit wall, are in the "Jornada style." I am impressed by what is before me. The figures appeal to my aesthetic sense and are interesting works of art in and of themselves.

Juanita at this point cannot contain her excitement. Her knowledge of archeology gives her a very different perspective of the rock art. We both are looking at the figures in the rocks but are seeing very different things. She begins to tell me that "the mere presence of the roadrunner track in prehistoric rock art was strongly indicative that the roadrunner and/or its track had religious significance in the prehistoric southwest." Barely taking a breath she continues, "The whole animal may be signified by a track, although in certain cases the track, or paw—in the case of bears—is imbued with specific ritual powers" (Morphy, 1989, p. 261).[3] I am speechless, for my newfound understanding of the figures is deeply enhanced by the ethnographic information Juanita so excitedly shares.

What I am experiencing is the way in which the work of an anthropologist or archeologist can inform my overall understanding of, and experience with, specific rock art. Although we can enjoy the artwork on its own, the subject matter background lends a context and foundation for interpreting the art in addition to reacting to it. In contemplating this notion I can make a connection to a similar experience during my forays into bird watching with fifth-graders. Though I often go bird watching at the lagoons in southern California when I go out with a real "birder," I become even more excited as I find that not only am I looking at a beautiful bird but my sighting is rare because the bird is endangered and a highly infrequent visitor to this particular lagoon.

On one of our class trips to the lagoon we were accompanied by Barbara Moore, an experienced naturalist and bird expert. Through a grant the school had acquired enough binoculars and bird cards so that each child had a pair of binoculars and an Audubon bird reference card identifying local birds most common to southern California. Bird watching came alive for us as Barbara identified a certain bird and told us about it (e.g., it was an adolescent, or it was nesting). We spent two hours on the lagoon with her, absorbing valuable information.

When we returned to the classroom we settled into our writing and sketching routine as a way to think about our experience. What interested me in reading the students' poems and journal entries that day was how much of the information Barbara had relayed was incorporated in the students' poems. Her knowledge of birds, offered to the students, made many of the poems more detailed in a scientific manner than previous poems. Here, subject matter had given the students more options as they reflected on their experiences through an art form. As a result, I feel that their poems were more interesting and rich.

A related example comes from a dance class at the university. A group of students were choreographing a new piece based on environmental issues. As a way to develop their piece they met with several environmentalists. As they met with the environmentalists, the students became more and more invested in the issue for its own sake in addition to it being a topic for a dance piece. When they finally performed their dance, it was clear that the work was far beyond a show of technique. Their understanding of the environmental issues informed their dance and performance.

---

[3] Juanita's information is taken from the book *Animals into Art*, edited by H. Morphy, London: Unwin Hyman.

ART AS SUBJECT MATTER

In this section we will consider the arts in and of themselves as a matter for study. First I will argue for their inclusion in the daily curriculum; then, following the formula of learning *with* and *through,* I will show how to use the arts to teach *about* the arts. So far we have examined the arts in relation to methods for learning. Now we explore their intrinsic value in and of themselves.

The arts serve to ground many students as well as allow them to experience accomplishment. By participating in artistic activities, students engage in transformative thinking. By studying works of art, students are introduced to a fundamental aspect of humanity and the history of humankind. The arts can set the stage for learning. They remind us that we are whole beings who can "experience" through multiple perspectives and lenses. As subject matter in and of themselves, the arts provide lifelong learning opportunities. They intersect with our lives every day, from music on the radio on the way to work, to literature we read when we have returned home, to movies we watch on the weekends, to murals we pass when we venture into the city. We cannot escape the arts in our daily lives.

Men and women have built monuments to artists. Consider the number of art museums and concert halls throughout the country. Where I live in southern California, the county has just opened up an $81 million arts facility with two concert halls, an art museum, four studios, and a conference center. Go into any city and visit the galleries or music shops; no doubt they are active places. Consider the parks in your city; many are sculpted with flowers and trees—or walk past the city hall and notice the sculpture by the entrance. As I have argued in earlier chapters, the arts are intimately connected to people and cultures, defining who we are to others and serving as self-expression within our own lives. Thus, as a topic of study the arts present a rich, if not overwhelming, source of knowledge and documentation.

Shaping the teaching of arts in schools, different initiatives have suggested courses of study. Perhaps the most well known initiative in arts education is the Getty Center for Education in the Arts, Discipline-Based Arts Education (DBAE). Proponents of DBAE focus on four areas of art: creating art, art history, art criticism, and aesthetics. "Why discipline-based art education?" one might ask. The following quote from Getty addresses their philosophy:

> We increase our understanding of the meaning of an artwork if we have worked with the materials and processes that artists use to create art. We also broaden our understanding if we know when and where a work was made, something about its creator, the function it served in society, and what art experts have said about it.
>
> Artists, art historians, art critics, and aestheticians contribute different perspectives about an artwork. These perspectives are instructive and useful because each one deepens our understanding and our appreciation of the various levels of meaning the work of art conveys. (Getty Report, 1985, p. 13)

DBAE offers a standard for arts education and includes many aspects of the artistic experience, from the perspective of both the artist and the viewer. It covers a broad scope of experience in its delineation of the role of arts in history and culture. Yet the question lingers: Should we teach *about* the arts in schools? Without a doubt, absolutely yes. Arts are a fundamental aspect of the human experience. They are basic. They not only teach us about history and culture, they enable us to have a sense of wholeness—a sense of aesthetic awareness in life and history as we pursue studies of various cultures. To diminish the role of arts in education is to rob our youth of valuable knowledge and experience that can shape their lives and futures.

Two important premises guide the Getty philosophy (Getty Report, 1985): (1) Art is a repository of culture, and (2) The study of art is a principal means of understanding human experience and transmitting cultural values. If a significant change is to occur in the way art is perceived and taught in the schools, we need to better understand how art should and can be taught. I think the Getty initiatives have broadened and structured the role the arts can play in schools, especially with regard to history, criticism, and aesthetics. The arts provide such an overwhelming landscape of opportunity that it can be difficult to identify what to do in specific instances. Getty begins to give us a direction.

It is my experience that when students are enabled to utilize the arts as a teaching and learning mechanism (learning *with* and learning *through*), they are in a better position to appreciate and understand the arts as subject matter themselves. My student-poets are interested in reading the work of poets. My math students who use paintings to study geometry are more likely to appreciate artworks outside of math class. The children who have used movement to depict the story of the Raven are more likely to be drawn into the ballet's performance of "Swan Lake" and appreciate it. Thus, broadening the classroom to encompass the arts on various levels also engenders an appreciation and understanding of the arts as a source of knowledge in and of itself.

LEARNING ABOUT ARTS WITH ARTS

I would like to point out a few ways in which one might teach about subject matter—in this case, the arts themselves—with and through other art forms.

Numerous works of art are concerned with artists. I would like to highlight a few to illustrate my point. Georges Seurat was an artist of considerable importance and notoriety. There is a musical based on him and one of his more famous works. The musical is called "Sunday in the Park with George"; it was performed on Broadway and later produced for PBS. It is widely available on videocassette. The musical presents aspects of Seurat's life, personality, and the sentiments of the era. Throughout the work, various figures in his painting come alive and reflect upon the action of the tale. It is a delightful introduction through music and drama to the impressionist period and to the painter himself.

Music can often provide lessons for understanding and identifying musical concepts. The music *Peter and the Wolf* provides the listener with a delightful introduction to musical instruments. Throughout the story, each character is depicted by a specific instrument. Not only is the story delightful in and of itself, but the music deepens our awareness of musical instruments.

Literature is a rich source for learning about artists and arts. So many books ae available in this realm that the few I highlight in this chapter should be taken as merely the tip of the iceberg. Readers interested in this area should turn to Nancy Lee Cecil and Phyllis Lauritzen's *Literacy and the Arts* (1994), for it includes a comprehensive bibliography of children's literature about the arts.

Not only are there numerous picture books concerning the arts written for young children, but many novels with artist themes are written for adolescents as well. We will begin our discussion with a book that itself serves as an introduction to the art of picture books. Sylvia Marantz's *Picture Books* for *Looking and Learning: Awakening Visual Perceptions through the Art* of *Children's Books* (1992) lends insight into approaching picture books that recognize the importance of the arts and artists. Her aim is to give teachers the confidence "to deal with the art aspects of [children's] books as well as . . . the literary aspects" (p. 5). She shows teachers how they can pay attention to art while introducing literature.

In terms of children's books themselves, let me highlight a few categories. First, some books are concerned with the lives of artists. For young children, *Diego* by Jeanette Winter (1991), text by Jonah Winter, is about the painter Diego Rivera. A bilingual book (English and Spanish), it is a celebration of the powerful art of Rivera and his home, Mexico. *Pish, Posh, Said Hieronymus Bosch* by Nancy Willard (1991) is a fanciful tale based on paintings and creatures of the imaginative (and even bizarre) Hieronymus Bosch. *The Painter and the Wild Swans* by Claude Clement (1986) is the story of Teiji, a renowned Japanese painter whose work is so connected to experience that he ultimately embarks on a magical search toward capturing nature on canvas. Christina Bjork and Lena Anderson's *Linnea in Monet's Garden* (1987) is a novel for adolescents that combines illustrations, reprints of paintings, and photographs. The reader joins Linnea on her adventure into Claude Monet's garden, where she learns about Monet the person and what it means to be an impressionist artist.

Books with artistic themes are numerous as well. A few examples: Claude Clement offers the reader *The Voice of the Wood* (1993), a story about an Italian craftsman in Venice, music, and instrument making. Cynthia Rylant offers *All I See* (1988), a story about Gregory, a painter by a lake, and Charlie, a young boy who becomes intrigued with Gregory's work. This is a wonderful story of an emerging friendship between a boy and a painter. *Little Mouse's Painting* by Diane Wolkstein (1992), wonderfully illustrated by Maryjane Begin, is also a story of friendship and art, but between Little Mouse, Bear, Squirrel, and Porcupine.

Books about art and literature include *Here Is My Kingdom: Hispanic-American Literature and Art for Young People,* edited by Charles Sullivan (1994). This diverse anthology spans history from Columbus to César Chávez through intertwining poems, text, illustrations, photographs, and reprints of paintings. For example, on the same page that we read "Border Towns," a poem by Roberto Durand, we view the painting *Undocumented* by Malaquias Montoya. On another page we find an excerpt from the short story "The Harvest" by Tomas Rivera, accompanied by the painting *Campesino* by Daniel DeSiga, depicting a worker in an endless field symbolizing "the work of the farm laborer, which comes to end only with the harvest" (p. 72). *Celebrating America: A Collection of Poems and Images of the American Spirit,* compiled by Laura Whipple (1994) with art provided by the Art Institute of Chicago, highlights the land, stories, people, and spirit of North America through poetry and paintings. It includes diverse voices and a historical perspective.

There are even books about children as artists. *The Young Artist* by Thomas Locker (1989) tells the story of a 12-year-old apprentice to a painting master. *Ben's Trumpet* by Rachel Isadora (1979) is one of my favorite books about a child who learns to play the jazz trumpet. *Rondo in C* by Paul Fleischman (1988) concerns itself with a young girl who plays Beethoven's Rondo in C on the piano while inspiring others to imagine all sorts of scenes. *I Am an Artist* by Pat Lowery Collins (1992) is a fanciful adventure of a child who, like all children, is opening up to the life of an artist by seeing patterns in the sand, seeing colors inside a shell, noticing the feathers on a bird and feeling them as the bird does.

Second-graders in Escondido, California, show the covers of books they have created to be given as presents to their dads.

Finally, *Cherries and Cherry Pits* by Vera B. Williams (1986), is about Bidemmi, an African-American girl who illustrates her own story.

Many children's books focus on artistic activities while incorporating wonderful artistic forms in their presentation. Gerald McDermott's (1975) *The Stone Cutter,* a Japanese folk tale about Tasaku, a lowly but happy stonecutter, is one such example. McDermott hand colored and then cut out design forms to create the collages on each page. A somewhat different take on this genre comes from Judy Collins and Jane Dyer (1989) in the book *My Father.* This book is an illustrated version of Judy Collins's song by the same title. It also includes the musical notation written for piano and/or guitar.

There are also novels for older students on artistic themes. *The Cartoonist* by Betsy Bryars (1978), is about Alfie, who often escapes to his attic—a place all his own—to draw cartoons, and where he dreams of becoming a famous cartoonist. *In Summer Light* by Zibby Oneal (1986) is about the relationship between a famous artist and his daughter as they spend a rich but emotional summer on an island in Massachusetts.

Pulitzer Prize–winning *Maus* by Art Spiegelman (1986), in a category all its own, is a comic-book depiction of the author's family struggle to survive the death camps of World War II. Appropriate at the high school level, this book is a compelling work of art that captures the experiences of a family in a way that readers will not forget.

LEARNING ABOUT ARTS THROUGH ARTS

In teaching about music, I actively listen to music with my students. I generally begin class with simply listening to music. At times I choose the music; at other times the students do. At the middle school and high school levels I establish a few rules—for example, profane lyrics are not appropriate. As we listen we identify instruments, rhythms, sounds that are new to us. We discuss what the music seems to express and what in the music creates that expression. For example, after listening to Stravinsky's "Rite of Spring" (my choice), many students noted that the beginning created an uncomfortable feeling. We then examined what aspect of the music gave that impression. Students discussed the uneven beats and harsh accents on certain beats. The rhythm, especially, created an uneasy feeling, they reasoned. They also had questions about specific sounds. The piece begins, for example, with a bassoon solo. Many students were not familiar with the bassoon or its sound. Here was a perfect opportunity to learn, through Stravinsky, about the bassoon.

Even the untrained listener can begin in this manner. You might not choose Stravinsky, as I did, but you can begin with music that you listen to at home. Perhaps you like the Chieftains. The next time you listen, pay special attention to the instruments. Can you identify any of them? The CD liner notes will help if you are stumped. Try to listen to a song and follow the bass throughout, or the violin. We can start training ourselves to be more active listeners simply by listening. Having in-class listening parties provides a wonderful atmosphere to become more acquainted with new and familiar music.

Throughout just one semester my students and I listened to a variety of music, including (1) reggae, from which we learned about the role of the bass; (2) klezmer, in which we focused on the sounds of the clarinet; (3) an excerpt from a Tchaikovsky ballet, after which we discussed with delight how we could imagine dancers twisting and floating; (4) music from Senegal, gamelan music from Malaysia, and gospel music, from which we began a historical discussion of the role of music in culture and a musical discussion of acapella singing, melody, harmony, and call and response in the African-American tradition. With each piece of music, the students learned more and more. They began to use musical terms. They became comfortable identifying musical instruments and concepts. They could express whether the music appealed to them or not. Their musical landscape was broadened.

Many people use visual arts to understand music. I remember the following exercise from my own early education, and many of my student teachers have done the same with their students: draw while listening to music. The activity of drawing helps focus the child on listening; the drawing provides a structure through which the child engages with a piece of music. Later, in talking about their drawings, the children can make connections to the sounds, emotions, and images the music evoked. The teacher can pursue the connections even further. What in the music inspired the picture? What aspect of the sounds made it seem angry or gave it a happy feeling? What aspect of the music gave the impression of a country setting? And so on.

An interesting idea about the introduction of paintings came up on a recent visit to the local gallery. A group of teachers on an afterschool field trip were exploring ways to relate the gallery to teaching about the arts in their classrooms. One suggested having the students create stories or poems to accompany paintings or sculptures. In this way, the students would have to closely observe the paintings. Movement would work as well, they discussed; have students create a movement that describes a particular painting. "You might even create a game," mused one of the teachers, "such that the students are presented with four or five reproductions and they have to guess which reproduction a given small group has represented through movement [or story]. In this way you have given the students a concrete way [through the arts] to connect with specific paintings and think about them."

SUMMARY

I am interested in balance. I enjoy turning concepts on their head, or upside down to see if they work in different directions. If ideas can work in reverse, then I generally think I've found something important. Thus, as I worked harder and harder on my notion of the arts informing subject matter, I stepped back and contemplated a twist: How does subject matter inform the arts? This led me to consider "awareness," manifesting itself in a reflection on aesthetic experience in education and its role in teaching and learning.

The arts are intrinsically valuable and basic. Like other academic subjects, they can be approached in a reflective and harmonious manner by creating active learning situations. Just as the arts can enhance other subject matter, subject matter can inform our understanding of the arts—both in creating art and in appreciating arts. Arts can set the stage for learning by creating conducive learning atmospheres. They can be inspiring, a thinking tool. Finally, by understanding and incorporating the aesthetic, students can become more aware. That awareness can lead to further wonder, inquiry, and discovery.

QUESTIONS TO PONDER

1. In what ways do you (or will you) incorporate teaching about the arts in your classroom?
2. Drawing upon whatever arts you already integrate, how can you make even better use of what you're doing?
3. Brainstorm ways to teach about dance through visual arts.
4. Brainstorm ways to teach about visual arts through movement or music.
5. Brainstorm ways to teach about music through an art form of your choice.
6. What books do you have in your own collection with artistic themes?

EXPLORATIONS TO TRY

1. *Learning through the arts: Music.* Choose a short musical selection from your tape or CD collection. For your first try, choose a piece without lyrics. Listen to it once carefully. Identify as many of the instruments as you can. What feelings does it communicate? How might it do that? Does it create an image? What aspect of the music gives you that image, as opposed to some other image?
   a. Now listen to it again; what more do you notice about the piece? Write down all the things you've noticed about the piece.
   b. Try this with a friend. What do they notice that you didn't, and vice versa?
   c. Now you are ready to try this with your class.
   d. You or your students might become interested in other aspects of the music. Who is the composer? When was it written? Where was it written? How long did it take to write? Is it written down, or is it improvised? Can you name all the instruments you hear? And so on.
2. *Learning about the arts: Visual art.* Choose a painting, poster, or reproduction of some artwork. Note your initial reaction in a journal.

Now look at it closely. List 20 things about the painting that you notice. Now list ten mathematical things you notice. You might also want to create a story to go with painting. After you're done, re-read your initial reaction toward the painting and consider how your thoughts about the painting have changed.

   a. You might become interested in other aspects of the painting. Who painted it. When? Where? How long did it take? What kind of paints were used? How did the painter get a certain effect? Were the colors pre-mixed? And so on.

   b. Try this with your students. How do their connections match yours?

3. *Setting the stage for learning.* See if you can "set the stage" for your own learning. Choose one of the questions above to ponder. Before writing a response in your journal, listen quietly to some calm folk music or classical music (harp music or guitar music will work well). Did the music set the stage for you? Try drawing to the music as well. What does this do for your thinking?

4. *Aesthetic awareness.* Look closely at an object on your desk. How many things do you notice about it? List the things you notice. Now list the questions you might have about the object. What is your level of awareness? How many things are you noticing about the object that you didn't notice before? Do the same as you walk outside of your school or front door at home.

REFERENCES

Bjork, Christina, and Lena Anderson. (1987). *Linnea in Monet's Garden.* New York: R&S Books.

Black, Janet. (1993). *The Effects of Auditory and Visual Stimuli on Tenth Graders' Descriptive Writing.* Jurupa, CA: Jurupa Unified School District.

Blanchard, B. Everard. (1979). "The Effect of Music on Pulse-Rate, Blood-Pressure and Final Exam Scores of University Students." *Journal of Sports Medicine and Physical Fitness,* Vol. 19, pp. 305–308.

Byars, Betsy. (1978). *The Cartoonist.* Pine Brook, NJ: Dell Publishing.

Cecil, Nancy Lee, and Phyllis Lauritzen. (1994). *Literacy and the Arts for the Integrated Classroom.* New York: Longman.

Clement, Claude. (1986). *The Painter and the Wild Swans.* New York: Dial Books.

———. (1993). *The Voice of the Wood.* New York: A Puffin Pied Piper book.

Collins, Judy. (1989). *My Father.* Boston: Little, Brown.

Collins, Pat Lowery. (1992). *I Am an Artist.* Brookfield, CT: Millbrook Press.

Fleischman, Paul. (1988). *Rondo in C.* New York: Harper and Row.

Getty Report. (1985). *Beyond Creating: The Place for Art in America's Schools.* Los Angeles: J. Paul Getty Trust.

Giles, Martha Mead. (1991). "A Little Background Music, Please." *Principal,* Vol. 71, pp. 141–167.

Greene, Maxine. (1991). "Texts and Margins." *Harvard Educational Review,* Vol. 61, No. 1, February 1991.

Hospers, John. (1982). *Understanding the Arts.* Englewood Cliffs, NJ: Prentice-Hall.

Isadora, Rachel. (1979). *Ben's Trumpet.* New York: Greenwillow Books.

Locker, Thomas. (1989). *The Young Artist.* New York: Dial Books.

Marantz, Sylvia. (1992). *Picture Books* for *Looking and Learning: Awakening Visual Perceptions through the Art* of *Children's Books.* Phoenix, AZ: Oryx Press.

McDermott, Gerald. (1975). *The Stone Cutter: A Japanese Folk Tale.* New York: Puffin Books.

Morphy, Howard, ed. (1989). *Animals into Art.* London: Unwin Hyman.

Neruda, Pablo. (1994). *Odes to Common Things.* Boston: Little, Brown.

Olshansky, Beth. (1994). "Making Writing a Work of Art: Image-Making within the Writing Process." *Language Arts,* Vol. 71, September 1994.

Oneal, Zibby. (1986). *In Summer Light.* New York: Bantam Books.

Russell, Lori A. (1992). "Comparisons of Cognitive, Music, and Imagery Techniques on Anxiety Reduction with University Students." *Journal of College Student Development,* Vol. 33, pp. 516–523.

Rylant, Cynthia. (1988). *All I See.* New York: Orchard Books.

Spiegelman, Art. (1986). *Maus.* New York: Pantheon Books.

Sullivan, Charles, ed. (1994). *Here Is My Kingdom: Hispanic-American Literature and Art for Young People.* New York: Harry N. Abrams.

Wall, Steve. (1993). *Wisdom's Daughters: Conversations with Women Elders of Native America.* New York: HarperCollins Publishers.

Whipple, Laura. (1994). *Celebrating America: A Collection of Poems and Images of the American Spirit.* New York: Philomel Books in Association with the Art Institute of Chicago.

Willard, Nancy. (1991). *Pish, Posh, Said Hieronymus Bosch.* New York: Harcourt Brace Jovanovich.

Williams, Vera B. (1986). *Cherries and Cherry Pits.* New York: Greenwillow Books.

Winter, Jeanette. (1991). *Diego.* New York: Alfred A. Knopf.

Wolkstein, Diane. (1992). *Little Mouse's Painting.* New York: Morrow Junior Books.

chapter 9

Seeing a Different Picture: Assessment and the Arts

I am struck with how often my fellow teachers reported that their supposedly lower functioning students came up with the most creative responses when engaging in art activities.

Angela Ennen, teacher Las Vegas, Nevada

[In writing haiku] I found the students who really shined were the ones that were considered "low" . . . the arts lend themselves to showing kids in a whole new light.

Leslie Brinks, teacher Las Vegas, Nevada

When students create poetry, visual art, dances, music, sculptures, and so on, they are not only exploring and expressing understandings of subject matter, they are also offering original "documents" that provide evidence for assessing their grasp of important concepts in the subject matter areas. Viewing the arts as an assessment tool may broaden the methods available to you as well as challenge some traditional notions of what constitutes a "lower" or "higher" functioning student.

This chapter addresses Principle 6 of the role of arts in multicultural education (p. 15). The arts can deepen teachers' awareness of children's abilities and provide alternative methods of assessment. "Expanding notions of assessment to incorporate the possibilities offered by the arts can create exciting opportunities for teachers and learners" (Goldberg, 1992, p. 623). The arts are "languages of learning" (Gallas, 1994) that offer a lens into a child's view of the world. Young children's ability to use languages, especially the languages of the arts, provides useful information about their conceptions of the world. By studying children's expressions through the arts, teachers can broaden their knowledge of a child's progress and learn something of a child's inner thoughts and concerns, dreams and hopes.

There are numerous ways to consider the arts and assessment. I will highlight three throughout this chapter:

1. *Content and Concept Assessment:* Art can serve as evidence for the assessment of children's understandings of concepts in the content areas. In this case, the teacher uses children's artwork to determine the degree to which they understand a particular concept in one of the subject areas.
2. *Incidental Assessment:* Artistic events can provide a fuller understanding of children's general intelligence and abilities. Incidental assessment occurs when a child exhibits something through the arts that leads toward a fuller understanding of the child and his or her general abilities. For example, in assessing a child's poem to ascertain understanding of a science concept, the teacher might also gain understanding of the child's ability to create metaphors, apply language, or empathize with another living creature. In all cases, the artwork offers a way to assess the child.
3. *Artistic Assessment:* One may assess a child's ability to play a violin, write a poem, or paint a watercolor. Because this book focuses on content, concept, and general intelligence, I will address—but not focus on—artistic assessment in this chapter.

There are many ways to approach each assessment. I will address the following: (1) identifying evidence of learning, (2) setting assessment parameters, and (3) creating strategies to collect evidence, including portfolio assessment, performance-based assessment, and effective ways to listen to children and interpret their responses. But first, it is important to consider why and to whom assessment is critical.

THE NEED FOR ASSESSMENT

In considering the arts as evidence of learning—and perhaps more important, as documents of a child's world—the teacher gains an accumulating and evolving picture of her students. But there are many reasons to assess students' abilities. They range from obligatory classroom grading for report cards, to the district's desire to be competitive in terms of state standards. A question to consider is: Who is the assessment for? Is it for teachers, parents, students themselves, districts, or states? Who does the assessment? The teacher? The student? I suggest that in the spirit of a democratic classroom *both* should be involved in the assessment process. Enabling students to enter into self-assessment trains them to be reflective of their own work. It is also a lesson in self-reliance. It can build confidence rather than creating a state of dependence whereby the student relies on the judgment of others for gratification.

Other questions emerge. What constitutes evidence of learning? What criteria should be used to judge competence, or learning? What is the role of a culminating activity in assessment? Can students apply what they are learning to another situation? Does the student *understand* what he or she is learning? What is the student's interest level in the subject activity, and how does that relate to assessment?

One of the pitfalls (or wonders) of the arts is that they can either be integrated in teaching and learning as curriculum events and strategies, or stand on their own as independent artistic learning activities. When you begin to incorporate art activities into your lessons, then, it is important to remind yourself of teaching and learning goals. Consider these questions:

- What are the children learning by engaging in this activity?
- Is this a project/activity, or does it have more long-range implications? Projects or activities can be fine, fun, and appropriate, but in an integrated thematic unit, how does the artistic event fit into the bigger picture?
- In what ways does the artistic event fit into the students' lives? How does it reach the interests of the child?
- Where can you go from here?
- In what way does the curriculum encourage children to be lifelong learners? In other words, does this curriculum create learners as opposed to focusing on what to teach? (I consider this one of the most important questions in teaching and learning.)
- How will you determine if the children are actually learning?

I believe that assessment is most important to the teacher and student in the class, and the student's parents or guardians. Debates over standardized local, district, and national testing are another story altogether, which I will address later in the chapter. There are numerous ways to document and assess a student's learning through his artwork. I will highlight a number of ways as they relate to the art-based activities reported throughout this book.

EVIDENCE OF LEARNING

The arts provide a unique forum for assessment because they constitute evidence of students' work and thoughts. As children work through the arts, they engage with ideas and create representations that express their understandings. Because creating art involves translating ideas into another form, the children's representations are especially important windows into their thinking. Their artworks form a body of evidence that can be assessed and even compared—both to the student's individual progress over time, and to others in the class.

In working with teachers and student teachers on integrating the arts as a methodology for learning, it is not unusual to hear comments like the ones at the very beginning of this chapter: that the supposedly "lower" student seem to shine when activities turn to the arts, or that the students who consistently test poorly seem to have the most creative insights in the artistic media of poetry, painting, dance, music, rap, and so on. Comments of surprise at once excite and sadden me. It excites me that the arts provide a venue for students who often test "low" to shine in another area. It saddens me that according to traditional assessment tools, many of these same children have been labeled as "low."

Left to their own devices, children will naturally express themselves through music, dance, and visual arts. It is more a matter of traditional schooling practice that has limited the expression of knowledge to the spoken and written word. Unfortunately, through that practice we have unwittingly closed doors to many children who, for one reason or another, work better through the languages of the arts than through only the spoken and written word. As I have written elsewhere, "as many teachers seek to reflect our multicultural society in the subject matter they present and in the questions they explore, I believe it is time to embrace the multifaceted ways of knowing and expressing knowledge" (Goldberg, 1992, p. 623). Incorporating the languages of the arts expands the possibilities for all children in the classroom to work with ideas.

A fifth-grader discusses his understanding of a poem with the author.

Teachers and students have multiple experiences, ways of knowing, and ways of expressing their knowledge. Limiting this knowledge to expression in a logico-mathematical manner (as is dominant in most school settings) prevents many children from demonstrating their abilities and creativity, thus placing them at a disadvantage. Incorporating the arts as a way of working with knowledge and as a standard for assessment levels the playing field for all children. By widening their vision of acceptable expression and ways of knowing, teachers can begin to create a community in which all students have the freedom to learn and be recognized for their contributions and insights.

Using the arts with second language learners can also allow students to express deep understandings without having to rely on words they are just becoming accustomed to using. Often second language learners are at a disadvantage when taking written tests because of their emerging vocabulary. These students' test results are a poor indication of their understandings and more an indication of their language ability. For example, although a student learning English may not be able to write about the life cycle of a butterfly, his dance or drawings might demonstrate his deep and detailed understanding of the concept. Restricting students from languages of learning through the arts, then, potentially prevents them from fully working with, constructing, and communicating knowledge.

As with second language learners, "lower-functioning," "higher-functioning"— indeed *all*—children in the classroom, the arts as a tool for understanding and assessment can bolster self-esteem and self-confidence. Once a child gains confidence that she can effectively communicate her understandings through means other than traditional forms, she becomes willing to do so on a regular basis. As a next step, she might attempt more standard exercises such as writing a paragraph in prose. Most important, the arts may set the stage for both teachers and students to reassess labels and prior conceptions of abilities and intelligence.

CONTENT AND CONCEPT ASSESSMENT

There are numerous ways in which to consider children's artwork so that it reveals their understanding of subject matter. Most simply, paying close attention to the artwork will give many clues about how children conceptualize a subject and the degree to which they are interested in details. In Chapter 7 I discussed sound and movement fractions. One method of testing a student's understanding might be to give him a written test. Other options, however, would be to have him perform the fractions in sound or movement. The following vignette demonstrates what I mean.

"Zeke," asks the teacher, "What might $1/3$ sound like?" Or, "What could it look like?" Zeke considers this for a moment (needless to say, it is also good to create situations in which children are challenged in their thinking) and then performs a piece in which he moves and makes a sound, jumping three times and whistling once per every three jumps (on the first jump). Other children come up with creative ideas inspired by Zeke's performance. Playing off of their excitement, the teacher suggests that students perform a fraction while the rest of the class tries to identify which fraction it could be. One student demonstrates $\frac{1}{2}$ by walking two steps and clapping every other one. Another student stamps her feet three times while clapping her hands to the first and second stamp (an amazing act of coordination!), demonstrating $\frac{2}{3}$.

Through this artistic "game" the teacher can observe the children's demonstration of their understanding of fractions. She can assess their understanding by observing their performances, noting each child's identification of the fractions (if it matched what she was seeing and hearing), and asking occasional questions for clarification.

Consider another math example. If your class is studying groups, patterns, or sets, ask the children to create the patterns in sound, movement, or visual arts. If a child creates a sound piece that clearly has a repetitive three-note pattern, she is demonstrating an understanding of repetition and sets of threes. If a child creates a visually consistent repeating pattern, he is applying and demonstrating an understanding of the concept of patterning. Successful (or unsuccessful) application in the art forms can be easily recognized and utilized as a measurement of understanding. In the end, the measurement of understanding in art is not only an adequate tool but usually an enjoyable activity as well.

INCIDENTAL ASSESSMENT

Children's art can provide a teacher with information that may go undiscovered through traditional testing mechanisms. Leslie Brinks, a second-grade teacher in the Las Vegas area, describes how through writing haiku with her students she was able to learn more about the students themselves and their ability to use words. The following are some of her favorite poems from the class, accompanied by comments about the children.[1] In order to write the haiku the students took inspiration from the outdoors, where they sat in the schoolyard observing their environment.

The first poem was written by Marta, an ESL (English as a second language) student who is considered "the shyest girl in our class." Because she is quiet and reticent, it is easy to overlook her abilities. This poem is a sweet reminder to offer her opportunities to express herself outside of traditional writing and speaking exercises.

I see bumble bees
buzzing in the summer sky,
Stay away from me!

---

[1] The children's names have been changed.

"Shadows on the grass" was written by Sean, who goes out of the room for two hours a day for language development. Because Sean is labeled as a "resource-room student," it is easy to dismiss his ability to participate in non-traditional activities often reserved for gifted students (such as poetry). However, we see Sean blossom in this circumstance rather than be confounded by it.

Shadows on the grass
The sun shining close to me
Fresh air around Sean.

"Children playing loud" was written by Karen, an almost non-reader who struggles with second-grade work. It is interesting that she uses so many verbs in her poem. It was striking to her teacher to see how clearly she expressed herself through this minimalist form.

Children playing loud
Jumping Screaming, running fast
I would like to play

The last example, "I see a shadow," was written by Kelly, an ESL student.

I see a shadow
I feel my mom hugging me
I see flowers

Leslie asked Kelly why she wrote the line "I feel my mom hugging me." Kelly answered, "That's just what it felt like when we were outside." Leslie then told me, "I loved that!" It was an opportunity for Leslie to share the magical association her student was capable of creating. Leslie learned something of Kelly's personal thoughts, but in addition she was introduced to Kelly as a poet creating relationships between images and feelings.

SETTING ASSESSMENT PARAMETERS

Content and concept assessment plans must be intimately connected to curriculum goals and standards. In fact, curriculum should ultimately guide assessment plans. Assessment tools must also be contextualized to individual students and situations. In other words, I am advocating assessment plans that can be utilized in the entire class while at the same time addressing the progress of individual students. Admittedly, in my own teaching I am more interested in following the progress of each student than in comparing them to a class standard.

The first priority in assessing any student's understanding of subject matter involves collecting evidence and/or data that will in some way indicate the student's progress. Consider the work of the fourth-graders in Chapter 4 who were exploring language through writing poetry. The teacher's curriculum goal in the poetry unit was to engage her students in writing and to increase their vocabulary. As evidence of their work, the teacher had each student keep all brainstorming and poetry in a journal. Therefore, a log of work was available when the teacher wanted to check on their progress.

The next step is to establish a way to interpret the evidence. This will vary according to both the activity and the individual student. In our language development poetry activities, the teacher and I established that we were interested in (1) the amount of brainstorming the individual student was doing: as evidenced by the amount and level of words they brainstormed and the seriousness with which they did this work; (2) the metaphors and similes they created, and the level to which they were abstract or concrete: as indicated by uniqueness; and (3) the level of success with which they applied their words, metaphors, or similes to a poem: as indicated in the drafts and final form of their poem. The curriculum goals and ensuing assessment go hand-in-hand. The following example illustrates how we approached one of the poems reported on in Chapter 4.

Simile: My mom is like a beautiful <u>flower</u> blooming in the spring
Brainstorm: flower
beautiful, smell good, bloom, rose, spring, red, bouquet, pollen, bees, garden
Poem

MY MOM

My mom is like a beautiful flower blooming in the spring
she is like the beautiful red rose in a bouquet
you could plant her in your garden and
she smells so good!
Anybody would like to plant her in your garden
she is beautiful!

Heather Mendez

1. Heather brainstormed over ten words for "flower." In addition, she went to the dictionary to look up "bouquet." Overall, in relation to her previous poetry work including other brainstorming exercises, she did above average on this task. Her words were more detailed and sophisticated than in previous sessions, and her interest in utilizing the dictionary was new.
2. Heather created two similes in her poem: "My mom is like a beautiful flower blooming in the spring" and "she is like the beautiful red rose in a bouquet." Both similes include descriptive words and modifiers that further the impact of the simile. Compared to her previous work and to other children's work in the class, Heather's similes were more

extensive and descriptive. As a result, I would judge Heather's effort on this poem as above average.

3. The level of success with which Heather used her words is good. She included all her brainstormed words except "pollen" and "bees." I imagine that given another editing session, she might be able to use those words as well. Her word order and usage was good—with the exception of the second to last line, which is grammatically awkward owing to her use of "your" rather than "their." Overall, however, I would say this is an example of a good application of words and ideas for Heather.

In assessing children's drawings (as opposed to language-based art activities), a similar method may be employed. The nature sketches mentioned in Chapters 6 and 7 constitute a body of evidence demonstrating children's understandings of nature and math topics. The trick is in interpreting the evidence. To begin, you might simply observe the sketch closely and make note of all the parts of the sketch. Again, I suggest setting up criteria to guide your judgments. This might include the level of detail. For example, if the sketch is of a Fibonacci pattern, then you would want to check how accurately the child has re-created the pattern. Other criteria: Does the child accurately depict the pointiness of the oak leaf? Does the child capture the ridges in the muscle shell?

The sketches provide information that can be translated into an assessment tool indicating levels of detail and expressing student understanding. One note of caution, however. It is important to pay attention to the essence and detail of the sketches rather than their "beauty." Some talented student-artists might produce lovely pictures but fail to provide accurate detail of the object. Conversely, some students who lack drawing skills might capture the details of an object more accurately than you think at first glance. Be a careful and close observer of your students' work.

STRATEGIES TO COLLECT EVIDENCE

To collect evidence the teacher can use a number of strategies, some more structured than others. A structured strategy might include checklists. For example, teachers may create conference checklists that guide conference sessions with their students. In keeping with the goals of a particular unit or activity, the teacher lists questions or discussion topics she will ask of each student during a conference. A less formal method involves a journal or log in which to record notes about each child. There are many options in keeping journals and logs: Some teachers prefer journals with a page or so devoted to each child; others keep index cards. I have found this to be a useful classroom method. Often, when I look back at the end of the week at my notes, I am surprised at the amount of or lack of notes about a particular child. This serves as a reminder that I must pay more or less attention to individual children.

Portfolio Assessment

A method of collecting evidence that is gaining popularity is the portfolio. In creating portfolios, students and teachers collect various items to judge individual progress. Portfolios might include poems, drawings, essays, reports, reflections on included samples, and so on. If the teacher is interested in quantifying collected data from the portfolios, journals, and logs over time, an easy way to do so is to create a rubric. In a recent issue of *Portfolio News* (1994), a newsletter devoted to portfolio assessment, the editors proposed a scale with five categories to judge the quality of each student's work over time. I have adapted that scale for our purposes:

> 4—*Outstanding Progress:* Portfolio shows consistent progress, and there is a significant difference between early and most recent work. The student's understanding of material has considerably broadened, and the student can reflect upon the changes.
>
> 3—*A Lot of Progress:* The student has expanded his notions of subject matter and is able to assess his own work. He is able to delve more deeply into subject matter as evidenced by his work, but not as evident as in category four.
>
> 2—*Some Progress:* The student's examples are coherent and easy to understand, but the topics and content have not changed much over time. There is less material than in a category three portfolio. It shows less application to real-life situations.
>
> 1—*Minimal Progress:* The portfolio contains little material. Little progress has been made over time as exemplified in the samples.
>
> X—*Ungradable:* The portfolio contains little material, and in that material no progress is evident.

Performance-Based Assessment

Performance-based assessment is highly touted. It often involves a culminating event whereby the student or group of students "perform" in order for the teacher to assess what they have learned. The activity also gives the students an arena to explore and work with their ideas. When I had my fifth-grade students create raps about photosynthesis and then perform them, I was able to assess their understanding of the concepts related to photosynthesis and the vocabulary they used in expressing their understanding. Culminating events might also guide the structure of your everyday class activities.

The following example from Chapter 1 illustrates the possibilities of assessing a performance or culminating event. "The Cliff" was written by Joey Strauss, a fifth-grader. It was composed as a culminating event following many class discussions, a visit to the ocean, and a series of note-taking and sketching activities.

THE CLIFF

It stands alone in silence
never losing its strength
except sometimes a wave
will come and dig beneath
the sandstone shell

It cannot lose more than a chip
but slowly it disintegrates from
all the time the tide has come and
all the time the wind has gone

Joey Strauss

In this poem we can find a number of indicators of Joey's understanding of the beach. In terms of vocabulary, he has incorporated words such as "sandstone," "disintegrate," and "tide" and used them appropriately. From the vocabulary, we can see that he understands and applies key elements of the science lesson. Although I don't feel the need to create a rubric to judge Joey's understanding on some scale in this case, in another circumstance I might be inclined to do so. Another circumstance might be if I were using the poems as a test. In that case, a scale would help in terms of grading more formally.

A caution concerning performance-based assessment: Sometimes a performance is a poor indicator of a child's understanding. This happens when a child lacks the "performance skills" necessary to undertake a performance. My dissertation research was in the area of musical performance. I was interested in investigating the relationship between performing and playing music. A question that concerned me was: Can a person play music but not be a performer? What became increasingly clear was that performing was a skill *added on* to one's ability to play music. The core activity was playing music. When performing, all sorts of other factors came into being such as the ability to express oneself in public (which has little to do with one's ability to play an instrument). I found this to be true as a music teacher. During class time my students would play their music unbelievably well, but in front of their parents and peers the music would sometimes evaporate into some other universe. It became clear to me that students could be wonderful musicians yet poor performers.

Performing is a skill added on to a core activity—whether it be playing music, understanding science concepts, or exploring a topic in mathematics. Thus, it is important to tap into the core activity as a measurable indicator of understanding rather than relying solely on a child's performance. I do not mean to imply that performances are not important or that curriculum units should not include culminating events. One of the reasons musicians perform before an audience is to heighten their ability to play the music. In schooling, a performance and/or culminating event might serve as motivation to push students beyond everyday limits. What I do mean to emphasize is that (1) not all students are terrific at performing, and (2) for those students, attention to the core activity itself will provide more reliable information on their understandings than an actual performance event.

The performing notion is also illustrated in the failure of standardized tests to adequately measure students' abilities. There are numerous reasons why a student may fail a standard test—ranging from lack of testing skills, to cultural differences, to lack of vocabulary. For example, the second language learners with whom I work inevitably score terribly low on standardized tests. The tests are not designed to reach their ability or general intelligence. When I interact with a 10-year-old who can read and interpret poems by Longfellow but scores miserably on a standardized test for comprehension, I am deeply saddened.

Here is where the arts can give us an alternative, if not a more rounded and authentic assessment of a child's abilities. In the case of the 10-year-old, it was clear that the child could think abstractly and interpret the Longfellow poem—a high-level thinking skill completely unmatched by her performance on the standardized test. If I were to rely on that test as a true measure of her intelligence, I would be doing her a severe disservice. She was an interested and thoughtful student who could demonstrate through her ability to comprehend poetry that she was able to think abstractly. Had it not been for the opportunity to prove her abilities, through the arts, she was at risk of being judged as less competent.

One final criticism of performance-based and culminating activities is that units rarely end with a period. Good curriculum units should end with more questions than they started with, and with enthusiasm for continuing adventure. In that sense, I suggest that a unique and very telling assessment tool would be to inquire of your students what their continuing questions are of any given unit. Recalling Piaget, the test of a child's thought and interest often lies in the questions they ask of themselves rather than the information they are willing to give back to us. Betsey Mendenhall and her social studies students, whom I presented in Chapter 5, provide a good example of ending a unit with more questions than it began. Her students became so interested in the conversations the puppet presidents might have that they created discussion topics that could fill a lifetime. Betsey, then, could judge—by the kinds of questions her students asked—the level of their engagement and their ability to conceptualize the role of a historian.

I suggest that students work closely with teachers to create their own assessment rubrics and tools to match curriculum units or activities. They should also be encouraged to critique each other's work after establishing ground rules for discussion. Giving children these responsibilities teaches them to be responsible and reflective learners. It is also a lesson that can be applied later in life in situations of judgment. I remember my own graduate work and a class in which I worked very hard. Because my conceptions of the subject matter did not match the instructor's, I was given a lower grade even though my ideas were carefully and thoughtfully constructed. Although disappointed with the grade, I was not disappointed in myself or my work.

Listening to and Observing Children

A way to assess students' understandings is to observe their actions and listen to what they say. But how can we know if our observations and conversations truly tell us what the children are thinking? To be sure to collect evidence and data while listening to children, the teacher may set up parameters that match curriculum goals. In other words, the teacher (perhaps in consultation with the students) decides what is important to record. For example, if the subject is understanding the skills of a naturalist and you are teaching these skills through the arts (i.e., sketching and writing poetry), you might consider the following questions to guide your observations, discussions, and note-taking:

- Can the child identify qualities associated with being a naturalist in conversation or writing (e.g., silence, close observation and identification, sketching objects in nature with detail)?
- To what extent does the child apply these qualities in the field?

When I go out into the field with children, I am tuned into their general awareness, interest, and curiosity about the setting. If the children begin to identify plants, I know they can apply some of our classroom work. If they spot a heron and become excited at the sighting, I know there is some measurable level of success. I can usually learn something about the class as a whole from simply being in tune with their behavior on a field trip. If, on the other hand, I notice a child who is uninterested or reticent, that is another clue I might consider in terms of my understanding of the child's learning.

In considering their artwork, I am looking for attention to detail and description. If I am looking at their sketches, I check to see that the sketch matches the label they have given it. For example, if a child sketches an oak leaf and labels it a maple leaf, something needs to be corrected. Conversely, if a child sketches a mud flat and then realizes it is an example of a fractal in nature and identifies that in her sketchbook, I have a sense that she is putting the pieces of our nature study together in a way that makes sense and is recognizable. In reading children's poetry, I am interested in their "making sense"—I am looking for descriptions that match physical reality, or appropriate use of words and concepts (e.g., a poem concerning finches' eating habits should have them eating seeds rather than small mammals).[2]

Jean Piaget outlined a number of interesting guidelines in considering the words and actions of young children. In *The Child's Conception of the World* (1976), Piaget was interested in understanding children's conception of the natural world. He discovered that children's actions and language are not always true indicators of their understanding of particular phenomena. Therefore, he

---

[2] Like all poets, some children take liberties in utilizing poetic devices whereby they juxtapose seemingly incongruous events or concepts. In these cases, rather than assume the children are missing some point, I ask them to tell me more about their poem and what they were thinking about when they came up with certain phrases.

started his investigation in an interesting manner. Rather than asking children about their conception of various phenomena to ascertain what they thought of it—such as what the sun does at night—he began paying attention to the questions children asked on their own, without any prompting from inquisitive adults. Thus, by collecting questions that the children themselves asked, he began to understand the issues that concerned them and began to formulate his own course of investigation. The *questions* that children ask provide important insights to their thought processes.

Piaget also realized that in assessing children's understanding of phenomena, he could not rely on accepting their answers at face value. He outlined five kinds of responses that children present to adults when they are asked about natural phenomena. I offer my interpretation of Piaget's five responses so that you may begin to consider the complexity of dialoguing with children:

1. *Answer at Random*—In this case the child is not particularly interested in the question and says anything to the questioner just to appease him or her. For example, if the questioner is interested in a drawing a child has created during a science lesson, she might ask, "Tell me about your picture." If the child responds, "I like to eat pickles," then the child has probably answered at random. Perhaps the inquiry did not make sense to the child, or the child was simply not interested in the question.

2. *Romancing*—Romancing occurs when the child is taken with his or her own ability to tell a story and perseveres at length in the retelling. Many of you with small children are familiar with this creative ability. In responding to the inquiry "Tell me about your picture," the child may begin, "Well, I see the moon and then the tree at the very top of the forest and the dinosaur likes that place and he eats bagels there with little oreo cookies and then the giant comes to the forest and eats the dinosaur and the . . ." In this case the child is interested in his own ability to tell the story, but we are not offered a lot of material about his conception of the science lesson as it relates to his picture. The child exhibits a creative flair for storytelling, but the information is not particularly useful in assessing his picture or his understanding of the science lesson.

3. *Suggested Conviction*—This occurs when the child answers to please the questioner. In other words, the child answers what she thinks the questioner wants to hear rather than answering what she truly believes. Sometimes this is the result of the way in which the question is asked. A leading question, for example, will often result in a suggested conviction. Therefore, the way in which a question is framed is very important. For example, the questioner may ask, "Is that a picture of the sea grass we were learning about?" Upon hearing that she might be onto something, the child could likely answer "Yes!" to please the questioner. What she was really drawing, however, was a picture of her family at the beach.

4. *Liberated Conviction*—This occurs when the child truly thinks about the question and answers it, having never considered it before. This is an interesting moment because the questioner is able to tap into the child's thinking as it is happening. You might find that the questions you ask inspire the child to think even more.

5. *Spontaneous Conviction*—Sometimes the child has considered the issue under question beforehand and answers right away, without having to think about the answer. If a child is asked to "tell me about your picture," having already considered and drawn what she set out to do, she will answer without having to reflect on what she has done.

In both liberated and spontaneous convictions, the children's responses are true to their thinking and reflect their beliefs. These responses are most valuable in assessing children's thoughts and beliefs. A note of caution, however: The answers need not match convention, nor will they in many cases. For example, a young child who has drawn a picture of the moon and is asked what the moon does when the child walks home at night, might very well respond with a spontaneous conviction, "It follows me, silly!" Although his answer does not match physical reality, the child no doubt had considered this question before and "knew" the answer already. Thus, whether the answer is "right" or "wrong" is independent of the kind of response the child offers.

SUMMARY

Students' artwork provides a rich arena for assessing their understandings. The artwork documents the students' world of contemplation and exploration. Because they are original representations of the child's thinking, the artwork is an authentic indicator of the child's understanding. Because the child has created representations of his or her ideas through the arts, the teacher gains a source that tests understanding rather than the ability to "give back" information (which essentially tells the teacher nothing of the child's ability to comprehend).

For students who have been labeled "lower-functioning" during their years in traditional schooling, the arts may contribute to a more informed view of their general intelligence and abilities. For many creative students, traditional testing has failed as the sole source and measurement of their abilities. Not only do the arts help inform teachers about their students' intelligence, learning styles, and personalities, but they offer a route to success that can heighten students' own sense of their abilities and self-esteem.

QUESTIONS TO PONDER

1. When you assess your students' work, for whom is the assessment meant (yourself, the student, parents, principal, etc.)?
2. What role do your students play in assessing their own work?
3. To what extent do you vary the assessment tools in your classroom?

EXPLORATIONS TO TRY

1. Create a list of the assessment tools you already employ (or plan to employ) in your classroom. After considering the examples in this chapter, what additional options might you try in your classroom?
2. Choose an example from one of the subject matter–related chapters in this book, and create a rubric for how you might assess the activity. Check to see if the curriculum goals and assessment rubric match each other.
3. Look at a sketch created by one of your students (or use one of the math/art sketches from Chapter 7). Describe the sketch in detail. How does your description inform you about the child's understanding?

REFERENCES

Gallas, Karen. (1994). *The Languages of Learning.* New York: Teachers College Press.

Goldberg, Merryl. (1992). "Expressing and Assessing Understandings through the Arts." *Phi Delta Kappan,* April 1992.

Piaget, Jean. (1976). *The Child's Conception of the World.* Totowa, NJ: Littlefield and Adams.

Portfolio News. (1994). Vol. 6, No. 1. San Diego: Portfolio Assessment Clearinghouse, University of California.

chapter **10**

A Lithograph in the Closet
and an Accordion in the Garage:
Connecting with the Arts
and Artists in Your Community

I'm by a blooming flower
and if you were little
you would look around that flower
and you would think you were in a jungle

I'm by a colorful flower
and if you were little
you would dream
that a bee was really a bear—by its sound—

My mind is by a flower
and if you were little
you would feel the flower
as if it was soft smooth cotton

I'm picturing I'm by a flower
and if you were little
you would picture that smell
as ten jars of honey

Adan Gonsalves, fifth-grader

In this last chapter I will address three topics: (1) getting to know the arts
resources in your community; (2) becoming familiar with connections to arts
and education through the World Wide Web; and (3) creating public school/
university/art center collaborations. I will begin by suggesting ways in which
readers can utilize community resources to support their arts initiatives. Then I
will introduce the possibilities of technology and the World Wide Web (Internet).

179

I end by reporting on a cultural partnership program in southern California that is fully operational and is based on the ideas outlined in this book.

UTILIZING COMMUNITY RESOURCES

Every community has artists and resident "art experts." Although your community might not have an Aretha Franklin, Derek Wolcott, Alvin Ailey, Bonnie Raitt, or Aaron Copland, no doubt there are many individuals who engage in artistic activities. Perhaps, there is even an arts center close by. Utilizing local arts centers and artists as you begin to conceptualize arts-based activities for your classroom will increase your opportunities for success. Finding creative and artistic individuals requires a little investigative work but can bring many wonderful surprises to your teaching.

To discover artists, creative thinkers and art activities, you must first be aware of your surroundings and the magic it holds. Often I have found that friends have artistic hobbies I never knew about, or acquaintances that unbeknownst to me have secret talents. Sometimes a relative may surprise you, as my Uncle Bill did when he pulled out of the closet a series of lithographs he had made. I didn't know he knew anything about the craft. But that didn't surprise me as much as my cousin did on a rainy summer day when she pulled out an accordion from her garage and started playing Irish folk songs. Indeed, lurking within in your own closets and family may be an accordionist, a mandolin player, a basket weaver, a potter, a watercolor painter. Be especially aware of those closets, garages, and basements for clues!

Almost every town has an art association or gallery. This is a good place to start looking for local painters, sculptors, and other visual artists. You might engage them to help you conceptualize an activity. Or you may simply be interested in inviting them to your classroom. Having artists visit your class introduces the students to people with special talents and provides a connection to people in the arts. Much like inviting a community officer or engineer to your classroom, inviting artists offers the students role models in the realm of the arts.

Artists can also be utilized to support ongoing programs. In one school I visited, a local artist who specialized in paintings of the local harbor was invited to show students her work as they studied local history. In another school, a teacher asked a local potter to demonstrate the process of tile making and glazing for a chemistry unit. Another teacher asked a parent who was a painter to help a class design a mural for the school.

Often I have met interesting people while visiting craft fairs or festivals, even at parties! At a powwow in southern California I met a Native American instrument maker who subsequently visited my music class to make drums with the students. At a party I met a guitar maker who agreed to visit my class to discuss how he made guitars. Community centers can also be wonderful resource centers. Many have folk dance clubs, art classes, or singing clubs. At a local Jewish center I was able to find a senior Yiddish folk song club willing to perform for children. Through a local PTA I found out about a Folklorico (of Mexico) dance ensemble willing to do school performances. Needless to say, the possibilities within your own community are probably limitless.

If there is a local college or community college in your area, you can contact arts instructors to see if their students might be available to visit your class. As part of the Musical Activities for Children and Adults class I teach at the university, I require all students to do an internship (teaching music lessons) in local schools. Each student works in an elementary classroom teaching musical activities to children for a total of 15 hours throughout the semester. The goal is for the students to gain practical experience in applying the ideas we discuss (and try) in class. Because none of the local schools have music specialists anymore, my students also perform an important service for the local school children. Some of my colleagues have set up similar programs whereby their students in theater and visual arts visit local schools to gain experience working with children. Even if there isn't a class structure as I have at my university, there might be arts majors who would be willing to help you on some project. A simple call to the university arts department will set you going on this potential opportunity.

A few more hints. Art supply stores, music shops, and dance studios are terrific resources for people and classes. Consider asking for their advice and help. Often there are parents who have hidden artistic talents (or know people who do) who might be willing to help on a project. In one class, a child's mother who was an architect helped the children construct a small town for a unit that combined history and mathematics. In another class, a mother demonstrated the art of

First-graders with their teacher stand behind the city they built and assembled with the help of a parent.

origami. Consider as well the talents of colleagues throughout your school and district. Perhaps the second-grade teacher can teach a few songs from a culture you have been studying. In return, you might read a favorite story of yours to her class. Work out some kind of trade of talents.

Many people in communities are willing to offer their time. This is especially true for parents, senior citizens, and school organizations. However, if funding for special guests in the classroom is problematic, there are many local organizations (including banks, realtors, supermarkets, and department stores) that might be willing to grant you a stipend for a specific project. Most art centers have funds for scholarships, and local organizations may be willing to negotiate special terms. PTAs might also be encouraged to support art projects or artists in the schools. In many states, there are opportunities to apply for artist-in-residence programs. Check at the reference desk in your local library for information concerning funding. All in all, with a little creativity and a willingness to investigate possibilities, you can connect with many artists and arts agencies in your community. Once you do, you will not regret your efforts!

THE WORLD WIDE WEB AND ARTS EDUCATION

A larger community to which you have access via the Internet is the World Wide Web. The scope of this technology is phenomenal. By simply searching "arts and education" you will find an arts education news and information network, arts curriculum and teacher training sites, grants and resources, and arts education research and assessment. The Association for the Advancement of Arts Education (AAAE) maintains a Web site that connects to many other sites. The address is http://www.aaae.org/ and it might be a good starting point.

In addition to arts education sites (of which you can connect to hundreds, if not thousands), you can access individual artists, musicians, sculptors, photographers, and so on. To access these individuals, simply search according to their name. Many museums also maintain sites on the Web, offering even more opportunites for enhancing learning and specific subject matter. Recently I accessed museums in Chicago, Florida, and Massachusetts by simply clicking a few buttons! "Yahoo," a search tool of Netscape, maintains an entire section on the arts including links to all kinds of art forms, artists, museums, cinemas, and programs.

SUAVE: A CULTURAL PARTNERSHIP FOR TEACHERS

Description and Overview

SUAVE (Socios Unidos para Artes Via Educación),[1] a Cultural Partnership Program for teachers, is a professional development project for teachers in the North County of San Diego, California. It is collaboratively sponsored by the California

---

[1] Translation: United Community for Arts in Education. "Suave" in Spanish is similar to the word "suave" in English.

Center for the Arts, Escondido; California State University, San Marcos; and three school districts: Escondido Union School District, San Marcos Unified, and Valley Center Primary. The program provides professional development for teachers through supported in-service training, weekly in-class coaching on ways to integrate the arts[2] into curriculum as a teaching methodology, and special workshops and performances with professional artists in residence at the Center for the Arts, Escondido.

Since its inception in 1994–1995, 30 elementary teachers from three schools in three school districts have participated in this innovative collaboration. In all three districts, state funding for arts specialists has long since been eliminated. Therefore, collaborative arts partnerships are appealing to school advocates. The school superintendent of each district chose the site schools, and the principals of the chosen schools selected teachers to participate in the program. Originally, the principals were chosen primarily because they each had a personal commitment to the arts. In one school the principal had recently completed a doctoral dissertation on arts magnet schools. Another principal is on the board of the California Arts Project (a statewide arts group); the third principal has advocated for her school to become an arts magnet school. Now, as the program adds new schools and districts, principals without arts backgrounds are requesting the partnership.

Of the approximately 1,000 students presently served by the 30 partner teachers, approximately 70 percent are minority. Each setting is culturally and linguistically diverse. The largest minority population represented is Mexican American, owing largely to our location about 50 miles north of the border and the fact that this region was actually a part of Mexico until about 100 years ago. Over half the current classes are bilingual, and all the teachers work with (or have worked with) language transitional students in their classrooms. Valley Center is a rural setting with a considerable Native-American population. Escondido is the oldest city in inland North County with well-established older neighborhoods. San Marcos is a new and growing community with a community college and a new state university branch.

California Center for the Arts, Escondido (CCAE), is an $81 million cultural arts center that opened to the public in the fall of 1994. It includes two concert halls, an art museum with four galleries and a sculpture garden, a full-service conference center, and four art studios. California State University, San Marcos (CSUSM), is also a new facility, having opened its doors to students in 1990. The university has a strong commitment to the arts and education through its programs in both the College of Education and the College of Arts and Sciences.

Background

Having arrived as a newcomer to CSUSM, I was anxious to become familiarized with the arts programs in the area. Unfortunately, it was not long before I realized that the level of arts education in the local schools was severely limited owing to budget cuts. Coinciding with my arrival in southern California was the

---

[2] Arts is broadly defined to include visual arts, music, movement/dance, literature and poetry, drama, photography, sculpture, puppetry, and so on.

completion of the California Center for the Arts, Escondido, a facility that was committed to an arts education program. The Director of Education and Institutional Access, David Humphrey (formerly of the Kennedy Center for the Arts), and I met early on and began collaborating to develop an educational plan.

I knew I was not interested in developing "recipe" workshops. I did not want to develop a model whereby teachers were given workshops with pre-prepared material that they could bring back and try in their classes. Although this model has advantages, it also limits the teacher's tools to what was covered in the workshop rather than focusing on the ongoing activities of each class. Also, David Humphrey was concerned that teachers might not be willing to come to workshops on their own time. So we were faced with the challenge of creating a program that could be worthwhile to individual teachers and at the same time not be a burden in terms of their personal time commitment.

My solution was to bring the workshops to the teachers—in their classrooms—rather than bringing the teachers to the workshops. A goal was to create situations whereby the teachers would gain skills that (1) directly applied to their individual practice, and (2) could be utilized in related situations, thereby training the teacher not to replicate designated activities but to become familiar with artistic methodologies that could be applied under various circumstances. Whereas most workshops deliver activities that can be replicated in classrooms, this program would encourage teachers to utilize the arts as a methodology for exploring the content areas.

It was clear to me that a solution was to place arts coaches (or specialists) in classrooms as partners with the teachers. Prior to developing this model, I had been working in a local school with a fourth-grade teacher, Michelle Doyle, on a poetry project. (Some of that work is discussed in Chapter 4.) The project enabled me to join Michelle in her classroom for about an hour each week. In our work together, I did not come into the class as a guest teacher or expert. Instead, Michelle and I worked collaboratively in every way—from planning what we would do, to working with the children. Michelle was the expert in her class, knowing her students and their abilities, and able to contextualize what the students were doing according to their previous work. I was an "expert" in various art forms (though admittedly not a poet), having the tools to conceptualize curriculum possibilities that integrated the arts. Together we worked as a team. Having achieved success in our partnership as exemplified in the children's work and responses to the poetry project, I felt confident the model could be expanded. Hence the seed and roots of SUAVE.

In effect, the SUAVE model revisits the role of the arts specialist in the school. In this model, the arts specialist (the arts coach) works *with* teachers and children in the classroom to integrate activities that are of importance to each class. In the SUAVE model, the arts coach does not take over the class to teach arts lessons. Instead, he or she works within the curriculum. Although I could argue that a perfect situation would be to have the integrated partnership and separate arts lessons for the children, if one were forced to choose among the two I would suggest the former. In the SUAVE model, which emphasizes integrated activities, children are likely to become genuinely interested in art forms as a result of working with them.

Philosophy and Theoretical Underpinnings

When Howard Gardner proposed his breakthrough theory on multiple intelligences, the arts—specifically visual arts, music, and dance—were raised to a new level of importance in the classroom. Teachers adapting their instruction to reach all the intelligences have been conscious of incorporating the arts into the classroom.

SUAVE teachers enjoy a movement exercise at an in-service day at the California Center for the Arts, Escondido.

SUAVE furthers thinking on the role of arts in education by taking a stance that departs from both Gardner's view and the traditional role of arts in the school. Learning subject matter *with* and *through* the arts is the focus of SUAVE. Its intent is to use the arts as a methodology for learning mathematics, science, social studies, literacy, and other subject areas in the multicultural and multilingual classroom.

Teachers in the program who are initially using the arts as a teaching methodology are not expected to have any expertise in specific art forms themselves. Instead, they are trained in utilizing the arts in ways that broaden their students' options for working with ideas and expressing knowledge. However, through association and familiarity with the arts, teachers and students also develop a greater knowledge of the arts and of artistic opportunities in the community. Thus, although a teacher may not be an accomplished poet, she can still utilize poetic forms through which her students gain skills in writing. She may thereby become more familiar with poetry in general.

In addition to weekly coaching and collaboration with the arts coaches, SUAVE teachers attend five in-service days at the Center for the Arts. Here they participate in professional and personal development activities, working with professional artists and educators and visiting with museum educators in the Center Museum Galleries. Each teacher also has the opportunity to attend a minimum of five performances and/or artist lectures presented by the Center for the Arts.

To broaden their use of art techniques in the classroom, teachers may take various Art for Children courses after school to gain further skills in art forms. These classes focus on specific artistic techniques that teachers may apply in their teaching. Courses change from semester to semester but include visual art techniques (watercolor, sketching), puppetry, music/singing, movement/dance, photography, and mural techniques.

Beginning in 1995–1996, participating SUAVE teachers were able to receive graduate credit from CSUSM for their work.[3] This credit may be applied toward a Masters degree in education at CSUSM. Finally, a unique aspect of the SUAVE partnership with CSUSM includes 25 student teachers who are placed in SUAVE classrooms. The students are all focusing on arts integration as they prepare for their teaching credential. Thus, they benefit from the training and weekly visits from the coaches along with their master teachers. The master teachers benefit as well by having student teachers with interests similar to their own.

Goals and Objectives

The philosophy that guides this program is that the arts are fundamental to education. By integrating artistic ways of knowing throughout the curriculum, teachers will further develop teaching and learning strategies to the benefit of

---

[3] To receive credit, participants are required to keep logs and journals, attend monthly seminars, and present curriculum projects to the instructor.

their students. The purpose of the program is to support classroom teachers so they can become comfortable in integrating the arts throughout all areas of the curriculum. This brings us full circle to the goals of multicultural education and the arts, as SUAVE focuses on the seven principles of multicultural education and the arts to guide its philosophy:

1. The Arts Expand Expressive Outlets and Provide a Range of Learning Styles Available to Children.
2. The Arts Enable Freedom of Expression for Second Language Learners.
3. The Arts Provide a Stage for Building Self-Esteem.
4. The Arts Encourage Collaboration and Intergroup Harmony.
5. The Arts Empower Students and Teachers.
6. The Arts Deepen Teachers' Awareness of Children's Abilities and Provides Alternative Methods of Assessment.
7. The Arts Provide Authentic Cultural Voices and Add Complexity to Teaching and Learning.

Specific methods and benefits relating to the implementation of the principles include the following:

1. Classroom teachers will be coached so that they will be able to incorporate the arts into existing curriculum as a method for encouraging student learning.
2. Teachers and learners will be helped to utilize arts resources in their communities by their coaches.
3. Anticipated student benefits from the program will include the following:
   a. students will be introduced to meaning-making and expression through the arts
   b. creative, critical, and imaginative thinking will be encouraged while working in content areas as well as in specific art disciplines
   c. learning through the arts meets the need to address multiple learning styles
   d. the arts provide concrete methods for second language acquisition
   e. artistic activity provides methods for authentic assessment, enabling teachers to better assess their students' progress.

Methods

The Role of the Coach. A coach is an artist-educator. This individual works with teachers in devising integrated activities. The coach works with each partner teacher in her or his classroom to uncover opportunities where the arts could be fundamental to learning. Each coach is assigned to one school, where she or he works with up to ten teachers on a weekly basis. Coaches have a

David Mackintosh, SUAVE teacher, holds up a math/art project he developed with his coach.

role in introducing and implementing arts-based activities with the children in the class.

- They might model an activity.
- They might work with individual students.
- They always work with the partner teacher to devise lessons, activities, and assessment tools.

Presently three arts coaches serve SUAVE participants, although that might increase as more schools are added to the program. In putting out a call for the coach positions, we were overwhelmed with the number of respondents. There is seemingly no shortage of artist-educators. Many who applied were former arts specialists. Choosing only three coaches proved quite difficult, because there are so many interesting and qualified artists.

The arts coaches meet for two hours weekly with the program director (coach-leader) and administrative assistant, in addition to spending time in the classrooms. To give a sense of who the arts coaches are, I include brief biographies of the original coaches here:

Mindy Donner, puppeteer, storyteller, performance artist, and mask maker, has over twelve years of experience working in schools. She began her career in art education as a Waldorf kindergarten teacher.

Eduardo Parra has extensive experience in conducting and designing art classes to introduce students to disciplines such as ethnic and social studies, language, and history. He has a strong background in music, theater, film, television, set design, and painting. Eduardo is a native Spanish speaker and has been working with migrant education for the last few years.

Marni Respicio has been a teacher of dance, movement, theater, voice, music, and poetry in local schools. She is a professional dancer who recently choreographed and performed in the musical *Hair*, presented at the Lyceum Theater in San Diego. Marni speaks Tagalog and is experienced in African drumming.

The Role of the Coach-Leader.   The coach-leader is responsible for overseeing (1) the evolution of the coaches' ability to conceptualize and act upon infusing the arts throughout the curriculum, and (2) the actual work in individual SUAVE classrooms. The coach-leader meets with the coaches (as a group) on a weekly basis. In these meetings the coaches brainstorm with each other to develop methods of infusing the arts in specific circumstances. They also reflect upon the work that is ongoing in their classrooms. In addition, the coach-leader provides an initial "training" for new coaches as they begin to observe classes.

Accomplishments of One Year of SUAVE

This section is meant to give the reader an idea of the structure and activities of one year of SUAVE.[4]

1. Weekly coaching of thirty teachers from three districts, October 1994–May 1995
2. Five in-service days
   a. October 11, 1994: Introduction to program and museum; arts as an integrated approach to teaching and learning
   b. December 6, 1994: Literacy and the Arts
   c. February 2, 1995: Science and the Arts (workshop with Tandy Beal Dancers)
   d. March 16, 1995: Math and the Arts
   e. May 2, 1995: Teacher presentations
3. Performance, lecture, and workshop offerings
   a. Performances
      i.   Anna Deveare Smith
      ii. Children's Theater of Minneapolis
      iii. Turtle Island Quartet
      iv. Bella Lewitzky Dancer Company
   b. Workshops and lectures
      i.   Tandy Beal Dancers movement workshop

---

[4] This report is for the 1994–1995 year of SUAVE.

    ii. Integrating museum experience and exhibitions into curriculum with Ellen Willenbecher, Museum Educator

    iii. "Drumming and Power: An International Language"

    iv. "Ute Lemper, Marlene Dietrich, and the Torch Tradition"

    v. "Mexican, Mestizo, Chicano: Arts and Cultural Identity"

4. Evaluations. Program evaluations occurred twice during the year to assess the participants' changes in implementing the arts and arts-based activities in their classroom. Attitude changes have been assessed as well.

5. Research proposal. CSUSM and the Education Department of CCAE have been working on a comprehensive 3-year longitudinal study to evaluate SUAVE. Proposals have been submitted to funding foundations.

Funding and Assessment

Funding is currently provided jointly by participating organizations, with the CCAE providing the major portion (coaches' salaries). Districts support fifty days of substitutes for their SUAVE teachers (attending in-service days at the CCAE: five days times ten teachers). CSUSM partially supports the time of the program director (myself) through course release time. Together, CSUSM and CCAE are exploring other sources of funding to underwrite SUAVE, including major educational funding agencies.

In assessing the program, data including evaluations, observations, interviews, video tapes, and documented activities were collected. Preliminary analysis indicates that participating teachers are increasing their modes of instruction of subject matter through the arts. Not only are their methodologies and teaching strategies being expanded, but their thoughts about learning and instruction are evolving as well.

Beyond the Pilot Year

SUAVE is ongoing in the original three school districts. It is expected that the program will add one more school in each of the participating districts as well as moving to new districts. After two years of "professional" coaching, it is anticipated that there will emerge from each school a teacher who may continue as a mentor in that school. We are currently in negotiation with the school districts to support the time of the mentor/coach. Upon becoming a mentor/coach, the teacher will attend the weekly two-hour coaching meetings with the program director and other coaches. Thus, every two years we will be able to increase the coached population by a minimum of 30 teachers (1,000 students).

At the time of this writing, consideration is being given to "SUAVE Membership" to participants who have completed a year in the program. Membership could include early notification of educational events, access to library and curriculum materials, special events (museum, lectures, workshops), and discounts for members and their students to performances and workshops. Past and present SUAVE teachers will also have access to an online newsletter that will be up and running in the fall of 1996.

Reflections on the Program

What has impressed me most about the program is the confidence and open-mindedness the teachers displayed as they progressed through the year. Near the end of the pilot year, participating teachers were asked to reflect on a series of questions. I have included a brief analysis of their thoughts, as well as a sampling of their responses.

1. Describe how your thoughts about the role of the arts have changed, evolved, or been enhanced as a result of your SUAVE involvement so far. For example: Do you think about curriculum differently? Has your teaching philosophy changed?

Responses to this question suggest that teachers are broadening their skills, methods, and philosophy of teaching and learning. Some teachers describe feeling "more well-rounded." The program has enhanced their thinking about integrated thematic units across the disciplines. Also, teachers report feeling that they are able to reach more students.

- It is becoming more clear that none of the disciplines are isolated or separated. On the contrary: They are intimately connected and they interact with each other. The power of the arts is that magic element that binds subjects together. Arts is like the ocean where all the elements come together.
- I can now see how you can integrate arts *throughout* the curriculum. I had never thought of using dance in math or in science! I'm excited about that. My philosophy has changed and I feel I can reach *more* students.
- I have never thought of myself as "artistic." However, I now feel quite differently. My teaching *methods* are changing and I'm having more fun—as well as the children! My philosophy, "I teach to learn," has been reinforced.
- I've found ways to incorporate art into very structured, sequential skill lessons that I would not have thought of before. For example, when teaching compound words, two "actors" each acted out a word and then worked as a team to demonstrate the larger word (such as football) while the class guessed the word.
- As we do more art in the classroom, I begin to see children differently because I see them do well when in other areas they did not seem to do so well. I see them more as valuable individuals because I am in contact with the *whole* person. I feel more well-rounded as a teacher.

2. Do you feel the SUAVE experience is making a significant difference in your own professional development? How so?

Teachers respond that their "perspectives" are being widened, the program "frees" them to experiment with different activities in the classroom, and they are finding more ways to apply what they are learning in the classroom.

- Definitely. It widens *my perspective,* and I'm able to carry that over not only to my classroom but to my family, friends, and other peers.
- It has freed me in many ways. It has given me permission to experiment with light, color, dance, sound, and measurement.
- I'm finding more ways to apply arts in the classroom, and I'm getting useful material, tips, practice, and experience to apply in the classroom.

3. Do you feel the SUAVE experience is making a difference in your students' education? How so?

Teachers report that the program has a significant impact on their students. Many discuss how their students' self-esteem has been "boosted" as a result of using the arts. Students have worked cooperatively with each other through the arts, and their confidence levels have increased. Students have also expressed interest in pursuing careers in the arts.

- It gives them a different way of seeing things. They feel more confident in presenting their ideas through music, dance, and art. This helps their self-esteem, especially bilingual students.
- I feel it has offered them a variety of ways to show me their understanding of concepts. I feel a sense of freedom, not that my classroom is totally unstructured chaos, but because I am open to responses in many forms—all considered and equally valuable.
- Yes. My children's self-esteem has been boosted in many cases. Other more logical children are being challenged to think/act in different settings.
- Students develop new skills and expand their perception channels. This directly enables them to integrate new ways of receiving, processing, assimilating, and using information. I have found that the students become more critical thinkers and more creative. They also have learned to work as a team and participate more.
- My students have told me several times that school is "fun." They look forward to SUAVE projects. They are more open to each other, more willing to discuss and debate better ways to learn. Cooperative learning is a daily process.
- It's definitely more fun. Kids are finding talents in areas that they never knew existed. It's amazing how many kids now want to be professional musicians, dancers, or painters. I've never seen this degree of excitement in any group, ever. They want to make these things their life.

Of particular interest to me in reviewing the program and its impact on classroom practice is that the changes in teachers and students are not related entirely to the arts. Teachers are thinking about teaching and learning in general. Students are working cooperatively, tapping into their creative abilities, and feeling good about themselves and others. Students and teachers both are challenged to think in new ways and inspired to pursue interesting questions. Also, through their thoughts and actions they are being artists, musicians, sculptors, writers, poets, and dancers creating unique and often profound works.

SUMMARY

Integrating the arts throughout the curriculum can create magic in the classroom—the ways individuals approach subject matter, and in the ways they view each other. The arts open doors to understanding and paths toward adventure. The arts can create change. Perhaps through those open doors, down those adventurous paths, and in the changes the arts release, students will be able to challenge life as it is and create ways in which it could be otherwise.

Through the arts, children may learn to empathize with others: in so doing, they might have the tools to envision the unexpected or how things can be differently. Education that integrates the arts sets the stage for making discoveries a reality. In providing art activities through which students practice their imaginations and creativity, teachers can influence the ways in which children approach their world. At the same time, teachers might be able to see their own world in new ways and with a keener understanding of the complexities that bind us together.

I hope this book has encouraged you, or even challenged you, to consider the arts in ways that broaden your teaching tools and languages of learning. I have written it with excitement and conclude it knowing that what I have written is but a slice of what is possible. Perhaps one of the most wonderful aspects of this journey has been in knowing that the destinations are limitless.

QUESTIONS TO PONDER

1. Make a list of all the potential arts connections (institutions and people) in your community. What sources might you tap in addition to the ones on your initial list?
2. If you had access to a folk singer, what might you ask him or her to do in your classroom? How about a ballet dancer? A rap singer? A graffiti artist? A bluegrass violinist? A potter?

EXPLORATIONS TO TRY

1. Revisit the essay you wrote at the end of Chapter 1 outlining your philosophy of education. How would you change it? What aspect(s) of your thinking has evolved?

2. Interview a local artist, musician, or dancer. What aspect of their work and life is relevant to culture? History? Mathematics? Science? Literacy? Your curriculum?
3. Do an Internet search on the arts and education. Where can you go? What sites can you explore?
4. Write a brief essay outlining five ways in which you imagine integrating the arts in your classroom (or future classroom). Include a rationale of what you hope the students will accomplish as a result.

Index

Acosta, Zulma, 97
Acquisition-Learning Hypothesis, 67
Action, aesthetic experience and, 150
Aesthetic experience, 147-150
Affective Filter Hypothesis, 67
Allen, Jeanette, 92-93
All I See (Rylant), 156
Anderson, Lena, 156
Anna, 78-79
Art
 form dictated by subject matter,
  151-153
 purpose of, 27-28
 as subject matter, 154-155
Assessment
 artistic, 164
 checklists/journals used for, 171
 content and concept, 164, 167-168
 incidental, 164, 168-169
 methods for collecting evidence,
  171-177
 need for, 164-165
 observation and listening to children,
  175-177
 performance-based, 172-174
 portfolio, 172
 setting parameters, 169-171
 of students, 15

Association for the Advancement of Arts
  Education (AAAE), 182
Australian Aboriginal, 88

Baldwin, James, 27
Banks, James, 13
Baptiste, H. Prentice, Jr., 13
Baptiste, Mira, 13
"The Beach Today" (Goodrum), 122
Ben's Trumpet (Isadora), 157
Berthoff, Ann, 27
*Beyond Words: Writing Poems with
  Children* (McKim and Steinbergh),
  76
Birnbaum, Emily, 120, 123-124
Bjork, Christina, 156
Boles, Martha, 128
Brinks, Leslie, 168
Bruner, Jerome, 26, 42
Bryars, Betsy, 158
Bullock, Cathy, 128, 136, 137, 141, 142
Burk, Donna, 134, 141-142
Burke, Karen, 137

California Center for the Arts (CCAE),
  183, 184, 190
California State University, San Marcos
  (CSUSM), 183, 186, 190

"Calvin and Hobbes," 140
"Canary, The" (Nash), 81
Carawan, Candie, 93
Carawan, Guy, 93
Cartoonist, The (Bryars), 158
Cecil, Nancy Lee, 60, 156
*Celebrating America: A Collection of
    Poems and Images of the
    American Spirit* (Whipple), 157
Cerros, Elizabeth, 74, 76–77
Chaplick, Dorothy, 132
Chea, Susanne, 114–115
Checklists, assessment, 171
Cherries and Cherry Pits (Williams), 158
Child's Conception of the World, The
    (Piaget), 18, 19, 175
Chomsky, Carol, 44
Chomsky, Noam, 44
Clement, Claude, 156
"Cliff, The" (Strauss), 172–173
"Clouds" (Laperdon), 125
Cockburn, Victor, 88–89
Cohen, Philip, 89
Collingwood, R. G., 42
Collins, Judy, 158
Collins, Pat Lowery, 157
Communication
    art used to form common languages,
        59–60
    sharing time, 60
    speech play, 60
Community resources, utilizing, 180–182
Comprehension, testing of
    dance and, 66
    drama and, 63, 65–66
    music and, 66
    picto-spelling and, 62–63
Concentration, aesthetic experience and,
    150
Connections, creativity and making, 43
Contemplation, aesthetic experience and,
    150
Content and concept assessment, 164,
    167–168
Contreras, Anabel, 141
Conviction
    liberated, 177
    spontaneous, 177
    suggested, 176

Creating Minds (Gardner), 49
Creativity
    as an action, 42
    defined, 42–45
    Gardner and, 42, 49–50, 52–53
    imagination and, 47–49
    imitation and, 44, 45–47
    improvisation and, 50–51
    invented spelling and, 44
    judges of, 51–53
    language usage and, 44
    making connections and, 43
    motivation and, 43, 49
    play and, 43, 50
    reflection and, 43
    stress and, 51
    technique and, 53–54
Creator versus participant, 54–55
Cultures, arts used to learn about
    different, 6, 11–13, 15–16

Dance
    used to document mathematics,
        132–133, 136
    used to document science, 108
    used to teach cursive writing, 61–62
    used to test comprehension, 66
Dandeneau, Casey, 118–120
Danto, Arthur, 9
Davidman, Leonard, 13, 14
Davidman, Patricia T., 13, 14
deArrieta, Tara, 110–111
Dewey, John, 26
Diego (Winter), 156
Discipline-Based Arts Education (DBAE),
    154–155
Donner, Mindy, 94–95, 188
Donoghue, Denis, 148–149
Doyle, Michelle, 69, 83, 184
Drama
    learning with the arts, 93
    used to document history, 93
    used to document mathematics,
        141–142
    used to test story comprehension, 63,
        65–66
Drawing, used to document science,
    108–112
Duckworth, Eleanor, 2, 23–24, 29, 43–44

Durrell, Gerald, 104
Dyer, Jane, 158

Education, purpose of, 27
Einstein, Albert, 49
Eliot, George, 50
Eliot, T. S., 49
Ellis, Catherine, 9
Emotions, imagination and, 48
Empowerment of students and teachers
    through the arts, 15
Engel, Peter, 137
"en-vi-RON-ment" (Hopkins), 90-92
"The Explosion" (Birnbaum), 123-124

Finley, Alicia, 113-114
Flanders, Michael, 81
Fleischman, Paul, 157
Fleming, Alexander, 50
Folding the Universe: Origami from
    Angelfish to Zen (Engel), 137
Freud, Sigmund, 49

Gallas, Karen, 5, 8, 11, 60, 67, 109
Gandhi, Mahatma, 49
Garcia, Eduardo, 140
Gardner, Howard, 24, 185
    creativity and, 42, 49-50, 52-53
Geography and papier mâché, 98-99
Gerard, R. W., 47
Getty Center for Education in the Arts,
    154-155
Gonsalves, Adan, 75, 76, 179
Goodrum, Darrell, 122
Graham, Martha, 49
Grallert, Margot, 109, 111
Grant, Carl, 13
Greene, Maxine, 10, 37

Haiku, 168-169
Hand in Hand: An American History
    through Poetry (Hopkins), 90
Hart, Mickey, 9
Having of Wonderful Ideas, The
    (Duckworth), 29
Henry, Edward Lamson, 92
Here Is My Kingdom: Hispanic-American
    Literature and Art for Young
    People (Sullivan), 156-157

History/social studies, methods of
    recording/understanding
    drama and, 93
    geography and papier mâché, 98-99
    learning through the arts, 93-99
    learning with the arts, 89-93
    mural making and, 97-98
    music and, 88-89, 92-93
    picture-drawings and, 88
    poetry and, 87, 88, 90-92
    presidential puppetry and, 94-97
    songs and, 88, 89-90
    visual arts and, 92
Hoffmann, James, 9
Holzer, Harold, 92
Hopkins, Lee Bennett, 90
Horton, Julie, 25-26
Humphrey, David, 184
Hunter, Diane, 25

I Am an Artist (Collins), 157-158
Imagination
    aesthetic experience and, 150
    creativity and, 47-49
    defined, 47-48
    emotions and, 48
    role of, 5-6
Imitation, creativity and, 44, 45-47
Improvisation, creativity and, 50-51
"I'm the Lagoon (after)" (Wise), 118
Incidental assessment, 164, 168-169
Ingram, Garret, 75
"Inside of Me" (Timinsky), 120-122
Intellectual development
    methods/role of translating ideas, 26-29
    theories of, 23-26
    what it means to be a learner, 29-37
Intelligences, Gardner's types of, 49
Invented spelling, 44
Isadora, Rachel, 157
"I See I Feel" (Birnbaum), 120
It's Elementary!, 89

Jaime, 77-78
Johnson, Mark, 27
Jones, Bill T., 12
Journals
    assessment, 171
    used for writing poetry, 77-79

Judges of creativity, 51–53
"Judging the Lagoon" (Dandeneau),
    118–120

Kagan, Jerome, 42
Kevin, 112
Knowledge, arts and, 2–4

Ladino musicians example, 6–8, 51
Lakoff, George, 27
Language
    art as, 8–11
    creativity and use of, 44
Language acquisition
    Acquisition-Learning Hypothesis, 67
    Affective Filter Hypothesis, 67
    by writing poetry, 66–69
Laperdon, Nicole, 125
*Latin American Art: An Introduction to
    the Works of the 20th Century*
    (Chaplik), 132
Lauritzen, Phyllis, 60, 156
Learner, what it means to be a, 29–37
Learning
    Acquisition-Learning Hypothesis, 67
    Affective Filter Hypothesis, 67
    art as a process toward, 6
    evidence of, 165–167
    factors affecting, 67–68
    how art sets the stage for, 150–151
    methodology for, 16–20
    Spanish Jewish music (Ladino)
        example, 6–8
Learning about the arts
    description of, 4, 5, 20
    literature and, 156–158
    music and, 155–156, 158–159
    through arts, 158–159
    visual arts and, 159
    with arts, 155–158
Learning styles, art used in working with
    varied, 14
Learning through the arts
    dance and, 108
    description of, 4–5, 17–20
    drawing and, 108–112
    geography and papier mâché and, 98–99
    mural making and, 97–98
    poetry and, 112–125

presidential puppetry and, 94–97
used to document history, 93–99
used to document mathematics,
    134–142
used to document science, 108–125
Learning with the arts
    dance and, 132–133
    description of, 4, 5, 17, 89
    drama and, 93
    literature and, 134
    music and, 92–93, 107, 134
    poetry and, 90–92, 107–108
    used to document history, 89–93
    used to document mathematics,
        130–134
    used to document science, 106–108
    visual arts and, 92, 106–107,
        130–132
Leff, Judy, 87, 88
Letter to Teachers, A (Perrone), 26
Lewitzky, Bella, 9, 10, 61
Liberated conviction, 177
"Life of a Wave, The" (Sieble), 103
Linnea in Monet's Garden (Bjork and
    Anderson), 156
Lippard, Lucy, 10
Listening to children, assessment and,
    175–177
Literacy
    methods of attaining, 60–61
    poetry and, 61
    sharing time, 60
    speech play, 60
    storytelling and, 61
Literacy and the Arts (Cecil and
    Lauritzen), 156
Literature
    learning about the arts with arts,
        156–158
    used to document mathematics, 134
Little Mouse's Painting (Wolkstein),
    156
Locker, Thomas, 157

McDermott, Gerald, 158
McKim, E., 67, 76
Marantz, Sylvia, 156
Mathematics, methods of recording/
    understanding

comparison of mathematician and artist, 127-130
dance and, 132-133, 136
distance estimation, 135
drama and, 141-142
fractions, 135-137, 167-168
games/constructs of the mind, 128-129
learning through the arts, 134-142
learning with the arts, 130-134
literature and, 134
mural making and, 140-141
music and, 134, 135-136
origami and, 137
painting and, 130-132
permutations, 135
points and coordinates, parallel lines, 140-141
shapes, symmetry, angles and geometry, 137-138
single-digit addition and subtraction, 139-140
visual arts and, 130-132, 136-137, 140-141
Math Excursions 1 (Burk), 134
Matias, Anain, 123
Maus (Spiegelman), 158
Mendenhall, Betsey, 15, 94-97, 98, 174
Mendez, Heather, 74, 170-171
Meno (Socrates), 18, 19
Metamorphosis/art exercise, 30-31
Metaphors, use of, 27
Methodology for learning
defined, 5
described, 16-20
Michelangelo, 12
Miller, Mary Britton, 80-81
Millman, Richard, 130, 132
Mind's Best Work, The (Perkins), 42
Mine Eyes Have Seen the Glory: The Civil War in Art (Holzer and Neely, Jr.), 92
Mirror metaphor, 9-10
Modeling, writing poetry and, 83
Montanto, Ladianni, 80-82
Monet, Claude, 156
Montell, Paul, 116-117
Moore, Barbara, 153
Morrison, Toni, 12
Motivation
creativity and, 43, 49
learning and, 67-68
Motter, Matt, 125
Multicultural education and the arts, goals of, 13-16
Mural making
used to document history, 97-98
used to document mathematics, 140-141
Music
how music can set the stage for learning, 150-151
as a language, 9-10
learning about the arts through arts, 158-159
learning about the arts with arts, 155-156
learning through the arts, 135-136
learning with the arts, 92-93, 107, 134
used to document history, 88-89, 92-93
used to document mathematics, 134, 135-136
used to document science, 107
used to test comprehension, 66
My Father (Collins and Dyer), 158
"My Mom" (Mendez), 170

Nachmanovich, Stephen, 50
Nash, Ogden, 81
Neely, Mark, Jr., 92
Neruda, Pablo, 124, 146, 147
Newman, Rochelle, 128
Nieto, Sonia, 6, 14
Nikki, 79-80

Observation of children, assessment and, 175-177
"Ode to a Cluster of Violets" ("Oda a un Ramo de Violetas") (Neruda), 145-146
Ogren, Lynne, 94
Olshansky, Beth, 151
Oneal, Zibby, 158
Origami, 137

Painter and the Wild Swans, The (Clement), 156
Paintings. *See* Visual arts
Parra, Eduardo, 135, 189
Participant, creator versus, 54-55

Perception, aesthetic experience and, 150
Performance-based assessment, 172–174
Perkins, David, 42
Perrone, Vito, 26
Peter and the Wolf, 156
Piaget, Jean, 18, 19, 24, 45, 175–177
Picasso, Pablo, 16, 49, 131, 152
Picto-spelling, 62–63
*Picture Books for Looking and
    Learning: Awakening Visual
    Perceptions through the Art of
    Children's Books* (Marantz), 156
Picture-drawings, 88
Pish, Posh, Said Hieronymus Bosch
    (Willard), 156
Play
  creativity and, 43, 50
  speech, 60
*Play, Dreams, and Imitation in
    Childhood* (Piaget), 45
Poetry
  attaining literacy through, 61
  haiku, 168–169
  lagoon, 117–122
  learning through the arts, 112–125
  learning with the arts, 90–92, 107–108
  ocean and beach, 122–124
  question, 124–125
  used to document history, 87–88, 90–92
  used to document science, 107–108,
    112–125
Poetry writing
  copying poems, use of, 79–82
  journals used for, 77–79
  key elements in, 83
  language acquisition by, 66–69
  language acquisition by, examples of,
    69–77
Pointillism, 131
Portfolio assessment, 172
Portfolio News, 172
Puppetry (presidential), used to
    document history, 94–97

Question poems, 124–125

Random answering, 176
*Random House Book of Poetry for
    Children,* 80, 107
Raquel, 73, 76

"Red Tailed Hawk" (Riel-Mehan), 123
Reflection, creativity and, 43
Respicio, Marni, 136, 189
Rich, Adrienne, 10, 12, 51, 52
Riel-Mehan, Megan, 123, 125
Rivera, Diego, 12, 156
"Rock" (Timinsky), 122
Rock art, 152–153
Romancing, 176
Rondo in C (Fleischman), 157
Rosales, Adriana Rosales, 114
Rubin, Ruth, 89–90
Rukeyser, Muriel, 52
Rylant, Cynthia, 156

Sand, George, 51–52
Schoenberg, Arnold, 16
Science, methods of recording/
    understanding
  dance and, 108
  differences between a naturalist and an
    artist, 104–105
  drawing and, 108–112
  learning through the arts, 108–125
  learning with the arts, 106–108
  music and, 107
  painting and, 106–107
  poetry and, 107–108, 112–125
  songs and, 107
  visual arts and, 106–107, 108–112
Second language acquisition
  Acquisition-Learning Hypothesis, 67
  Affective Filter Hypothesis, 67
  poetry writing and, examples of, 69–77
Second language users
  art and, 14
  writing poetry used to help, 67
Self-confidence, learning and, 68
Self-esteem built through art, 14–15
Sendak, Maurice, 134
Seurat, Georges, 130–131, 155
Shakespeare, William, 9
Sharing time, 60
Sieble, Michael, 103
Silverstein, Shel, 61
*Sing for Freedom: The Story of the Civil
    Rights Movement through Its
    Songs* (Carawan and Carawan), 93
Sleeter, Christine, 13
Smith, Bradley, 88

Socrates, 9, 18, 19
Songs
  used to document history, 88, 89-90
  used to document science, 107
Songs of Earth, Water, Fire and Sky, 107
Special needs, 112, 163, 169
Speech play, 60
Spelling, picto-, 62-63
Speranza, Ramona, 130, 132
Spiegelman, Art, 158
Spontaneous conviction, 177
Steinbergh, J. W., 67, 76
Stern, Deb, 132
Stone Cutter, The (McDermott), 158
Storytelling, literacy and, 61
Strauss, Joey, 172-173
Stravinsky, Igor, 49
Stress
  creativity and, 51
  learning and, 67, 68
SUAVE (Socios Unidos para Artes Via
    Educación) project
  accomplishments of, 189-190
  background of, 183-185
  description and overview of, 182-183
  funding and assessment of, 190, 191-193
  future of, 190
  goals and objectives, 186-187
  philosophy of, 185-186
  presidential puppetry, 94-97
  role of the coach, 187-189
  role of the coach-leader, 189
Subject matter
  art as, 154-155
  art form dictated by, 151-153
Suggested conviction, 176
Sullivan, Charles, 156
Summer Light (Oneal), 158
*Sunday Afternoon on the Island of La
    Grande Jatte, A* (Seurat), 131
"Sunday in the Park with George," 155

Tchaikovsky, Pyotr Ilich, 9
Teamwork, art used to enhance, 15
Technique, creativity and, 53-54
Tewa, 148
Theory of Harmony (Schoenberg), 16
Timinsky, Jenna, 120-122

Tlamatini, 88
Tolley, Kimberly, 104
Translation of ideas, methods and role of,
    26-29

"The Universe" (Miller), 80-81

Villanuevo, Kekoa, 74
Visual arts
  drawing and, 108-112
  geography and papier mâché, 98-99
  learning about the arts through arts,
    159
  learning through the arts, 94-99
  learning with the arts, 92, 106-107,
    130-132
  mural making and, 97-98, 140-141
  painting and, 106-107, 130-132
  presidential puppetry, 94-97
  used to document history, 92, 94-97
  used to document mathematics,
    130-132, 136-137, 140-141
  used to document science, 106-107,
    108-112
"Voice of the Turtle" (Leff), 87, 88
Voice of the Wood, The (Clement), 156
Vygotsky, Lev, 24

Warnock, Mary, 48
Where the Wild Things Are (Sendak), 134
Whipple, Laura, 157
White, Katrina, 127
Whole Language classroom techniques,
    60-61
Willard, Nancy, 156
Williams, Vera B., 158
Winter, Jeanette, 156
Winter, Jonah, 156
Wise, Carson, 118
Wolkstein, Diane, 156
Wordstormings, 83
World Wide Web, 182
Writing
  dance used to teach cursive, 61-62
  See also Poetry writing

Yamada, Mitsuye, 28-29
Young Artist, The (Locker), 157